Denali Journal

DENALI JOURNAL

A thoughtful look at wildlife in Alaska's majestic national park

Tom Walker

STACKPOLE
BOOKS

Published by
STACKPOLE BOOKS
Cameron and Kelker Streets
P.O. Box 1831
Harrisburg, PA 17105

Cover photo by Tom Walker

Cover design by Mark Olszewski

Printed in the United States of America

First Edition

10   9   8   7   6   5   4   3   2   1

Library of Congress Cataloging-in-Publication Data

Walker, Tom. 1945–
    Denali journal : a thoughtful look at wildlife in Alaska's
majestic national park / Tom Walker. — 1st ed.
        p.   cm.
    ISBN 0-8117-2437-9
    1. Natural history — Alaska — Denali National Park and Preserve.
2. Mammals — Alaska — Denali National Park and Preserve.   3. Birds —
Alaska — Denali National Park and Preserve.   4. Denali National Park
and Preserve (Alaska)   I. Title.
QH105.A4W365   1992
508.798'3 — dc20

                                                        91-29381
                                                        CIP

To the memory of Charles Sheldon, Adolph Murie,
Joe Hankins, Bill Ruth, Jim Shives, and Maggie Yurick,
as well as to all who have loved this great park

CONTENTS

Acknowledgments

Over the years several current and former Park Service employees have provided an inside look at both the park and government service. Deanne Adams, Gary Brown, Steve Buskirk, Tom Griffiths, Liz Hutson, Steve Kaufman, Rollie Ostermick, Charlie Ott, Bill Nancarrow, Jim Shives, Tony Sisto, Mike Tollefson, Will Troyer, Bill Truesdale, and Joe Van Horn have all added immeasurably to my appreciation and understanding of the park. My failure to mention others is a mere oversight, albeit an unpardonable one.

Professional reports and wildlife censuses and studies, along with the accumulated monthly superintendent's reports, have aided in the preparation of this book. Important background data: L. Adams, K. Armitage, M. Baker, V. Van Ballenberghe, B. Barnes, R. Beasley, J. Beattie, A. H. Brooks, T. Bundtzen, T. Burch, S. Buskirk, S. Capps, R. Chapman, J. Dalle-Molle, F. Dean, J. Dixon, D. Dolson, B. Evison, L. Keith, L. D. Mech, T. Meier, F. Glaser, D. Gudgel-Holmes, G. Haber, L. Johnson, J. Kari, G. Machlis, C. McIntyre, S. Miller, A. Murie, O. Murie, D. Orth, B. Shults, F. Singer, W. Troyer, J. Van Horn, B. Washburn, R. Weeden, C. Zabel. Any errors in interpreting professional works are the author's own. Because some reports deal with ongoing surveys and studies, conclusions drawn from them should be viewed as both tentative and partial.

Jim Rearden provided his transcripts of interviews with, and the field diaries of, Frank Glaser. Additional Glaser material was provided by the National Archives.

Rose Speranza and Marge Naylor of the Alaska and Polar Regions Department, University of Alaska, Fairbanks, were invaluable assistants in accessing the Adolph Murie papers. Louise Murie-MacLeod and Charlie Ott provided additional insight into Adolph Murie's McKinley Park career.

Park Service historian William E. Brown reviewed portions of the text for accuracy. Colleen Matt, former naturalist, deserves recognition for taking the time to read an early draft of this manuscript. Her observations and insights redirected the book in a most positive manner.

INTRODUCTION

In sharp contrast to most books about Denali National Park, which at least in part center on climbers and climbing, this work focuses on the wildlife and natural history of the area adjacent to the Park Road, where most visitation occurs. Some historical information is offered to provide background and perspective. The book focuses on the peak visitor months of June through September, the brief seasonal respite from winter.

A brief look through the pages will quickly reveal that this book is not a standard diary treatment. For the most part, it is a derivative of a journal kept sporadically for over twenty years, fleshed out with gleanings from government reports, field diaries, and interviews. A few dates have more than one entry.

The journal format allows the reader the opportunity to begin reading anywhere. A visitor to the park in July, for example, could read the entries corresponding to his visit, perhaps gaining a sense of place and season, which may in turn lead to further reading and investigation. One of the great joys of Denali is this opportunity for discovery.

Charged with great excitement and expectation, I first visited Denali, which was then called Mount McKinley National Park, in 1969. The writings of Adolph Murie and Charles Sheldon had ignited my original interest, and that spark was fed by the stories and photographs of an acquaintance who drove a tour bus there in the early 1960s. He showed me pictures of jaegers, foxes, ptarmigan, grizzly bears (he called them "Toklats"), moose, caribou, wolves, and Dall rams. Even now I recall his picture of a person sitting within feet of a magnificent Dall ram. To a budding wildlife photographer, the image was gasoline on the fire.

Despite rain and snow, lack of time, money, and proper equipment, despite a suffering companion and a dilapidated, untrustworthy vehicle, my first visit was more than memorable. Perhaps for the first time in my life, I'd found something that met — and exceeded — my expectations. I would come back again and again, spending as much time as I could, in all kinds of weather and circumstances.

Over the last twenty years I've been fortunate to be able to support myself through a variety of uniquely Alaskan seasonal occupations that bear little resemblance to the usual nine-to-five workday of the modern world. Because free-lance writing and wildlife photography have become both vocation and avocation, I've spent a rather generous amount of time in the park.

My initial visits to the park were camping trips to the various campgrounds along the Park Road. Soon I was hooked on more remote backcountry areas. Indulging my passion for the area, I moved my family to a log cabin I built on the edge of a remote lake near the southeast boundary of the park, in the very shadow of Mount McKinley. For many years, I awoke each clear morning to a stunning view of the mountain looming in the distance. In recent years I've built another cabin near the park entrance. I've explored the park in various ways — by airplane, skis and snowshoes, private vehicle, and shuttle bus — but the most satisfying method is still on foot with a backpack.

I've seen many changes since 1969. By far the biggest change has been in the number of human visitors. The park had fewer than 100 visitors in 1942; 7,000 arrived in 1952; then 17,000 in 1962; 89,000 in 1972; 322,000 in 1982; and 600,000 in 1989. At times, it seems we threaten to overwhelm what we're attempting to protect and appreciate. Limiting access along the Park Road to bus traffic is a gallant effort to protect the unique wildlife values and viewing opportunities.

Most visitors to Denali stay but a brief time. Some of these visits are satisfying — yes, even thrilling — others are disappointing. Denali has its complex problems and issues, some without obvious solution. Greater minds than mine have agonized over the issues and have yet to come up with answers. Though I touch on some of the issues here, I have no miracle prescriptions. Instead, this book offers a contemporary look at the park for the armchair traveler or casual visitor, as well as for those more personally connected to the park.

Natural History Calendar

January
    Temperatures fall to annual lows (minus fifty-four degrees
Fahrenheit)
Northern lights are visible
Days are short
Wolverines are born (into March)
Bear cubs are born in dens
Resident birds remain (nine to twelve species)
Ravens begin courtship

February
    Snow and extreme cold continue
Northern lights are still visible
Days remain short
Wolves, foxes, and coyotes mate (into March)
Beaver mate in lodges
Red squirrels mate
Ravens continue courtship

March
    Snow continues (with April, the driest month)
Temperatures become less extreme
Northern lights are still visible
Daylight hours increase

Snow buntings arrive
Lynx mate
Porcupines are born
Ravens nest
Golden eagles return
Owls begin territorial hooting and calling
Vernal equinox occurs

April

Snow continues
Daytime temperatures moderate
Days grow longer
Breakup begins
Willow catkins appear
Snowshoe hares mate
Weasels, ptarmigan, and hares begin color changes
First bears emerge from hibernation
Nonpregnant cow caribou shed antlers
Ravens' eggs hatch
Martens, foxes, beaver, and arctic ground squirrels are born
Grouse begin courtship
Golden eagles lay eggs
Marmots mate
Moose and caribou antlers bud
Bird migrations begin
Pasqueflowers bloom (last week of April)

May

First spring rains and snow squalls occur
Daytime temperatures increase
Days grow longer
Breakup continues
Bird migrations peak
Avian courtship and nesting begin
Plants leaf out
Eggs of golden eagles, goshawks, and owls hatch
Caribou begin calving
Cow caribou lose antlers (near time of calving)

Moose begin calving (into June)
Pikas mate
Marmots, wolves, lynx, and hares are born
Ptarmigan begin courtship and territorial defenses

June

Summer rains begin
Days are warmer; last freeze occurs
Longest day (twenty-one hours of daylight) is the
    summer solstice
Wildflowers bloom
Tundra and taiga green up
Mosquitoes hatch
Birds hatch (155 to 161 species)
Bears mate (delayed implantation)
Moose and caribou antlers grow rapidly
Dall sheep begin lambing
Caribou begin migration
Wolverines mate (into July)
Grayling spawn and migrate upstream

July

Frequent rains continue
Temperatures reach eighties (warmest month)
Days are long
Wildflowers abound
Mosquitoes and other insects abound
Waterfowl molt
Yellowlegs migrate south
Caribou continue migration
Martens mate (delayed implantation)
Pikas begin storing plants

August

Frequent rains continue
Days become cooler and shorter
First freeze occurs
Insect populations diminish

Last wildflowers bloom
Plants go to seed
Berries ripen
Ptarmigan and grouse pick gravel
Moose and caribou shed velvet from antlers
Bird migration south increases
Red squirrels gather and store cones
Pikas gather and dry plants
Beaver build feed caches
Sharp-shinned hawks, merlins, and golden eagles
    begin migrations
Autumn colors appear (at month's end)

September

Rain and snow mix
Freezing temperatures at night are common
Northern lights return
Daylight wanes; darkness returns
Autumn colors peak and fade
Animal pelage reaches prime state
Animal winter preparations continue
Insects become inactive or die off
Bird migration peaks
Canid pups disperse
Moose begin rut
Grayling migrate downstream
Weasels, ptarmigan, and hares begin color changes
Marmots den
Caribou reach rutting grounds
Autumnal equinox occurs

October

Snow and freezing rain fall
Freezing temperatures are common
Northern lights are still visible
Daylight wanes
Watercourses and ponds freeze
Golden eagles migrate

Bears, wood frogs, and arctic ground squirrels hibernate
Caribou begin rut
Weasels, ptarmigan, and hares turn white

November
Snow and cold continue
Northern lights are clearly visible
Days grow shorter
Caribou bulls shed antlers
Moose shed antlers (into December)
Dall sheep rut
Porcupines mate
Resident birds remain (nine to twelve species)

December
Snow and extreme cold continue
Northern lights are visible
Shortest day (four hours of light) occurs at the winter solstice
Sundogs (ice crystal "rainbows") appear
Wildlife suffers winter mortality (cold, starvation, and
    predation)

DENALI NATIONAL PARK

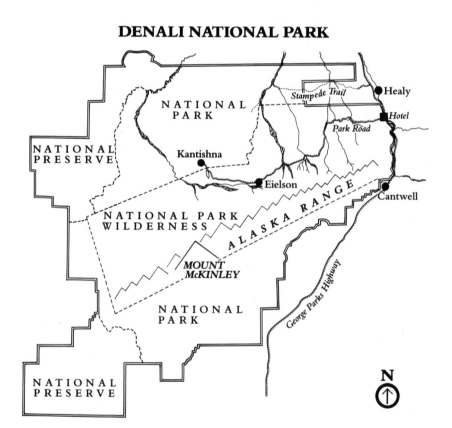

Out of Darkness

Out of winter, into the light.

MARCH 19, 1990. In the darkness, at the hour of false dawn, silhouettes of distant mountain peaks separate from the night as the faint dawn light snuffs out the stars and recaptures the sky. Blue washes the horizon, revealing a landscape of snow-drowned thickets, forest, muskeg, and meandering river surrounded by crenellated summits.

From the cabin window I can look across the Nenana River and into the park. Soon the light will be strong enough for me to see through the spotting scope the herd of caribou wandering the ridge above Triple Lakes, their many trails spreading through the snow like fissures in ice.

What strikes me most about late winter, now that the worst days of cold and darkness are behind us, is the *color*. On a clear morning like this one, night surrenders in pastel hues of claret, ruby, gold, even jade. The peaks and ridges to the west will awaken in a crimson wash of alpenglow, of sherbet colors you can almost taste. Each evening the process is reversed, but the colors are no less intense.

Midday on the tundra, the sun blasts off the ice and snow with an intensity that can blind. Except for the trees and brush that rise above the snow, the land indeed suffocates under a white blanket. Earlier in winter, there seemed little hope of ever seeing the sun again or feeling its warmth; now the strengthening solar heat is almost shocking. Soon the snow will fade and disappear under

1

lengthening daylight. For animals and humans alike, it is none too soon.

MARCH 21, 1990. Vernal equinox dawned clear and calm. This is the day the sun crosses the equator, and our night and day are now of equal length. Banished is the typical day of winter: in the extreme, nineteen hours of darkness and five hours of dawn.

Just after nine P.M. and after full dark, I stepped out on the cabin porch. I looked up. A brilliant aurora washed the sky, sweeping away my sleepy yawns. I rushed back inside. Soon, dressed in parka and snow pants, I snowshoed to a point of the ridge overlooking the valley of the confluence of the Yanert and Nenana rivers. Diaphanous green auroral bands spanned the horizon from Mount Healy to Mount Deborah. Broad vertical brush strokes rained light on Mount Fellows and turned its serrated summit into a phantom tiara.

In the maturing night, the colors died one place, only to flash alive somewhere else, often silhouetting the peaks. Three brilliant green bands tinged with yellow and pink appeared simultaneously. When they faded away, a faint crimson blush began to glow in the east and west. For perhaps over an hour the blush intensified, and I felt as if I were watching an approaching fireball. Sometime after midnight the crimson cloud billowed across the sky, obscuring faint stars. To the west, where Orion guarded Denali with brandished sword, two coyotes yip-yapped into the night, heralds of the first hours of spring.

APRIL 1, 1974. Minus twenty-two degrees. The cold snap continues, but the sun is returning. Solar heating has brought the temperature up to zero the last two days, yet it is hard to be patient. I want summer. I want to see jaegers coursing over the tundra, to hear the whistle of wings over the ponds and the cry of loons. It's the absence of birds—their variety, their abundance, their songs and calls—I miss most in winter. (Each species has only one song but several calls to announce arrival, territory, feeding, and breeding, and to summon the flock or young.) How many bird species migrate north each year—150? 160? In early summer the taiga is alive with avian melodies, but winter brings a deafening silence. What have I seen or heard recently? A horned owl. Gray jays. Boreal and black-capped chickadees. Some redpolls, crossbills, grosbeaks, woodpeckers. And the ubiquitous ravens. That's it.

Spring arrives soon—by air express, I hope.

APRIL 2, 1978. Minus ten this morning. Parked my truck at Headquarters and hiked past the locked gate across the Park Road. The road has already been plowed to Savage, but it will take many weeks of effort to open the road all the way to Eielson; it won't open to the public until sometime in mid–May and then only as far as Teklanika. I carried my pack instead of sledding it. Seemed odd to walk the dry, plowed road carrying a huge pack with snowshoes strapped on top. I didn't see a single maintenance vehicle or another person. No skiers. No dog drivers. Huge snow drifts choked the road into the Savage campground, and I needed my snowshoes.

I set up my tent in the extreme upriver end of the campground in sparse timber, where the wind scours down to bare ground. There is no snow within a twenty-five-foot radius of my tent. This site will be fine until the wind blows. Judging by the ski and dogsled-runner tracks that led here, I am not the first to use this site. When finally I crawl into my bag, it is calm, clear, and plus sixteen degrees.

APRIL 3, 1978. After melting snow and boiling it on my backpack stove, I ate a hurried breakfast of instant oatmeal washed down with black tea. Afterward I walked downstream through the willows along the river. A mile from camp, small oval bird tracks, looping in strings from bush to bush, led me along. I had no idea that I had encountered anything unusual until I saw the holes the birds had burrowed into the snow for overnight protection from the cold. By their size and depth I knew that they were made by white-tailed ptarmigan, which are not common in the park, the northern limit of their range. Just beyond the Savage River bridge I found the flock.

Of the three kinds of ptarmigan, only the white-tailed turn entirely white in winter. The willow and rock ptarmigan, although also white in winter, have black tail feathers, and male rock ptarmigan have black eye stripes. Huge obsidian eyes are the only break in the white-tailed ptarmigan's complete winter camouflage.

Here and on the north side of the Talkeetna Mountains, all three species of ptarmigan share portions of the same range. Willows usually keep to the flats and thickets, and white-tailed and rock ptarmigans to the summits and tundra hillsides. During severe weather, or times of deep snow that buries mountain plants, the latter two species move downhill. In Canada rock ptarmigan have been known to migrate eight hundred miles or more to their winter range. Willow ptarmigan may also go on long annual treks, but whitetails usually shift only altitudinally. The three species have different shaped and sized bills, as well as perhaps different alimentary systems, each adapted to specific foods. With its more generalized bill, the whitetail has somewhat more versatility and can shift diet and is not so often forced to compete with the others for scarce winter forage.

This flock no doubt lives in this general vicinity both winter and summer. Tolerant and unafraid, the birds allowed me to approach. I sat down in the snow near one bird. A dark eye blinked at me, but the bird did not move. Through my camera lens I studied the luminous eye, the black bill, and general shape of the resting bird. Each tiny feather across the back and over the feet was exquisitely formed. A bird the color of winter.

Although I could feel only slight warmth from the sun, it seemed the birds had deliberately picked an exposed location. Ptarmigan can withstand tremendous cold—in experiments captive birds have been subjected to temperatures as low as minus eighty without suffering adverse effects—but I can't help but wonder if these birds anticipate the warmth of summer as much as I do.

APRIL 5, 1978. Minus five and clear. The wind blew all day, lowering the effective temperature to below zero. In the afternoon I surprised a richly colored, full-furred red fox napping near the sled trail just beyond Savage River. It lay curled in a ball on a little knoll fifty feet from the trail, fluffy tail wrapped over its legs and muzzle up to the eyes. When I stopped moving, the fox was up in an instant, but when I didn't approach, it curled back into a ball. I'd had a long day on snowshoes looking for ptarmigan. Tired, hungry, and cold, I headed for camp, leaving the fox glowing with the fire of the scarlet evening light.

APRIL 5, 1976. While driving north on the Parks Highway, I spotted a large bird perched in the top of a small spruce by the lake next to the railroad crossing. I turned around and went back. My first glance was correct: a bald eagle, an uncommon sight here. Most bald eagles congregate along the coast or along interior rivers or lakes where fish are abundant. On the other hand, golden eagles usually inhabit mountainous regions where they hunt rodents, hares, and birds, rather than fish. Just recently the goldens have returned from their winter migrations. At a distance, immature bald and golden eagles can be misidentified; goldens have fully feathered legs, bald eagles don't. No mistaking this mature bird, however: white head and tail, golden legs and eyes.

All too soon the eagle wiggles its tail, flexes its wings, then flaps into the air and away across the forest. I wish I could see it soaring in front of the mountain.

APRIL 6, 1980. Awoke early this morning to a terrific caterwauling coming from the slope behind the cabin — a sound like that of a child in pain. Once my mind cleared, I recognized it as the wailing of a lynx.

I leaped out of bed, got dressed in everything handy, and went out. The new-moon darkness was complete. A light breeze soughed through the spruce. Motionless, I tracked the lynx by sound as it moved along the ridge parallel to the cabin. Then its yowling, although much amplified, sounded like that of a housecat in heat. Knowing that lynx are sometimes called by hunters, I tried imitating its call. Silence. Then a loud wail startled me. I remained silent as the lynx continued. After a while the sounds died away, and I slipped back inside, uncertain whether I was shivering from the cold or from the preternatural night cry.

APRIL 7, 1980. Awake and dressed at first light. After feeding the stove, I went outside to discover oval lynx tracks crisscrossing the yard, one print on the woodshed step. I backtracked onto the ridge before following the winding trail through the yard. Just as I was about to go back to the cabin, movement beyond the shed caught my attention.

Under a spruce not fifty yards from the outhouse, the lynx lay watching me. My pulse quickened as we exchanged extended stares. Although it seemed unlikely that the lynx would stay long enough for me to get my camera, I backed away toward the cabin. I was inside only a minute. With camera and telephoto lens, I hurried back, expecting the lynx to be gone, but it was still there. I stepped off the packed trail into the soft snow and moved cautiously forward. When the lynx stood up, I squatted down, braced my camera and focused. Through the lens I gazed into the hooded, golden eyes.

The lynx was almost silver in color, its guard hairs tipped in black. A shaggy, black-streaked, silver ruff framed its oval face. Long, delicate whiskers extended from either side of the pink nose. Tufts topped the ears.

Soon enough I remembered to snap a few pictures, but photography was oddly an afterthought. In one easy movement the lynx stretched, turned around, and padded away on its oversized paws. Just before it ducked under a spruce limb, it paused for one last look back, its stubby, black-ringed tail twitching. Then it was gone.

Over breakfast tea I looked up a passage that I partially remembered from *Arctic Prairies*, Ernest Thompson Seton's great book. "Of all the northern creatures none are more dependent on the rabbits than is the Canada Lynx. It lives on rabbits, follows the rabbits, thinks rabbits, tastes like rabbits, increases with them, and on their failure dies of starvation in the unrabbited woods."

APRIL 8, 1980. Plus six and snowing. Still thinking about the lynx's supple grace as it glided atop the snow. A consummate hare catcher. It was surprising then to read Charles Sheldon's account of a young Dall ram brought down by a lynx. Because of the disparity in size—the sheep weighed 115 pounds and the lynx 20—if Sheldon hadn't caught the lynx in the act, a natural assumption would have been that the lynx had merely happened on a ram carcass. In Alaska such attacks on large mammals must be considered rare and usually occur after the dramatic crash of the hare population, when is little else for the lynx to eat. It is somewhat surprising how easily people convict an animal seen feeding at a carcass as its killer. Certainly a gray jay or magpie that feeds on a dead moose cannot be considered responsible for the death, but if a wolf or lynx is seen feeding there, it is accepted as irrefutable proof of guilt. Many reports of predation are nothing more than acts of scavenging. Additional circumstances, such as cold, snow, ice, disease or injury, youth or old age, usually play a part in most predation.

In 1986 on Riley Creek, John Burch found evidence that a lynx had killed a full-curl ram. The lynx had chased the ram down a steep gully and onto the ice, where the ram broke through a dry hole. As the ram came up out of the hole, the lynx jumped on its back. John found the carcass soon after the kill. A hole had been eaten in the back of the ram's neck and the animal was still warm. Later, both a lynx and a wolverine fed at the carcass.

APRIL 9, 1979. Finally. The white moose. For over two years, I've searched both inside and outside the park for this unusual cow. Many people have seen her, including a few photographers, but until today, she remained a legend for me. John Hewitt and I were driving back from a ptarmigan hunt when we saw the white moose and her yearling calf feeding in the willows about one-quarter mile from the Parks Highway just north of Healy. She was even more remarkable than described. She stood out like a neon sign, her whiteness stark against the drab brown willows. We watched her from the road for a while, then Hewitt dropped me off with my cameras, promising to come back later.

I approached as carefully as I knew how, walking in a slow zigzag, never in a direct beeline. Each time one looked up from feeding, I'd stop moving and look in another direction. It was hard to suppress the desire to rush right over. Even around bears, I've seldom been so on edge. I'd heard that the cow was shy of people; perhaps she knew she was vulnerable. I had my 400mm lens on the camera. Even so, I'd have to be fairly close for a good picture.

I crouched behind my tripod. Through the lens I got my first good look at the cow and yearling and solved one big mystery. She was not an albino but a true white moose. Albinos have pink eyes; hers are brown, and her snow-white coat is dotted with several brown spots, including one the size of a small tangerine on her right side, just behind the right foreleg. Her nose is pink and her ears salt-and-pepper. Her hooves are black. She's a large, mature moose that, judging by her paunchiness, seems to have wintered well.

Her yearling is a bull and a real marvel. With white blaze and brown ears, he's marked somewhat like a pinto horse. His lower body is brown and black, but his shoulders and saddle are salt-and-pepper.

This is the third spring in a row that a white moose has been seen in this general area. Probably this adult is the same animal that has been seen in the park near Savage River each of the last two Septembers. Her range easily could be this large: calving near Healy in the spring, moving into the Savage drainage for autumn breeding season. Sightings of white moose are not infrequent here. *That autumn, Johnny Johnson saw a white cow near Savage River. In April 1990 a white cow moose, most likely a different one, was seen often along the Parks Highway north of Healy. In mid-October 1989 a patrol ranger saw a white cow at Mile 17 of the Park Road. "I thought somebody's horse had gotten loose," she said. North of the park, white moose are now protected by law from hunters.* They have been seen along the Park Road, mostly near Wonder Lake and Kantishna, as well as north of the park between the Parks Highway and Stampede. Park Service biologist Will Troyer published a report that listed sightings back to 1927.

He estimates at least two or three different white moose could be present in the population at any one time and theorizes that such animals are more susceptible not only to human hunters but to predators as well, despite the possibly protective winter camouflage.

I exposed several rolls of film before the pair browsed into the heavy timber and lay down. At one point, the yearling and the cow fed within thirty yards of me. Maybe the extra care given the stalk had paid off. A little later in the spring, with a new calf at her side, I doubt she'll be quite so tolerant.

Hewitt returned, and I walked away, leaving the moose to their sleepy ruminations.

APRIL 10, 1988. Minus five. Clear. Faint light in the western sky at midnight last night. Today we enjoy fourteen-plus hours of daylight. I arose early to watch the hares in the willows surrounding the cabin. Each morning this week, pairs have chased each other in circles through the willows. Yesterday four ran single file in winding loops through the bushes and around the cabin. When two hares come face to face, they stop, stare a moment, then bound high into the air as if spring-loaded. The chase then begins again. Breeding season is at hand.

At peak numbers hares struggle to find enough to eat. Gnawed and half-eaten spruce boughs litter the snow. A few hares are even chewing on the outhouse door built of cedar.

What wonderful names describe the same animal: *varying hare* and *snowshoe hare.* Their elongated, furred hind feet enable them to travel easily over the deepest snow, where other animals would flounder. And twice a year, when hormonal output waxes and wanes in response to changing daylight, hares change color, white to brown, brown to white. In just the last three days, some hares — about half of those I've seen — have begun to turn color. Each pelage phase is actually a mixture of colors. A winter hare has dark underfur, as well as a few colored guard hairs. A summer hare's pelt is a mixture of white, brown, and tan.

Lately I've been observing one particular hare, or at least I *think* it is the same animal. Always, at the same time of day, it is in the same exact covert. Four days ago it had a few brown hairs showing about the back; today it is one-quarter brown. Soon, even though snow will still cover the ground, the varying hare will be as brown as the exposed ground. Not uncommonly, however, hares are out of synch with ground cover—white on bare ground or brown on the snow. Chinook winds that bring early thaws can make hares as vulnerable to predators as early snows.

APRIL 11, 1973. We are now at the peak of the hare population cycle. Everywhere in the forest, and along forest edges, are the signs. Near Mile 9 on the Park Road, I paced out the boundaries of an acre plot of ideal habitat, spruce mixed with willow and birch. I could not find a section of snow larger than four square feet that did not have hare tracks crossing it, plus droppings in astonishing quantity.

When populations peak, prime habitat becomes saturated, forcing hares into marginal areas where food is scarce and survival tenuous. Hares were numerous in 1913 when Archbishop Hudson Stuck's expedition made the first ascent of Mount McKinley. A snowshoe hare followed the party's trail to the 10,000-foot level before turning back, subsisting off bark gnawed from the willow wands used to mark the trail. Stuck speculated that the hare had taken a wrong turn in its migration from the crowded valley below. "Unless the ambition for first ascents have reached the leporidae," he wrote, "this seems the only explanation."

Hare populations can build quickly. Hares breed at one year of age. Although few live past three and a half years, a female will produce two to four litters a year: two on the decline of the cycle, four on the upswing. Research in Alberta documented birth rates of 18.6 young per female during the upswing of the cycle and 8.6 per female on the downswing. After a gestation period of thirty-five to forty days, the baby hares are born in an unlined "form," a mere hollow in the ground. Unlike rabbits, the leverets—as baby hares are called—are born fully furred, wide-eyed, and able to walk soon after birth. Within one week they are eating vegetation. Females breed shortly thereafter. Even considering such remarkable fecundity, it's amazing to learn that in Alberta, populations reach a density of 5,900 hares per square mile. (Two male and two female Arctic hares were placed on Brunette Island in Fortune Bay, Newfoundland, and six reproductive seasons later, there were 1,000 hares on the island.) Near Fairbanks, hares recently peaked at an estimated 1,900 hares per square mile. In the prime habitat of the park, densities may reach those documented for the Fairbanks area. It is commonly believed that hares cycle every eight to eleven years, but localized cyclic fluctuations occur within that time span.

APRIL 12, 1973. Plus ten, overcast. The road opened to Savage River a few days ago, and I've been out watching hares every morning. Because they are mostly nocturnal, I have to be out early to see any activity at all. This morning I found the oval prints of a lynx crossing and crisscrossing the thicket. Sometime last night it had come up from the creek bottom and hunted the forest edge. Although I tracked and backtracked, I could not tell whether it had made a kill. Its tracks were a good five or six inches across, bigger than tea saucers and lightly pressed into the snow. On snowshoes I sank eight inches deep.

Hares can do a phenomenal amount of damage to their habitat. In this thicket, almost every woody plant shows damage to a height about twenty-four inches above snow level, or about as high as a hare can reach. The brush is girdled and in some cases broken. This habitat degradation, not disease and predation, is now believed to be the most probable reason for the sudden crash of hare populations.

Overabundance results in habitat destruction and leads ultimately to starvation. With poor nutrition, reproductive success falls off, litters get smaller, the breeding pairs suffer, predators become more successful, and cold and winter storms become more dangerous. All the predators whose numbers have increased along with hares will suffer population crashes, too: lynx and great horned owls especially, but also goshawks, foxes, and coyotes. Wolves are affected less. After the hares crash, perhaps as soon as one year later, fewer owls, fox, and lynx will hunt the taiga and tundra.

APRIL 13, 1979. Calm and minus two yesterday morning. This morning a slight breeze and plus ten.

The sun rises over the mountains earlier each day now. Like bears rousing from winter sleep, people seem more alive, vibrant, and happy. Although it is still cold, the sun makes all the difference.

This morning I decided to ski up Riley Creek. To enjoy the sun I stayed along the timber's edge, avoiding the wind. Except for a few open places where the current runs strongest, the creek was still frozen, buried in snow. In some places I could hear the creek rumbling over the boulders below, stirring wistful memories of open water purling over gravel.

Two spruce grouse interrupted my ski. (Perhaps if I had a more perfect mastery of cross-country skiing, I'd have missed them. I was picking myself up when I saw the grouse at the edge of the timber.) A cock was strutting before a hen. Both were almost gunmetal blue, but the hen paled next to the cock's flamboyance. His feathers were richer and edged in vibrant white. He strutted with fanned tail and stiffened wings held at his side. A distinct rustle of fluffed-out feathers accompanied each movement. Closing in on the hen, he stopped, preened, then rushed closer. He scratched at the ground like a common barnyard rooster showing his toughness.

With what seemed complete disinterest, the hen pecked at the duff under a tree and turned away. When he rushed her, she took off through the timber, dodging and weaving through the trees, her ardent suitor in close pursuit.

APRIL 13, 1976. Reached Savage Campground after a long, cold trek in. Though it was well above zero, the head wind the last six miles lowered the effective temperature.

Before setting up the tent, I had to clear away several inches of loose snow. It took very little effort to reach bare ground. In the shelter of the trees the snow had yet to compact, but snow conditions are changing. It is still cold at night, often above zero. By midday, however, there's sufficient solar heating to melt the surface layer. A few more days of this kind of weather (plus ten degrees at six A.M., forty at two P.M.) and I'll be able to walk on top of the concrete-hard snow for at least a couple of hours each day. Perhaps as of yet the subnivean world of the vole and shrew is unaffected by the approach of thaw, but soon life there, too, will change as water flows into their hideaways.

When the sun dipped behind the mountains, I crawled into the tent and hurriedly wriggled into my bag; the nylon was shockingly cold on unprotected skin. Soon my shivering eased, and I dozed off, only to awaken to the sounds of something passing by in the snow. I looked out and saw two moose moving through the timber, browsing willows. I drifted off to sleep to the sound of their feeding.

APRIL 14, 1976. Clear and calm this morning. I have no thermometer, but to judge by the frost on my bag and on the inside of the tent and by the sharp tingle in my nose when I inhale, it must be below zero. Here at Savage, winter hasn't loosened its grip much — the elevation makes a difference.

It is hard to get out of my sleeping bag. I toss and turn and play mind games. "Five more minutes and do it." Five minutes pass. "It's not that bad. Just get dressed, and you'll be warm." Time drags. "Sun'll be up, and you'll still be in bed." I roll over. "It's so *warm* in here." A ptarmigan's calling nearby works better than an alarm clock. When a second bird joins in the reveille, I brutally unzip the bag three-quarters its length. "Get dressed or freeze, turkey."

I hurry to melt snow for my tea and instant oatmeal. There is very little moisture content in the snow, and it takes many scoops to fill a quart pot with water. The air is cold enough that the gasoline stove requires preheating. I eat my oatmeal, but I am still cold and shivering. I make a second cup of tea, and it goes cold in what seems seconds.

It doesn't take long to find the ptarmigan. In fact, they are everywhere. Large numbers have concentrated in the thickets at the confluence of Jenny Creek and Savage River. Long skeins of oval tracks lead from one bush to another, one thicket to the next. Curled droppings littering the snow indicate that the birds have been here for some time. I move easily on my snowshoes but not as easily as the birds do on theirs. My snowshoes give me support on the snow but no warmth. In fact, the bindings are constricting and often cause my feet to be cold. A ptarmigan's full-feathered feet and toes not only act as snowshoes but also insulate from the cold.

On Jenny Creek, a hundred yards upstream from the Savage, I locate a covey of willow ptarmigan. They are moving through the brush, nipping buds and twigs from the willows. It's always such a pleasant treat to encounter them. First, there seems to be nothing ahead but snow and ice; then the snow begins to move. Sometimes it even flies. "Oh"—the dull-witted mind connects—"ptarmigan."

They are so beautiful and delicate looking in their white winter plumage. One bird, a male, already has begun to molt, and a few dark-colored feathers show on his neck. All the other birds in this covey of fifty or more seem to be unchanged. Soon, of course, they will begin the transformation from winter white to summer brown. The males change first, then the females. This molt, just like the pelage change of hares, is hormonal, triggered by increasing daylight.

Not one of these ptarmigan has flown an inch since I first spooked them. They prefer to run from danger. Flying takes too much precious energy in a habitat that allows little margin for waste.

In too short a time, the wind begins to blow, and despite the sun's feeble heat, I am chilled through. I head toward camp to build a small warming fire.

APRIL 15, 1976. Late last night the wind picked up, threatening the tent. I struggled out of my bag and into my clothes. In the dark I placed the rocks from the campfire ring on top of the tent pegs — a bitterly cold exercise. Back in the tent I shivered into my bag but not to sleep, kept awake by the cold and the loud flapping nylon. Later I awoke to silence. The wind had ushered in a weather front and with it a silent snowfall.

Because of thick snow and reduced visibility I stayed in camp this day, in the tent and by the fire. At least it is warmer and the wind is calm.

APRIL 16, 1976. High overcast this morning, six inches of new snow. Brisk breeze. Snowshoed out to the Park Road, stashed the snowshoes in the willows, and walked the road to Savage Canyon. In the narrow point of the gorge, where it was compressed by the natural venturi of the canyon walls, the wind blew hard enough to knock me down. I struggled from rock to rock, avoiding sections of ice in areas that otherwise would have been easy walking. Not too far uphill were the Dall sheep (named for naturalist William H. Dall). They moved in a ground blizzard, seeking refuge in the lee of rocks. I had intended to photograph them, but it would be next to impossible today, so I turned back. Hiking toward the road was more work than coming down-canyon. I had to really lean into the wind. On the ice I slid backward one step for every two gained. By the bridge where the canyon widens, the wind lessened somewhat, but I was chilled to the bone.

With most of the morning gone, I decided to pack up and head out of the park a few hours early. On the long walk back I was struck by the significance of what I was doing. The ability to *leave* always seems the most potent difference between animals and human visitors to the park. We humans can always go someplace else (for shelter, relief, or amusement), but the animals haven't the luxury. On the long slope just above Headquarters, where I'd parked my truck, I thought about a hot meal and shower. I thought, too, of the sheep crouched in the rocks, waiting for the wind to die away, so they could more easily paw through the snow for something to eat.

APRIL 17, 1986. Near Mile 9 I saw the first porcupine of spring. One hundred yards from the road, a spruce tree about twelve inches in diameter and perhaps twenty feet tall was debarked nearly from snow line to crown, a remarkable degree of damage. A porky clung to the far side of the tree, busily gnawing away at a patch of bark. The ground below was littered with droppings, bits of bark, small boughs. Tracks radiated outward from the trunk, not just those of the porcupine but the imprints of a fox and a small wolf, as well. Probably the fox and wolf had been attracted by scent or by the sound of gnawing.

My approach unnerved the porcupine, and it climbed higher, its long claws digging into the near-barkless trunk, the bristly underside of its tail offering support as it inched upward. Porcupines are generally nocturnal and spend the day sleeping in crevices or hollow trees. Perhaps this one was a little more nervous than usual because of its daylight foray. When I halted, it stopped climbing to peer down myopically, its nose twitching for scent. I remained motionless, and the porky soon began gnawing on another bit of bark. It looked to be a large porcupine, perhaps twenty-five pounds.

Thousands of tooth marks covered the bare wood. I wondered what singled out this tree for such attention. In winter porcupines feed on needles and bark. Winter home ranges are small, about thirty-six acres, and porcupines stay close to preferred trees and shelters. During the summer, porcupines feed more on the ground, eating roots, stems, leaves, berries, seeds, nuts, and flowers. But they eat bark at all times. Most seem to gnaw from different trees at random, but this tree was about as bare as a log in a log cabin. Near the Toklat River, in an area called the Porcupine Forest, there are many trees peeled like this one. I picked up a few quills from beneath the tree, fingered their backward-pointing barbs, then skied on, leaving the porky to its task.

APRIL 18, 1981. Igloo Campground. Plus eight and clear. Walked the road to the rise above Sanctuary, then skied across country until rejoining the road just before the Teklanika bridge. In spite of the flounderings I call skiing, it was rather easy crossing the rolling tundra between Sanctuary and Igloo: a good, solid base to ski on and to drag my sled over. I'd have kept to the road despite the extra distance if cross-country travel had meant backpacking the load. I saw several flocks of ptarmigan and some old tracks that might have been wolverine.

After setting up the tent, I walked a short way up the road, feeling the soreness in my legs and shoulders. What won't a person go through sometimes just to watch a few sheep? It has been a long winter with many personal demands and little exercise of this nature. Does this type of activity toughen me up, or does it just wear out the flimsy human machine? Right now my machine feels like it could use an overhaul.

There's little snow on the slopes in Igloo Canyon. The wind blows hard here, and the road and hillsides are mostly bare. In a few places the road is lost beneath enormous drifts. Plows are just now working this way from Teklanika. It was nice to get here first. There are lots of old runner and sled dog tracks on the road. Perhaps those of a wolf, too, or maybe it was just a loose dog following a team. Moose have been in the campground. Lots of tracks and droppings. Every willow in the campground has been browsed by them. The timber offers good shelter from the wind and blocks some of the snow.

There's little snow under the thick spruce in the rear of the campground, and my tent awaits me there. I could camp anywhere this time of year, but because I am traveling alone, I prefer to set up in predictable places. Before turning in, I look at the ranger cabin, obviously much used this winter by dog drivers. Nail-studded "bear boards" shutter the windows. For perhaps the hundredth time, I wished I could winter in this cabin and watch the seasons change. Later I fell asleep to an owl hooting from a tree nearby.

APRIL 20, 1981. Just before first light I heard wolves howling in the distance. Their song came faintly at first, hidden as it was by the wind, but in a lull it came vibrantly to life. To the east beyond the frozen, muted stream, over the sparse timber thickets and snowy swales, perhaps as far as the Teklanika itself in the very shadow of Double Mountain, two, maybe three, wolves sang at the fading stars.

Today's hike to Tattler Creek from Igloo was made easy by yesterday's late afternoon passage of heavy equipment. It has taken the crews two weeks to work from Savage to Igloo. No matter how much snow falls each winter, the concretelike drifts are always bad on Primrose Ridge, Sable, Polychrome, and Highway passes, Stony Hill, and the approaches to Eielson visitor center. Clearing the road is neither easy nor safe. Tracked and wheeled vehicles can skid on ice. On April 29, 1964, bulldozer operator R. W. Cullers was killed during snow removal operations when his D-8 bulldozer went off the road at Mile 51. One of the drivers told me that it may take two weeks to clear huge drifts off the road from Tattler Creek to the East Fork River, a distance of about six miles.

Just a quarter of a mile from the road, I found a band of sheep to photograph, mostly yearlings and ewes, and two very young rams. In their winter pelage the sheep look much bigger than they do in summer, but in fact, after coping with the cold and winds of winter, these sheep now must be at their annual low point in body weight. I am very careful moving around them, not wanting to disturb them in the least or add to their stress. Although spring still seems a long way off, lambing is only a little over a month away, and many of the ewes are likely pregnant. As soon as the snow is gone and the threat of severe weather is past, the lambs will arrive; the summer ahead will be their chance to grow strong before winter once again descends on the mountains.

The sheep wander and graze on exposed vegetation and paw through the snow for buried feed. Although it is sunny and only a light wind is blowing, I find it hard to stay warm. In late afternoon when I finally do head back to camp, most of the sheep are ruminating in their beds in the snow. After the long, dark winter, this day must seem almost tropical to the sheep.

APRIL 21, 1972. All winter the willow ptarmigan have been silent, but now they are both visible and vocal. The cocks call from almost any conspicuous location. They are in the tops of willows and spruce crowns, on rock promontories, and on the road edge. Not only are they attempting to attrack hens but to protect and identify their territories as well. Unlike the females, which molt quickly from white to brown, cock willow ptarmigan retain the white wings and body through the spring. But their necks and heads turn a beautiful chestnut. Perched high on a willow or spruce and silhouetted against the azure boreal sky, the cock ptarmigan in spring breeding plumage is one of Alaska's most beautiful birds. His croaking call on an early spring morning heralds the joy of survival and birth.

APRIL 22, 1988. Forty-five degrees above zero today. Three weeks ago, the low was minus twenty. Five weeks ago, minus forty. Today, then, is eighty-five degrees warmer. Snow has turned to slush, and everything is dripping or running water. Travel off the road is impossible now. So begins the transition from snow and ice to bare ground and open water. In some of the higher elevations, depending on annual snowfall, this transition can make backcountry travel difficult or impossible into mid-June. Both humans and animals find the thaw difficult. Large animals like moose must use incredible amounts of energy to power short distances through the chest-deep slop. Foxes and other small predators flounder, and in the subnivean world, the mice, voles, and shrews often die in their flooded burrows and runways. Even the spring thaw here is another test of survival.

APRIL 24, 1975. Plus twenty-eight and snowing. Winter again. It's difficult to accept this wind-driven snow blasting through the trees, these whiteouts on the tundra. No wonder the worst cabin fever comes this time of year. A taste of spring and summer, days of sunshine and solar heating, then a midwinter storm. Terribly confining in the cabin. I spend the morning splitting wood and shoveling snow that I know will melt in a few days, perhaps even tomorrow. Anything to be outside. I almost ache with anticipation. *Will this winter never end?*

APRIL 26, 1978. Another clear day. Snow soupy and the dirt roads turned to muck. What a difference a few clear days make. I saw a moose bedded in the willows near Riley Creek when I drove to park Headquarters this morning for a long chat with chief Ranger Gary Brown. (We talked about a code of ethics for professional wildlife photographers, one designed to eliminate obvious wildlife harassment without punishing concientious photographers. As is often the case, these types of regulations come about because of the actions of a few and usually end up being written for the lowest common denominator.) Six hours later, the moose was still lying in the snow. "What patience," I thought. *Patience?* The word was hollow. Perhaps the moose didn't have the energy to rise and travel in the soft snow. Maybe it was injured. Or perhaps it was just chewing its cud through the warm afternoon. There could be any number of reasons for its immobility. Patience, however, connotes waiting, a concept related to the passage of time. Time is man's invention; its passage is unrecognized by animals. One dictionary's definition, however, seems appropriate to animals: "quiet perseverance."

APRIL 27, 1978. Overcast. Horned owl songs ringing through the woods each night this past week. The snow has melted enough to permit limited travel in the timber now that the snow shadows under the trees have expanded and joined. But the underlying soil is so thoroughly frozen that the water stays on the surface and does not soak in. Even small rivulets are in flood. Many voles and shrews, which spend their lives beneath the snow or under the grass and in the soil, are forced out. Boreal and great horned owls are not the only ones to take advantage. Yesterday I saw a gray jay pounce on a shrew as it scurried across the snow.

Today, despite yesterday's snowfall, from the timber came the sweet song of the ruby-crowned kinglet, its rich melody another harbinger of summer.

APRIL 29, 1979. Snowy tracks crossing the road near Mile 5. *Grizzly.* When I saw the tracks, snow fallen from its legs and paws was still melting on the warming tarmac, so I guessed that the bear must have crossed within the last hour or so. Just down the hill are the remains of a moose that wolves have fed upon. A local who has kept an interested but infrequent watch on the kill told me there was nothing left but bones. He showed me a deformed jaw that he thought might be evidence the moose was a winter kill, not a wolf kill. The grizzly was probably attracted by the scent. Even though the bear was headed away from the kill, I didn't go down for a look. No telling when that bear, or another, would come back.

APRIL 30, 1984. Plus forty-eight, clear and calm. It seemed downright hot today. Went on a walk in the woods near Riley Creek looking for hares but instead found a huge squirrel midden at the base of a spruce. Shredded cones and shards, piled two feet deep in the middle, tapered twelve feet out from the tree. Lots of holes where the squirrels had tunneled into the midden. Not a bad idea, living in the middle of your winter's stores. These stockpiles may contain mushrooms, buds, berries, and the bark of woody plants, but their main ingredient is spruce cones. In one study, Fred Dean fed captive squirrels a monodiet of white spruce cones; each consumed about 144 cones per day. Although it wasn't the largest midden I'd ever seen, I wondered how many cones went into this cache—and how many squirrels shared it. People talk about the industrious beaver, but beavers have nothing on squirrels when it comes to winter preparedness.

Spring

Just as the cock ptarmigan crows its spring benediction,
willow catkins herald the rebirth.

MAY 1, 1976. Broken, scudding clouds. Plus forty-eight at eight A.M., sixty-two at two P.M., the snow disappearing fast, almost before our eyes. Trumpeter swans and Canada geese are passing overhead, a few of the swans swinging low over the inlet to the lake. This is the spring waterfowl migration north through the mountains. Some flocks of geese appear to pass quite close to the summit of Denali itself. The few cranes I've seen going north seem to aim for the mountain as if it is a navigational aid. I wonder what it would be like to be a climber on a glacier or on the long pull up the ridge to the mountain's summit and see flocks of geese honking by. Climbers tell of ravens on the mountain that raid food caches and garbage pits. But ravens are birds of mystery and magic; geese are birds of migration and movement, symbols of flights to far places. How confining it must be to tie into a rope and with labored breath inch up an icefall, only to witness such freedom. All I know is that each morning that I awaken to the sound of passing waterfowl, I'm swamped with an overpowering urge to follow.

MAY 2, 1980. Clear and calm. Although it's only forty-five or fifty degrees, the day seems hot. Dodging snow patches, I hiked in a T-shirt. In late afternoon, after spending the day photographing ptarmigan, I noticed two white cumulus clouds puffing up above the southeastern summits. *Cumulus.* Would the significance of this be lost on all but those who spend the winter in Alaska? All winter the clouds advance in flat streaks and great gray fronts. Those now rising on the horizon are very different, more typical of Interior Alaska summers. What a fine gift so early in May: summer clouds in a summer sky. T-shirt weather.

MAY 3, 1980. Only a few snow patches cling to the shadowed forest thickets around Horseshoe Lake. Looking for spruce grouse, I found instead a moose antler dropped sometime last fall. Already porcupines and small rodents have gnawed craters and gaping holes in the palm, their source of phosphorous and calcium. Nearby I found a number of quills, not the huge pile that would be the porcupine's mortal remains, but enough to indicate some struggle. Perhaps a coyote or wolverine had tested this dangerous prey. I've seen quill-injured specimens of both, as well as foxes and, once, a female brown bear. Sourdoughs claim that wolves seldom attack porcupines. Smaller predators face death from starvation with a mouth full of quills. I suspect this porcupine escaped under its armor and eventually climbed to safety in a nearby tree.

MAY 6, 1973. Willow catkins are now blossoming everywhere. A close look reveals delicate shades of red, yellow, purple, and blue. Silken tips almost glow when backlit by the sun. I spent hours today attempting to capture on film both the highlighting and the colors hidden within a catkin's flower cluster. The faint breeze stirred the willows, wiggling them at the wrong moments.

There are forty-three species of willow in Alaska, but because there are many hybrid forms, they are often hard to tell apart. Today I worked on the catkins of the felt-leafed willow. In one was the nest of a redpoll, a small tundra finch, lined with willow silk.

A superficial look at some willow thickets would give the impression that willows are of even height and branch structure, as tidy as some cultivated, pruned shrubs. And *pruned* is exactly the word. Moose, the gardeners, are primarily browsers. That is, they live off the leaves, twigs, and stems of woody plants, rather than graze on grass. They depend heavily on willows for sustenance. But at certain times of the year, even the grazers, sheep and caribou, utilize this nutritious plant. (On Kodiak Island, I once saw a brown bear eating them.) Ptarmigan and hares also rely in part on willows. All of this heavy cropping, especially in winter when moose break down some of the tallest stems, keeps the willows from growing very tall. Without the heavy use, many willows would grow taller and fuller. An examination of the plants themselves often gives resource managers an indication of seasonal usage, the quality of the habitat, and population estimates. It seems rather fitting, then, that the one plant that more than any other is responsible for sustaining life here blooms first.

MAY 7, 1977. Overcast, light rain falling. There seem to be three other campers at Teklanika Campground, probably early-arriving Park Service seasonals and hotel staff.

Just behind my campsite, there's a ground squirrel community. One squirrel was busily gathering and hauling to its burrow huge mouthfuls of fireweed fluff. Back and forth it went from fireweed patch to den, carrying load after load, pausing only to check for danger. Perhaps this squirrel has only recently ended its seven-month-long hibernation and is either renewing the insulation or preparing a chamber for its young. Despite such arch enemies as foxes, wolves, eagles, and bears, the squirrels must appreciate the sunshine and freedom after so long a time spent underground.

A recent landmark study by Dr. Brian Barnes revealed that a hibernating arctic ground squirrel can lower its body temperature below thirty-two degrees F. for as long as three weeks without its blood freezing. This phenomenon has been observed in cold-blooded vertebrates such as frogs, fish, and turtles, but never before in any warm-blooded animal. For an animal that may hibernate eight to ten months, this supercooling is a mechanism for increased winter survival. Body temperatures have been measured as low as twenty-seven degrees F. in wild populations and twenty-four degrees in the laboratory.

MAY 8, 1987. Nice quiet day wandering the thickets along the Nenana looking and listening for birds. Varied thrushes were the most easily noted. Many birds have beautiful, descriptive names, like warbler. One can almost hear the call when saying the name. Arctic warbler. Beautiful. Other bird names, though, have no poetry: Crow. Grackle. Scaup. Cowbird. But more often than not, bird names are lyrical. Ruby-crowned kinglet. Harlequin. Wandering tattler. Chickadee. Peregrine. Jaeger. (*Peregrine* means "coming from abroad," a traveler, and is the root of the word *pilgrim. Jaeger*, in German, means "hunter.") Old-squaw. Redpoll. (So true! The male has a striking scarlet forehead and chest in spring.) Turnstone. Even the ubiquitous gray jay has another name, one most attested to by summer visitors: camp robber.

MAY 8, 1980. On the bluff above the Nenana, near a small pond, goshawks nest in a stand of old poplars. It is a typical nest area. I take care when approaching the nest to avoid disturbing the birds but also to avoid becoming a target. Goshawks will attack people; biologists rate them as the world's most aggressive defenders of nests. A goshawk, which derives its name from the Anglo-Saxon *Gos* for geese and *havoc* for hawk—a hawk that hunts geese, is also an aggressive hunter, attacking its prey in the air and on the ground.

Both birds are in the nest vicinity. The female is on the nest, the male close by in a dead tree. Perhaps he has just brought her food—as he will throughout the incubation period. How long they have been incubating the eggs, or how many eggs are in the nest, I don't know. I'll check on them every few days (staying at least at binocular distance) and note the proceedings.

MAY 9, 1980. Once again both birds are near the nest. The female molds herself into the twig nest. It was she that took the lead in courtship. First she chose this site, then screamed to attract a mate. As egg-laying approached she grew ever more defensive of her nest site.

Perhaps because their eyes are almost scarlet, goshawks look incredibly fierce. The back, tail, and wings are glaucous; white chest and head are tipped and streaked with gray. They have black beaks and talons, bright yellow legs. The wings are stubby and the tail long for speed. These birds are ideally suited for twisting flight through woodlands.

MAY 11, 1974. Bird songs from the timber, brush thickets, and tundra swales. Juncos, white-crowned sparrows, kinglets, and robins. Not long ago winter's silence was broken by the sharp, burry whistle of the varied thrush, or the "telephone bird," as a neighbor describes it. I always wonder which I'll hear first, the kinglet or the thrush. Amid all the bird songs now in the forest, the thrush's has, for me at least, the most impact. I almost sigh in relief upon hearing it, glad for the spring tidings it carries.

MAY 12, 1985. Sat by an unnamed creek watching it flood over the rocks. Instead of the easy sluice of water around and over the jumbled stones that I'd see later in summer, the turbid stream crashed and fumed in an almost frantic effort to get down-canyon and mingle with the runoff flooding the plain. It was as if the meltwater could not contain its joy in being loosed from winter's iron grasp.

At one point I jumped up from my contemplation and swung around. *What was that?* I looked left and right, expecting a bear. But no, it was not an animal, or anything seen, but something felt—the sun's warmth on my shoulders. Just as a sleeper can be awakened or aroused by the warmth of a person leaning close over them, the sun, with its unaccustomed warmth, startled me. I sat down, smiling.

MAY 14, 1988. Can it really be sixty degrees today? It feels colder in the wind. Snow patches persist in the shade, but south-facing slopes are bare. Already pasqueflowers are in bloom, even in places where the ground has been exposed only a short while. These exquisite purple blooms look too delicate to withstand the cold spring nights. A closer examination reveals a special adaptation: Tiny hairs cover the stems, a pubescence to ward off the cold. Vernal equinox may have been March 21, but nearly two months later this is truly my first day of spring.

Another sure sign of spring: A motor home with out-of-state plates stopped in the pullout at Mile 11; no doubt its occupants were looking at the mountain.

Spring's pace is quickening. As fast as the ice goes out, water-fowl appear. Goldeneye and scaup on one pond, a common loon on another, a pair of mallards near the outlet to Horseshoe Lake. Today I saw a pair of harlequins on Savage River. They bobbed along in fast water just above the bridge, the river still turbid with runoff. I've often thought of harlequins as sea ducks, for the male's blue plumage with gorgeous russet sides seems associated more with coastal waters than with inland streams. Yet it is mountain streams such as these that they seek out for nesting and the rearing of their broods. Later in the summer, flotillas of harlequin duck-lings will trail the drab hen as she works the fast water that stirs up the larvae and insects they feed upon.

MAY 15, 1977. First mosquito bite of the year. Although for two weeks big blue-black flies have been buzzing around the cabin, inside and out, last night the mosquitoes appeared. Not many, just enough to ruin sleep. These are the extra-large variety that emerge first in the spring, having overwintered as adults by taking refuge under bark, leaves, and duff. They are slow and easy to swat, and except for their drone that disturbs sleep, they are not particularly annoying. Next month (almost always, it seems, on June 10), when the first big hatch of the tiny, fast fliers with the vicious bite descends on us, I'll wistfully recall this first bite and the ease with which I dispatched my tormentor.

MAY 16, 1974. Teklanika. When I awoke at five-thirty, the honey light of dawn was already dappling the spruce. Over breakfast I watched a cow moose work through the almost empty campground, stopping every now and then to stare at the few silent tents and vehicles. She trotted across the last open ground and into the timber. She is not the first moose that I've seen here. Just down the road last night were two cows and a young bull.

After breakfast, I drove west toward the Teklanika bridge. Less than a mile from the campground, where the road swings close to a riverside willow thicket, I stopped for two moose. A cow and yearling stood looking back at me. When I shut off the motor, they turned to face one another. The cow's hackles were raised and her ears back. The yearling held its head low and to the side, its eyes expressive of both surprise and entreaty. Suddenly the cow charged and struck at the yearling with her front hooves. The youngster dodged the vicious kick and ran to the cow's left. For some moments the two circled and feinted before the cow again lashed out, this time striking the yearling in the shoulder. The blow and the accompanying grunt of pain were audible on the road. The yearling crashed through the brush as fast as it could go, the cow in close pursuit. In seconds they were gone into the timber.

Although it seems harsh, all deer, in sharp contrast to mountain sheep, exhibit this violent separation of mother and young. Just prior to calving, the female becomes less and less tolerant of others, even its own progeny. After almost a full year together, the cow turns on its offspring. It may take several aggressive encounters to get the message across. The yearling has enjoyed the full benefit of its mother's protection and knowledge, and it is loath to separate. But leave it must. Soon the spring calf will be born, and all the cow's attention must focus on it. A clumsy yearling hanging about might also draw predators.

MAY 17, 1985. When the snow is first gone, the landscape looks bleak and unattractive. Soon a green blush will enliven the ground cover, but just now the drab tundra slopes are mottled with lingering snow patches and dull green, almost brown, timber thickets. Despite the overcast that seems to mirror the landscape's somber mood, I'm ionized with anticipation. Exciting reports are coming in from the maintenance staff working beyond the Teklanika road closure: of bear sightings, of spring cubs trailing females. Of caribou and big rams on the road. Of wolves. Anita Stelcel saw a pack of six wolves chasing a band of ewes on the slope below Polychrome Summit. *How I wish I could be out there.* The flimsy cable across the road seems a monumental barrier just now.

Each morning, with the sun already shining in the cabin window, I rise earlier than the previous day. It isn't really dark at all at night now, just an hour or two of twilight. Late last night there were only a few stars visible in the pale blue sky, a sharp contrast to winter's seething heavensful. I sleep fitfully, but I can't say why. Is it my incredibly impatient desire for summer? All I know is that I awaken eager to be outside. Soon moose will begin to calve in the forest thickets, and the grizzlies will come searching for them. Then each day, spurred by that one-in-a-thousand chance, I'll be out early, hoping to witness, and perhaps photograph, one of these rarely seen incidents.

MAY 18, 1974. Great horned owls are nesting in the same spruce tree as last year just a short walk from park Headquarters, in an abnormal growth of branches that is caused by a rust, or fungus. At first I didn't think anything was in the nest built atop this so-called witch's broom in the crown of the spruce, but a slight movement compromised the tenants. I got out my binoculars. An owl was tucked down in the nest; only the top of its head and its eyes were visible. It will be impossible to tell how many eggs or young are in the nest until the owlets are quite large. Lots of feathers and pellets at the base of the tree. I must remember to come back later, after the fledglings are gone, to examine the pellets and see what the owls have been eating. Last year many of the pellets contained bones of snowshoe hares.

MAY 19, 1987. Spent the morning hiking the bluffs along the Sanctuary River, ostensibly out for photographs but mostly seeking exercise. Thick shelf ice persists in places at the edge of the flooding river. It would be difficult, if not life-threatening, to attempt to cross the river now.

I saw very few cock ptarmigan and no hens. Probably the hens are hidden on their nests. Returning downstream through the timber, I spooked a spruce grouse. Or rather, it spooked me — scared the hell out of me. Bears were on my mind just then. When the grouse flew up from the base of a small spruce literally inches away, I must have jumped a foot. While catching my breath, I noticed a shallow nest at the base of the tree. In it were seven mottled eggs. It wasn't much of a nest really, just a leaf-lined depression with a few downy feathers. Unlike ptarmigan nests in thickets, this nest was completely exposed except for the overhanging spruce boughs. It was the first grouse nest I'd ever seen.

Not wanting to keep the hen from her nest, I hurried away. While eating lunch back at my vehicle, Gordon Haber drove into the campground. He's been studying park wolves for better than twenty years. I listened to his stories, then decided to see whether the grouse had reclaimed her nest and eggs.

The nest was difficult to find. At first I thought I was searching in the wrong place. I expected to see the nest and the eggs but saw only what I took to be bare ground at the base of the tree. Then with a jolt I realized I was looking directly at the hen. *She was on the nest.* So complete were her camouflage and immobility that she blended right into the duff. Her plumage pattern matched last year's fallen leaves and withered spruce needles. Only an occasional blink of the eye gave her away. I backed off and left her in peace.

MAY 20, 1980. After much searching I found a good vantage point from which to observe the goshawk nest. From a rocky outcrop on a nearby ridge I could look down on the nest and its two downy chicks. When I arrived, the male was feeding them. In its talons it held the remains of a small, brown-furred mammal, perhaps a tree squirrel or young hare, and was tearing bits of flesh away with its hooked beak. Both chicks begged with gaping mouths, but they were not always fed equally. The more aggressive one took most of the flesh from the adult's proffering beak. I can only guess at how long they've been hatched, but clearly, though both are smaller than robins, they already possess a hawk's appetite and demeanor.

MAY 21, 1988. Awaken at five to clear skies, calm winds, and sunlight streaming through the cabin windows. These past few days have brought a greening to the spruce. They are called evergreens, but they do vary in color. In winter, their muted green appears at a distance as gray or brown. In spring, the softening needles turn almost lime green. Crushed in the fingers, they smell rich and fresh after the olfactory sterility of winter. Needles steeped on the stove fill the cabin with a pleasant outdoor fragrance.

More and more birds return each day to the tundra and taiga. Some have come a long way to breed and nest here. Wheatears from Africa. Jaegers from the South Pacific. And though I haven't seen one yet this year, arctic terns back from Antarctica. Savannah sparrows and Lapland longspurs also make impressive migrations, traveling here from as far away as Texas, Kansas, or northern Mexico. Mew gulls are other migrants. These diminutive sea gulls spend the winter along the coast but return to inland waterways to nest. I've seen them perched along the Parks Highway, on the edge of the Park Road, the Savage River bridge, and floating above the Savage, Sanctuary, and Teklanika rivers. If gulls weren't so common, they'd be considered lovely, but they are so ubiquitous, I seldom notice them. I don't know how long they've been back, but their cries are a welcome part of the spring avian concert.

MAY 22, 1974. Although golden eagles long ago returned from their southern wintering grounds, with most pairs now incubating eggs or tending nests, two birds put on an aerial display above Igloo Creek this afternoon. I stopped to watch one eagle's undulating dive, then spotted the second circling high above it. The first eagle would free-fall on folded wings, then brake with a sudden extension of wings, the energy redirected in an upward swoop. At the apex of its upward loop, it would fold its wings for another free-fall. All at once the second eagle, a feathered bomb really, rocketed down upon the first in a lightning stoop. Just as they seemed about to collide, the one eagle banked hard to its right, while the diving bird opened its wings to roll hard left. They then circled into one another, twisting onto their backs to lock talons. With fluttering wings the two went into a spin and fell toward earth. After a hundred-foot fall through several spin rotations, they pulled apart, each going into a series of dives and swoops, gaining and losing altitude in fifty-foot swaths. Finally, in long wingbeats they went out of sight behind the summit of Igloo Mountain.

MAY 22, 1980. Five A.M. Partly sunny. Saw the first calf moose of this spring. About a mile from Teklanika Campground, it was following its mother along the edge of the pond that the bus drivers like to call No Moose Pond. Both stopped to stare at my truck, but when I didn't get out or make noise, they continued around the pond. The russet calf was newborn, wobbling on its spindly legs as it tried to keep up with its long-legged mother.

Watching it struggle over and around twigs and sticks—even the grass was a hindrance—I guessed it to be hours old. The cow stopped to wait for her lagging calf on the north side of the pond. The calf interpreted the halt as a breakfast summons, for it hurried into nursing position. Stepping over her calf, in effect saying no, the cow walked off into the timber.

Almost sixty degrees in early afternoon. Decided to visit the goshawk nest before heading home. One of the adults stood on the nest shielding the young with its fanned tail. For a time each day, the nest is exposed to the direct sun. Without its full foliage the tree offers little protection, so the adults must shield the young not only from cold and storm, but from heat as well. The adult held the pose for almost an hour.

MAY 24, 1980. Spent the evening at Horseshoe Lake. A few thin ice pans floated near the outlet, driven there by the wind. Below the old dam I saw a beaver in the creek, so I hid in the timber as it came closer. In the early 1970s beaver were numerous here, but recently, perhaps because of diminished forage, few have been observed. At one point, some park staffers, thinking the beaver were gone for good, proposed removing the dam so that visitors wouldn't hurt themselves crossing it. Wiser minds prevailed, and the dam was left in place. Beaver disperse [move out] once the accessible forage is removed from near their ponds and waterways, but transients often utilize old lodges. Colonies also have been known to reoccupy previously used sites, even if just for a short while in summer. My suspicion is that the entire colony never really abandoned the lake completely.

To my surprise the beaver crawled out on the bank just six feet away. It came with caution, sniffing the air and squinting into the shadows. Satisfied that no danger lurked nearby—I was downwind and hidden—it wriggled under a blowdown. Through the screening branches I watched as it began to groom, working its paws over its head and muzzle, chest and flanks, oiling its fur with secretions from the castor glands located in a pouch at the base of its tail. Much like a cat grooming itself, the beaver worked its paws, over and over, back and forth, until its auburn fur began to gleam. After grooming, it curled up and appeared to sleep. I slipped away.

On the walk back, I found fresh cuttings by the old lodge on the peninsula. Although I saw very little new willow, aspen, or cottonwood growth near the lake, I hope beaver will again become active here. Perhaps in a few years we will see beaver knifing the water and cutting willows on the bank, and we'll hear the loud *smack!* of a tail warning the colony of danger.

MAY 25, 1984. Half-filled buses roll by on the road newly opened to Toklat. In summer the verdant sward is more easily appreciated, but now the brown hillsides, dotted with patchy snow, roll away under an unrelenting overcast. A cold east wind adds an almost threatening touch. Wildlife activity near the road was nil earlier this morning. These visitors, perhaps on their only visit to Denali Park in a lifetime, are likely to leave with so little.

Because it takes special attention to appreciate the park now, I wonder how many bus passengers will be content with a sighting of a ptarmigan, raven, or caribou. I would bet most want picture-postcard views of the mountain, which isn't often visible this time of year, or of a grizzly by the side of the road. On days like today they are not likely to see either one.

Spring *is* an exciting time, not only because of the new calves, lambs, and cubs, but also because at no other time of the year is there more *life* here. Most of the birds, migrants from around the world, have returned to breed and rear their young. Yet it is possible to do a round trip and see very little. Much wildlife activity occurs early and late in the day, and good wildlife observation is seldom done at thirty-five miles an hour. Also, what passes for abundance here may seem like dearth to visitors from milder latitudes. The subarctic supports very few animals on a per-acre basis. Many visitors are disappointed when they don't see an animal behind every bush. One tour passenger told me that he never expected the park to be so desolate, with so few animals. Denali is not the Serengeti. To expect the same sort of spectacle is the first step to disappointment. As I watch the buses roll by, I hope the passengers see something of great excitement. There is always that chance.

MAY 26, 1977. Up at five A.M. but failed to see a single calf moose. Drove all the way to the Toklat roadblock and saw only a few scattered caribou, ragged in their spring pelage. On the spur of the moment I hitched a ride with a friend to Highway Pass to look for ptarmigan. The road is mostly dry with a few soft spots. It has been plowed free of snow almost to Eielson, many huge drifts having been bulldozed in weeks of work.

On a south-facing slope still partially buried in snow, I hiked a circuitous route from one patch of bare ground to another, in places wading through slushy, knee-high snow. A lot of work just to watch rock ptarmigan. Rock ptarmigan cocks, still dressed in winter white, were perched on a number of tussocks and promontories in defense of their hens and territories. Most were obvious on the bare rock and grass. Some were quite vocal, uttering their peculiar froglike call. It's difficult to understand how the cocks in spring avoid predators, but rarely do they escape gyrfalcons.

Today I saw a ptarmigan avoid a golden eagle. I first saw the eagle soaring over the ridge on which I sat. In the valley below were several conspicuous ptarmigan. Although lacking the speed of a gyrfalcon or the agility of a peregrine, the eagle has an inspiring blur of a stoop. Down the canyon this eagle dived toward a cock ptarmigan perched on a boulder. The ptarmigan saw the eagle and flushed. Instead of flying away, it gained altitude and went into a fast circling maneuver, thwarting the attack. The eagle pulled up, made a couple of tight turns to watch the ptarmigan, then banked and headed away. It apparently had little chance to catch such a speedy bird as a rock ptarmigan. The rock set its wings and sailed to its boulder.

MAY 27, 1986. Prior to five A.M. I walked all the roads around the hotel complex and airstrip. Out of respect for both moose and bears, I stayed out of the brush and timber. The forested areas around the developments are attractive not only to humans but to moose as well. Often, it seems, there are more moose here in spring than in other areas. The land around the hotel and depot once was a vast, open field, cleared first by homesteaders and wood gatherers and then by wildfire. Willows, birch, and other moose food replaced the original climax forest. Good browse is still available but growing scarce as the forest ages. One biologist theorizes that moose may congregate here because, until recently, many bears avoided these developed areas.

My goal this morning was to find a tolerant cow moose with newborns. Cows are likely to feel threatened by a person's approach and charge to protect their young, but that's only part of the reason I was being cautious. The moose are on edge, defensive of their young, because many bears are now in the area. One biologist describes the bears as being in a "heightened predatory state." As the moose population in this part of the park declined in the early 1980s, grizzlies seemed to be ever more common in the developed areas.

Although not all bears are adept predators — some are intimidated by cow moose — a few are expert. Sounds in the brush (just *sounds*) could be enough to attract a bear. The dangerous aspect of the area around the hotel and by park Headquarters is chiefly the lack of visibility that can result in a surprise meeting. That is why I walk the roads, even though that is no guarantor of safety. No matter where I walk, I never forget that grizzlies can be encountered almost anywhere.

My search was a success. I photographed a cow with two calves within a stone's throw of the hotel. The cow was kneeling to nibble newly sprouted grass, probably so sweet after a long winter of woody browse. (Moose consume forty to sixty pounds of forage per day, so the spring grass is a welcome, nutritious supplement to the regular browse diet.) The two calves watched me, perhaps curious about the clicking of my camera, but the cow ignored me. The arrival of a tour bus and a few early risers soon had the moose family moving back into the timber.

MAY 28, 1978. At three-thirty P.M. in the brush above the Hogan Creek bridge, I saw a cow moose stagger and fall. At first I thought that she'd been injured, but when she stood again, a calf fell to the ground. I drew only slightly nearer, anxious not to disturb her in this delicate moment. I watched through field glasses as another calf squeezed into life and made the long fall to the ground. The wobbly cow turned to lick the tiny, reddish calves. One struggled to its feet for a moment but fell back when the cow licked it. The cow seemed weak, able to stand only with difficulty. Several times she slumped to the ground — a shocking frailty, vulnerability. While lying down, she ate the translucent white afterbirth, then stood to finish licking the calves clean. She was consuming not only energizing tissue but probably also much of the scent that could betray her and her calves to wolves and bears. Around four-thirty the calves took their first few steps, already looking stronger. By five they were crow-hopping around their recumbent mother when Will Troyer, park service biologist, drove up. I pointed them out, and he decided to get a closer look. I went on, still unwilling to disturb them.

MAY 29, 1979. Nearly sixty degrees today. Almost summer. In a way, summer is Alaska's off-season, for no matter how much travel publicists try to minimize our harsh winters, ice and snow are the reality here for almost two thirds of the year. Winter is the favorite time for many rural Alaskans. Travel is easier: the frozen rivers and lakes offer easy, unlimited travel by snowmachine, skis, snowshoes, and dogsleds. And there are no bugs. Except during the darkest part of winter, when circadian rhythms are most upset, or in a prolonged cold snap, winter is an active time for many people. Summer, with its extended daylight, is a much more hectic season, primarily because, for humans and other animals alike, it is a time of preparation for winter.

Perhaps nowhere else in the natural world is the connection between sunlight and life so apparent as here. The brief summer is a respite that allows all life to continue. It is the season for breeding and rearing young, for flowering and spreading seeds. The seasonal exposure to the sun in the arctic and subarctic is a contrast of extremes: in summer, nearly twenty-four hours of daylight; in winter, nearly twenty-four hours of darkness. One nagging fear that I suspect haunts many people in the deepest part of winter is that our world will never again see the sun, that everything will stay dark and cold. Just now, winter seems a long way away. In just three weeks it will be the summer solstice, a day to celebrate.

MAY 30, 1981. Memorial Day weekend. The first big crowds of the summer. I had to laugh this morning, thinking of the naturalist I met last week in the visitor center who said that the job wasn't as bad as she'd heard. I told her to just wait a week.

Until yesterday the road was open to anyone; today the restrictions are on and a permit is needed to drive into the park. In the past few days there have been few cars on the road and hardly any campers in the campgrounds. Hotel and Park Service staff, other important spring migrants, easily outnumbered the visitors. But now people from Anchorage and Fairbanks are arriving. This weekend and Labor Day are the two times here when Alaskans dominate park visitation. Soon the motor homes, muddy or dusty from the haul up the Alaska Highway, will begin showing up.

Because of the crowds, I stayed off the Park Road today. Instead I hiked over to the goshawk nest. Just since May 18 the goshawks have tripled in size. Large, white, ungainly birds now fill the nest. It seems a prodigious growth rate—hunting must be good. Although I watched for about an hour from a considerable distance, neither adult returned.

MAY 31, 1987. Cloudy today and warm. Snow has mostly gone from the open spaces but persists in the mountains and sheltered areas.

Important changes this year. No longer will visitors with Igloo Creek or Wonder Lake reservations be allowed to drive their private vehicles to those campgrounds. A new "camper bus" system is being implemented. Campers will have to transport everything they wish to take with them on special camper shuttles. Almost every visitor, it seems, wants to overnight at Wonder Lake at least once. Even though the Wonder Lake campground does offer spectacular views of the mountain (as well as vivid and memorable encounters with mosquitoes), for many visitors it is the drive not the camping, that is the attraction.

This campground-access change is but a first step. All private vehicular access to park campgrounds is being phased out, because private vehicles are thought to affect wildlife behavior and diminish the wildlife-viewing opportunities along the Park Road. Many visitors stop to approach animals or operate their vehicles in a way that disrupts wildlife movement across the road. Bus traffic is assumed to have negligible impact. In a few years, the Teklanika and Sanctuary campgrounds also will be closed to private vehicles; Savage River and Riley Creek will remain open. These and other changes are mandated by the park's General Management Plan, approved in 1986. Some of the recommendations are based upon a 1982–83 park wildlife study, which concluded that, although vehicle traffic did not have a significant effect on overall wildlife *populations*, wildlife *behavior* may have been adversely affected. According to the plan, as private vehicle access is reduced, bus access may be increased. Consequently, this year both additional commercial tour buses and public shuttle buses will be allowed into the park.

As expected, the campground closures and other associated restrictions have not been greeted with universal approval. Most of the criticism centers on the crowded shuttle system, but a few critics of the campground closures see a hidden agenda. A new hotel, owned by a large package-tour company, opened this spring. It seems obvious, say these critics, that a successful corporation would not invest millions in a hotel without some guarantee that its patrons would be allowed into a park whose access is limited, often wait-listed. *Perhaps the critics had a point. In 1987 only 85 more shuttle buses, an increase of 2.5 percent, were allowed into the park during the season, but 476 additional tour buses made the trip. The imbalance in these figures can be explained away by formulas, contracting limitations, and the like, but in simple language, little was done to relieve the crowding on the public system, while the for-profit system increased by 25 percent.*

All the restrictions are a far cry from the days before the George Parks Highway opened and visitation boomed. Anyone who survived the drive on the old Denali Highway deserved to be here. A visitor then could drive in without a permit, camp in any campground, and experience the park in near solitude.

Early Summer

*A vernal blush suffuses the land, painting the
verdant tundra and forest with life.*

JUNE 1, 1989. The hotel is fifty years old today. Or more precisely, this is the golden anniversary of the hotel *site*. On June 1, 1939, the Mount McKinley National Park Hotel opened and served park visitors until it burned to the ground in 1972. Today, seventeen years later, the "temporary" modular hotel that replaced it is still in use.

"If adequate facilities exist or can feasibly be developed by private enterprise to serve park visitors' needs for commercial services outside park boundaries," reads the Park Service policy guidelines, "such facilities will not be expanded or developed within the park." Various justifications for violating these guidelines have been offered, but the proposed twenty-five million to thirty million dollar new hotel to be built by 1995 still sparks controversy both within and without the Park Service. Corporate favoritism, increased human impact, and loss of wildlife habitat are chief concerns. Much important moose-calving habitat would be lost along with cover for the grizzlies that hunt the calves. Instead of the proposed 140-room hotel, critics favor removal of the current structure and development outside the park. Such action would have profound effects upon concessioner contracts including tour bus access to the Park Road.

The 1939 hotel was built for its operator, the federally owned Alaska Railroad, by the Civilian Conservation Corps under the Work Projects Administration, the federal agency that instituted public works to relieve Depression-era unemployment.

Until the mid-1950s the railroad offered the only access to the park other than arduous overland travel or limited air service. On

35

March 12, 1914, three years before establishment of the park, Congress authorized the president to build a railroad to Interior Alaska. By February 1922, the Riley Creek bridge was completed, and all that remained for the final hookup of steel rails running from Seward to Fairbanks was the construction of the 701-foot, single-span bridge over the Tanana River. On a hot July 15, 1923, President Warren Harding drove the golden spike completing the railroad and making the park but a few hours' easy travel from both Anchorage and Fairbanks.

"The location of the hotel (at Milepost 347.9 on the Alaska Railroad) is somewhat puzzling because it is impossible to see Mount McKinley from anywhere in the hotel area," wrote Edwin M. Fitch in his 1967 history, *The Alaska Railroad*. "The first good view . . . is at Savage River, 12 miles in from the park station. There is a particularly magnificent view 60 miles in, and a close-up view at the Wonder Lake end of the road that defeats attempts at description."

Many visitors still arrive by train and often offer comments similar to Fitch's. Geography determined the route of the railroad, and proximity to the railroad, in part, determined the hotel location.

In the early years, neither the hotel nor the railroad was profitable. Hotel charges were high for the time, but so were the costs of operation during the short visitor season. Special promotions were common. In 1941, with visitation lagging, the Alaska Railroad offered its annual Labor Day Excursion, a two-day trip via rail from Fairbanks including meals, lodging, and "deluxe sightseeing bus," for twenty-five dollars per person. These promotional events failed to stem the red ink. The National Park Service was given control of the hotel at the end of 1952, on the recommendation of the General Accounting Office. McKinley Park Services, Inc. (MPS) took over the park concession on June 15, 1953. In November of that year, the Alaska Railroad properties were officially signed over to Oscar Dick, acting park superintendent, who in turn transferred the property on a twenty-year lease to MPS. A string of concessioners have since operated the hotel with ever-growing success, thanks first to the Denali Highway, completed in 1957, then to the Parks Highway, in 1972.

From 1943 to 1945 the hotel was used as a military rest-and-relaxation center for the World War II troops stationed in the territory. From 1950 to 1953 the hotel also was operated October to May as the Air Force Mount McKinley Rest and Recreation Center. All military personnel were welcome at a cost of two dollars per night per room, single or double occupancy, and sixty cents per meal.

The Mount McKinley Park Hotel was not the first to offer services and accommodations to park visitors. Maurice Morino, who moved to the area in December 1910, ran a roadhouse on the land he homesteaded in 1915. His business was assured of success when the railroad right-of-way crossed his homestead. Duke E. Stubbs operated a trading post from 1925 to 1936 on an adjacent thirty-five acres. Morino's early competition, Pat Lynch on Riley Creek, faded with the completion of the railroad bridge in 1922. But Lynch's Roadhouse lived on, in a sense: The relinquished homestead became the site of the first park Headquarters, and the structure offered salvage building material.

In 1923, only thirty-four visitors made the trip from the train station to Savage River. An early visitor to "Morris Moreno's [*sic*] Mount McKinley Park Hotel," the large, two-story log building that Morino had built, wrote, "Half-page advertisements in the various Alaskan papers had prepared us to expect a somewhat more elaborate structure, though we could see that the electric lights which the advertising had emphasized were a reality." Typical fare included moose meat and beans, Dall sheep steak or stew, a variety of locally grown vegetables and potatoes, sourdough muffins and rolls, and blueberry or dried-apple pie. Dozens of dogs were tied up near the hotel; their barking cacophony upset guests as well as proprietor Morino, who is said to have disliked sled dogs — a handicap for an innkeeper in a country where dogsled travel was a major form of transportation.

Just south of the hotel on a wooded rise above the Morino Loop Trail are three graves. A simple plank cross marks the resting place of Jerry McClarty, 1872–1934; an adjacent cross is unidentified. A short distance south of them is Morino's iron-fenced grave. Morino was born October 27, 1870, near Milan, and in 1900 he came to Nome, then a gold-rush boomtown. Besides being an innkeeper, Morino was the area's first postmaster. His 120-acre homestead became an inholding during the 1932 park expansion, but he did not receive patent to his land until 1934, just three years before his death. According to news accounts, Morino planned his own funeral and ordered a steel casket. He died March 6, 1937, in Everett, Washington. His remains traveled north by steamer, were transferred to the railroad, and finally arrived by wagon at the chosen site overlooking his home of twenty-seven years. In 1947, the Park Service acquired rights to the land from Morino's heirs. Much of the current development is sited on, or near, Morino's old homestead. A transient who apparently fell asleep while smoking caused the fire that destroyed Morino's abandoned, deteriorating roadhouse at eleven-thirty P.M. on May 30, 1950.

JUNE 2, 1985. Mile markers are up again. Wooden mileposts once marked the road and offered a method of locating points of inter-est. In the 1970s they were removed to minimize human intrusion, to prevent people from flocking to known wildlife hotspots and scenic areas as publicized by various trail and road guides keyed to the mileposts. Now flexible, synthetic posts have been set out. Even such a simple thing can be controversial.

Park policies sometimes change along with personnel. Not unlike the military, where officers are rotated from one command to another, park administrators serve a tour of duty in one park before moving on, often upward, to another. The idea is, essen-tially, that new people bring new ideas, new concepts, and new management principles. Such staff changes also tend to counteract the tendency of government representatives to become clients of the entities being monitored or administered. This blurring of allegiance, sometimes called clientism, can be a problem in parks where monopolies, the concessioners, are providing visitor ser-vices under Park Service supervision.

Nevertheless, it takes time to grasp the complexities of a particular park's natural and human resources, and often just as administrators become fully trained and effective, they transfer.

The new mile markers and the quasi-official road guide being developed come from the new regime. The markers are intended to provide visitors with reference points — even if they are often hid-den or too small to be seen from the bus. They are also said to offer accurate measurements for maintenance and ranger activities. However, someone, apparently a Park Service employee, dislikes the new markers. Last summer, within two weeks of their em-placement, and again recently, many turned up missing.

JUNE 2, 1989. After an unsuccessful search for calf moose, I walked downstream from Teklanika Campground to the old dig on the bluff overlooking the river. This site, as well as the one on the ridge across the road from the campground, was not restored when the archaeologists finished work. On the perimeter of the pit are several dead spruce, killed when their roots were cut during site excavation. Other than a few willows, a profusion of fireweed, and a few tiny spruce, surprisingly little has grown here since the site was excavated in 1961.

Perhaps regeneration has been slow, not only because the ground is rocky and bereft of topsoil, but also because so many people visit the site. There wasn't much of a trail in the early 1970s; now many footpaths converge here. The spruce trees below the bluff have suffered from campers scavenging firewood. Many trees are limbless to ten to fifteen feet, others are dead.

Archaeologists unearthed stone spear and arrow points, scrapers, knives, hammerstones, adzes, and blanks. The site was both game lookout and tool-flaking station, perhaps even a habitation site, though no hearths or dwellings were found.

Before firearms spread across Alaska, the Athabascans subsisted with ingenious hunting and fishing techniques. Above game trails or near mineral licks, a blind would be built in a tree. When a moose or caribou passed underneath, the hidden hunter would kill it with spear or arrows. One such blind was still standing in the 1920s near a lick on Savage River. The blind was built without tools. "They'd taken little dead spruce — no chopping at all — maybe eight or nine of them," Frank Glaser said, "and lashed them into a platform between trees with spruce root."

In the early 1800s it was said that the local Indians traded in a circuitous manner with others in the Copper River area, swapping furs for coveted goods. Long birchbark canoe trips were made to an island located near the confluence of the Yukon and Tanana rivers, a historically safe trading location.

Indians also used willow funnel traps to catch fish. In the spring, when the fish were migrating upstream, the Athabascans arranged underwater sticks to direct the fish into the woven trap. In autumn the sticks and trap were reversed to catch the downstream movement. One old village just north of the park was built near a creek known for its large run of fish. Shelters, dug into the ground and built of wood and sod, were abandoned before 1890; by 1926 only rotting wood betrayed the site.

Not far from the Teklanika campground, an interpretive sign says that the Ice Age hunters who lived along the river left "scant evidence" of their passing — just a few tools, datable to 10,000 years ago. Modern man's passing won't be described so kindly.

JUNE 3, 1978. From the road I watched three grizzlies, a female and two cubs, grubbing peavine roots on the East Fork gravel bars.

Boar *and* sow *are the common terms for male and female bears. Because bears are not swine, I do not use these terms.* A raven landed near one cub, surprising it. The cub cringed as if attacked, then bluff-charged the raven, which hopped away. The cub charged again, and again the raven retreated. Over and over the little dance continued. Since the cub was now in full pursuit, the raven had to fly a little to keep its distance. Time and again, just when the cub seemed about to pounce, the raven would escape, only to land a short distance away. Finally the raven tired of the game and flew off, the cub trailing for some distance before it seemed to realize the chase was over. (This chase looked to be a great strategy for separating a young animal from a protective mother.)

The cub, now more than five hundred feet from its family, looked around with seeming alarm and raced back. Its sibling spotted the running cub but bolted in the opposite direction, spooking its mother in the process. Upon seeing its family in flight, the cub sped up. This accelerating charge only increased the other bears' panic. The fiasco ended when the female turned to face her pursuer. The cub slammed to a stop and began to slink submissively forward. Soon all were once again placidly grubbing roots.

In late afternoon I stopped at the Hogan Creek bridge. The cow moose that I saw calve here last week has finally moved on. It seemed a long time to stay in one place. Will Troyer has been keeping an eye on her and her two calves and said they were gone this morning. He said he thinks the biological reason for this stationary behavior is not so obvious as allowing time for the calves to strengthen. There's a lot of scent associated with calving, Troyer told me, and perhaps by being stationary there's less of a scent *trail* for predators to follow.

JUNE 3, 1988. Two indistinct white stains on the rock cliff by the Toklat River bridge are all that's left of the plaques in honor of Charles Sheldon and Harry Karstens. Sheldon's plaque was donated by the Boone and Crockett Club and dedicated in 1951 by club member Robert C. Reeve, founder of Reeve Aleutian Airways. In 1958, Grant Pearson, accompanied by Park Superintendent Duane Jacobs, Assistant Superintendent Samuel King, and Mrs. Harry Karstens, dedicated the Karstens plaque, donated by the Pioneer Society of Alaska. A few years ago the plaques were repositioned on stands in front of the cliff. They were then removed during construction of the new bridge. Their future placement is under discussion.

Harry Karstens was appointed chief ranger for Alaska in April 1921 and became the first superintendent of McKinley Park in July of that year. His headquarters were in Nenana, sixty miles from the park. An article in the June 9, 1921, *Nenana News* presciently, and perhaps futilely, called for local cooperation:

> *When the railroad is completed . . . it will render [the game haunts] easily accessible to market hunters and wanton slaughterers of game. . . . In the meantime Alaskans can help the work by cooperating in every possible way . . . By observing of the park regulations, assistance in the preservation of game within the boundaries . . . help to speed the development of the park.*

In 1922 Karstens moved park headquarters to the existing settlement of Riley Creek.

Karstens left Illinois at age nineteen and headed north. After working as a packer carrying 125-pound packs over the Chilkoot Pass, he reached Dawson City at the peak of the 1897 Klondike gold rush. Later he wandered down the Yukon River and mined on the Seventy Mile Creek before helping lay out the town of Eagle, which in 1901 became the first incorporated city in Alaska. With his partner Charlie McGonagall, Karstens, by then famed as the Seventy-Mile Kid, broke the first dog-team mail route from Valdez to Fairbanks. (McGonagall was a member of the "Sourdough expedition," which scaled McKinley's north peak in 1910. McGonagall apparently turned back at 16,000 feet, although some accounts have him reaching 19,000 feet.) In 1905, while carrying mail to the Kantishna stampeders, he saw several dead Dall sheep freighted to the mining camps from the nearby mountains. It would prove a significant discovery. In 1906, then again in 1907–8, Karstens assisted Charles Sheldon in extended forays for Dall sheep and exploration of the area that later became the park.

In 1913, as coleader of Episcopal archbishop Hudson Stuck's expedition, Karstens, then thirty-two, became the second man to reach the south (true) summit of Mount McKinley. Hudson Stuck praised Karstens as the "real leader of the expedition especially in the face of difficulty and danger," and named the ridge they followed to the summit "Karstens' Ridge" in honor of a "brilliant piece of mountaineering." (Stuck's praise masked the little-known conflict between the sourdough and the preacher that marred their grand achievement. The animosity was exacerbated when papers trumpeting "Stuck's Conquest" barely mentioned his companions.) Walter Harper, a twenty-one-year-old half-Athabascan, was first to the summit. He and Karstens were closely followed by Stuck and Robert Tatum. Harper led the ascent on the bitterly cold day perhaps because the night before the attempt he had been the cook, and all the members of the party except Harper suffered "internal pains." (Karstens lost twenty pounds on the trip. Stuck and Tatum also suffered from severe, altitude-induced headaches.) But by no means should Harper's achievement be dismissed as a fluke. "Walter was a good one," Karstens later wrote Charles Sheldon, "21 years old, strong, fearless, and as fine and loveable disposition as I ever saw in a man. He was my main standby . . . he would do anything asked, and more."

With little or no money, this tough, seasoned Alaskan, whom Stuck described as "strong, competent, and resourceful," began the first efforts to patrol, protect, and develop the new park. Aside from Karstens' and one ranger's salary, the total park operating budget in 1921 was said to be twenty-four dollars—twenty-three dollars for a wood stove to warm headquarters and one dollar for hinges.

Arriving at Riley Creek in 1922 with his staff of one ranger, Karstens found a small settlement upstream from the railroad bridge and another along the tracks on the bluff to the north. Much of the construction camp was deserted, but a few hangers-on—miners, railroad workers, trappers, market hunters, home-steaders, and, yes, bootleggers and shady ladies—remained. Karstens transformed abandoned buildings and Lynch's Roadhouse into his headquarters before setting about ridding the park of poachers. With the establishment of the post office in 1922, the settlement's name was changed to McKinley Station.

Poachers were a problem. Karstens lost court cases because most local people viewed hunting in the park as a noncriminal activity. Locals would not witness against accused poachers and would not convict them. On February 12, 1924, a Healy jury found Jack Donnelly innocent, even though he had been caught all but red-handed inside the park with sheep and caribou meat. Several times in court and during the brief deliberations, Donnelly threatened Karstens. Grant Pearson, who described Karstens as absolutely "fearless" in confronting lawbreakers and protecting the park, said Karstens was not intimidated.

Part of the poaching problem stemmed from the language in the park's establishment act that allowed miners and prospectors to hunt within the park for their personal use. A poacher could simply claim to be a miner and go free. Congress repealed this provision on May 21, 1928.

Karstens also had trouble with his independent-minded rangers. In 1924 Ranger McFarland threatened to shoot Karstens "full of holes" in a confrontation over what Karstens saw as McFarland's dereliction to duty. Karstens also thought that McFarland had been tipping poachers off to ranger patrols. The two had many other battles before McFarland was fired.

Grant Pearson, whom Karstens hired and tested on a solo dog-team poaching patrol, described Karstens as having "a temper that could erupt like a volcano." Frank Glaser, who trapped on the Savage River just outside the park, said Karstens was a "violent-tempered man who nobody much liked." "Nobody" referred to the trappers and market hunters Karstens evicted from the park.

Glaser and Harry Lucky, a market hunter who had operated on the Teklanika River, delighted in tormenting Karstens. Late at night, whenever they were camped near Headquarters, one or the other would howl like a wolf to set the sled dogs barking and ruin Karstens' sleep. Soon after things settled down, the trick would be repeated.

To escape the festering conditions at McKinley Station and the bureaucratic infighting, Karstens moved Headquarters two miles west of McKinley Station. "I have in mind the selection of a site with a commanding view, drainage, water, and sufficient room for expansion." Clearing of the site on Rock Creek began on June 18, 1925, and construction began on September 7. Old buildings at Riley Creek were dismantled and hauled to the site, logs cut, and cabins built.

Without much doubt, in the rip-roaring days of 1920s Alaska, the fearless, experienced Karstens was the right man to develop and protect the fledgling park, but his mercurial personality was not suited to a maturing park and bureaucratic niceties. He stepped down in 1928.

Without Charles Sheldon, there quite likely would not have been a park at all. This wealthy, eastern, hunter-naturalist came here in 1906 to explore and to collect specimens for the American Museum of Natural History's biological survey. Sheldon, with Karstens' help, built a cabin on the Toklat River and spent parts of two years studying and hunting local wildlife. Five-ten and 170 pounds, and said to be "possessed of physical strength and endurance beyond belief," the self-effacing Sheldon fell in love with this remote country and its white sheep. C. Hart Merriam and E. W. Nelson edited Sheldon's field notes into book form, *Wilderness of Denali*, and published it in 1930, three years after his death at sixty on September 21, 1928.

Some of what Sheldon saw greatly disturbed him. The 1905 Kantishna gold rush lured hundreds into the hills near Mount McKinley. Sheldon and Hudson Stuck noted the destruction of wildlife wrought by the stampeders. Market hunters visited Sheldon's cabin. They had killed twenty ewes and lambs, most of which their dogs had consumed. Six years later, Stuck recounted the "wholesale destruction of game," with poison used in the "most reckless way."

The Alaska Game Law of 1908 established closed seasons and bag limits but did not prohibit the sale of wild animal meat. In 1912 sheep, moose, and caribou could be hunted from August 1 to December 10. Each person was allowed two moose and three each of caribou and sheep. Well into the 1920s the game laws were largely ignored. Almost every major drainage had a market hunting operation, many of which flourished even after the park's establishment. Market hunters supplied wild meat not only to mining camps and construction crews but also to settlements as far away as Fairbanks. Without transportation or a local livestock industry, market hunting was the only way to procure meat in Interior Alaska. It was said that both the Alaska Railroad and the Richardson Highway, the main route from tidewater into the Interior, were built on sheep meat. Ironically, it was the completion of the Alaska Railroad in 1923 and its link to the outside world that brought an end to market hunting. The Alaska Game Law of 1925 banned market hunting except for individual roadhouse use.

By then, however, market hunters had had a devastating impact on wildlife. Market hunters shot every calf, cow, and bull moose they saw, often without regard to season. But with work gangs of two hundred to three hundred men to feed, it was the plentiful Dall sheep that were hit hardest. Several sheep commonly were shot at one time. Some sheep were so tame it was possible to kill eight or nine before the survivors fled. One hunter shot twenty-two sheep at one sitting. Hundreds of sheep were killed in the drainages near Mount McKinley.

Big Herman and Little Herman Ketzler hunted the Savage River; Harry Lucky and Tom Steel hunted the Teklanika River; *After the park was established, former market hunter Harry Lucky guided tourists for the park concessioner, Mount McKinley Tourist and Transporta-*

tion Company. Bill the Turk hunted the Savage River; a group of Indians and another of whites hunted the Toklat. A Cherokee Indian, Tom Savage, for whom Frank Glaser said Savage River was named, reportedly killed 120 rams in one fall in cliffs along the Nenana River.

Tom Steel, a crack shot, and Harry Lucky, a hardy six-three outdoorsman, reportedly killed more game for the Fairbanks market than any of the others. Often the two would leave Fairbanks in the fall with dog teams or travel on foot and by water to the Savage River camp of Bill the Turk, who cared for forty to sixty of the market hunters' sled dogs. O. J. Murie and Frank Glaser visited the abandoned camp in 1922 and found the remains of a hundred big rams, some of which were killed for dog food. "We didn't even count the small rams," Glaser said. Adolph Murie found another camp on the East Fork River and counted the horns of seventy-one rams.

At the head of the drainages, marketers killed two to three tons of sheep, mostly rams averaging about 125 pounds gutted, head and lower legs removed but hide on. Once they'd gathered the frozen carcasses into a pile, they'd scatter strychnine-laced fat pellets around them, poisoning foxes, wolverines, ravens, eagles, and occasionally wolves, then scarce in the area. In short, they killed every meat eater that came to the caches. When conditions were right, they'd load their huge freight sleds and, behind ten to fourteen dogs, begin hauling meat the 150 miles to Fairbanks, where it sold for twenty-five to fifty cents a pound. It took a lot of wild meat to feed the fifteen thousand to twenty thousand people then said to be in the Fairbanks district. Stephen R. Capps of the U.S. Geological Survey, who explored the region in 1916, reported that from 1913 to 1916 market hunters took fifteen hundred to two thousand sheep each winter from the basins of the Toklat and Teklanika rivers.

Market hunting worried Sheldon. With the coming of the railroad, he foresaw the total destruction of his game paradise. A millionaire from his early years as a railroad general manager and from investments in Mexican mining, he had retired in 1903 at age thirty-five. He had all the right contacts within the eastern establishment, including Teddy Roosevelt. His membership in the influential Boone and Crockett Club and his untiring efforts in Washington, D.C., where he moved to facilitate his work, made the park possible. Despite the emotional appeal and support to save the game, it took eleven years before Sheldon's work and the work of others (notably Stephen T. Mather, Belmore Brown, and James Wickersham) paid off. On February 26, 1917, Woodrow Wilson signed the act, which Sheldon had hand-carried from Congress, that established the park "for the benefit and enjoyment of the people."

The year 1917 was momentous: Alaskan papers were full of news of the awakening Russian Revolution, U-boat sinkings, and plots by Germans against the United States. One headline in the Fairbanks *Daily News-Miner* blared, "Only Miracle Can Prevent War Now." And so it was that the establishment of the new park made little news. A one-column inch story under the headline "Mount McKinley to Be Park" appeared in the February 20, 1917, issue of the *News-Miner*. The article reported the U.S. House of Representatives passage of the park bill and predicted that it would be signed within the week.

JUNE 4, 1985. Moose calves are in the timber thickets all along the road from the Nenana to Igloo Creek. Twins seem even more common than usual this year. The amount of predation witnessed is astounding—predation not by wolves but by bears. Several busloads saw a calf being killed in the willows along Hogan Creek. Another calf was taken in the Sanctuary campground. Just the other night at park Headquarters, a radio dispatcher looked up to see a grizzly pursuing a calf across the lawn. The bear caught, killed, and ate its catch on the street in front of the administration building. Later, again on Hogan Creek, a female bear and her yearling easily outmaneuvered a cow and killed its calf. While they ate the twenty-five- to thirty-five-pound calf, the agitated cow lingered nearby.

JUNE 4, 1980. A visitor and a concession employee were injured by bears in two separate incidents last night in the vicinity of the hotel. Neither person was badly injured. There are many moose in the area now, and the supposition is that calving has attracted several bears.

The first incident occurred at midnight when a twenty-two-year-old man out for a late-night walk encountered three bears on a brushy, unmaintained trail along Riley Creek, east of the railroad bridge. When one of the smaller bears approached, the man shouted. The bear charged from forty feet, inflicting a minor bite or a claw wound to the man's left hand. Earlier a ranger had warned him of these bears.

Less than an hour later three hotel employees walking on the Park Road near Riley Creek Campground saw two moose run in front of them, pursued by two bears. When the three people tried to run to safety, the larger bear gave chase and pulled one man from a tree he was attempting to climb, inflicting a single puncture wound to the left ankle. The bear moved off, allowing the victim to get up the tree before it returned and unsuccessfully tried to reach him again.

It is not dark at night now, and evening twilight walks are popular. Moose are crepuscular animals and are likely to be encountered late in the day. Grizzlies can also be very active at night. If nothing else is learned from these incidents (aside from the obvious lessons of never running from, or surprising, a bear), they should serve as a reminder that all of Denali Park is grizzly country.

JUNE 5, 1980. Early this morning near Riley Creek, a goshawk flew up from the willows and crossed the trail with what looked to be a small hare in its talons. Prompted by this incident, I went to the goshawk nest in the afternoon. Again, there were no adults present. The downy white chicks had almost doubled in size since I was last there. Without disturbing them, I collected a few bones and fur scraps from beneath the nest—rodents and perhaps a red squirrel. The chicks have been fed well, but once on their own, life will be hard. Only one-third of all goshawks survive their first year. Most starve.

JUNE 6, 1975. Dall sheep are lambing now; each day more lambs appear on the hillsides, tiny lambs trailing ewes through the cliffs on Igloo, above Sanctuary and Toklat rivers, even on Polychrome Pass. Two days ago there were no lambs on the cliffs; today there are many—tomorrow, even more. This concentrated lambing has obvious benefits. If born earlier in the year, the lambs might succumb to late winter storms; born later, they would not be strong enough to survive the winter. This lambing-calving spurt may also be a defense mechanism. If lambing and calving were spread out over a longer period, predators could pick off the helpless newborns one by one. But because all the young are born at one time, their predators are unable to get them all.

Just prior to giving birth, a ewe leaves the band and seeks out the most rugged cliffs. Lambs meet the world in rocky aeries. Ewes accompanied by newborns seldom stray very far from escape terrain. Wolves would have a hard time killing a lamb in such locations. Perhaps an eagle or, more uncommonly, a wolverine will be the first to "test" a lamb and its protective mother.

Adolph Murie documented wolf-predation on sheep and found that impact varied according to sheep numbers, the presence of "buffer" species, forage, terrain, weather, and other factors. When sheep populations were high, large numbers of wolves could neither keep the population from increasing nor cause a decline. But on two occasions after severe winter weather exacted a harsh toll on park sheep, wolves lowered the population by killing the old, diseased, and the very young.

Observing lambs is an enjoyable pastime. I especially enjoy watching them signal their hunger. If the ewe is lying down, the lamb circles her and perhaps paws her. If that fails, the lamb climbs onto the ewe's back until she gets up. Immediately the lamb will suckle, working the teats with upward thrusts of its muzzle. This thrusting helps generate milk flow, but sometimes the ewe walks away from the abuse. In just a few days the lamb will join its fellows in gambols about the cliffs and meadows. Older lambs gather into "nurseries" often watched over by a single ewe, and their play will be vigorous and nonstop.

JUNE 7, 1989. On Stony Hill, I saw my first lesser golden plover of the year. As always I heard its call before I saw it running across the tundra. The speed with which its legs move is almost of cartoon quality. The head and body remain still, but the legs are a rapid blur. After two short dashes the plover took off and whistled downslope. I don't know why I'm always surprised by their flight speed, for after all, they migrate here from beyond the Argentine pampas.

A plover on its nest, which is nothing more than a slight hollow on the tundra, uses its camouflage coloration to elude detection. But if a predator or human should get too close, it employs a masterly rendition of the broken-wing trick, feigning injury as it draws the predator away from its eggs or young. It's definitely an act that no fox could ignore. The plover, like most ground-nesting birds, must be constantly alert. Threats can come from anywhere, including above. Jaegers share the same general terrain and will take the plover's dark, mottled eggs or its young if given the opportunity.

JUNE 8, 1988. Sixty degrees, rainy, broken clouds in afternoon. Windflowers and avens beginning to bloom on some tundra slopes. New shoots appearing in moist swales and along watercourses and rivulets. Last night the low was plus twenty-three at Teklanika, breaking a string of six straight nights when the temperatures stayed above freezing. Certainly more flowers will appear when the threat of frost has passed.

Today I hiked to a marmot colony on a slope above East Fork. While I was still at a distance from their rock pile, a marmot's shrill whistle warned of my approach. I could see a flurry of activity as marmots ran for their burrows, one scurrying across a vast open space to reach safety. On the slope below the den I sat down to watch. Soon a marmot's head emerged from a tunnel between the rocks. After a brief look around, it crawled out into the open and sprawled on a large rock. Soon other marmots were moving about, seemingly oblivious to my presence. Six marmots, all of similar size, were in sight at once. Two nibbled grass, two lay in the warming sun, and two chased each other in and out of various den openings. I laughed aloud at their comic movements. For these low-slung creatures to get up speed, they must throw their front quarters into the air in a kind of abbreviated hop, while pedaling hard with their hind feet. It doesn't take much to slow a marmot down. At one point, the pursuing marmot high-centered on a ludicrously small rock, its hind legs thrashing the air until it wiggled over the rock with the aid of its forepaws.

The two involved in the chase abruptly came face to face when they emerged from adjacent crevices. They rose to hind legs and began to wrestle, pummeling each other with forepaws. Gaping mouths revealed formidable scimitar incisors. After parry and thrust, they locked incisors and shook each other. They tumbled to the ground, rolled madly about, then stood again, their mouths still clamped together. A forward thrust by the larger marmot and the two went over, the attacker thrown as if by judo. The smaller one was up in an instant and the chase resumed. This wrestling continued for the next half-hour.

Marmots are true hibernators. While they sleep, their metabolism slows down; heartbeat, body temperature, and respiration rates drop. An entire family unit, up to fifteen animals, retreat in the fall to their den where they sleep huddled together through the winter. The last animal into the den, usually an adult male, plugs the entrance from inside with vegetation, stone, and earth. Marmots mate in May just after the end of hibernation and while still in their burrows. After a five-week gestation, the young are born hairless, toothless, and with eyes closed. At six weeks they are fully furred and venture out of the burrow for the first time.

Finally the warm sun seemed to exert its influence and the colony slowed down. When I left, two marmots lay sunning in the rocks. A grizzly had dug for squirrels on the slopes below the marmot colony, but there was no evidence that the bear had attempted to root out the marmots from their rock-protected densite.

JUNE 8, 1989. "Teklanika means 'river of much gravel' in Athabascan," declared the naturalist at last night's Teklanika Campground campfire talk. An interesting translation, one I'd first read in Grant Pearson's biography as "much river bed, little water." I've researched the origin of the names of many prominent features but primarily the origin of Teklanika and Toklat, about the only major features along the Park Road that bear original Indian names.

Most of the landmarks in the park were named by pioneering geologists, miners, prospectors, and climbers. Since most physical features around the turn of the century were unnamed and the region unexplored except, of course, by the land's original people, the Athabascans, both prominent as well as nondescript landmarks were named by almost every newcomer for almost any reason. The Teklanika was often called the Steel Fork by locals, for Tom Steel, a market hunter. Even the mountain was named after a president who never saw it, ignoring the lyrical *Denali*, from the Koyukon word *Deenaalee*, which means "high" or "tall," and not "the great one," as is often said. Hudson Stuck vigorously championed the retention of the mountain's original name. Many Alaskans prefer it because they believe Alaskan native languages are more expressive of the northern landscape. "Call it Denali, dammit," you'll often hear under the breath.

The name Teklanika was first reported in 1910 by geologist Louis M. Prindle, part of Alfred Hulse Brooks's 1902 exploration. Prindle, who explored the area from 1902 to 1911, offered no translation. The *Dictionary of Alaska Place Names* says Teklanika means "Tekla Creek," which isn't much help, but did offer a translation for the Toklat River. Army lieutenant Henry T. Allen, who passed through the region in 1885 on his remarkable fifteen-hundred-mile-long exploration of central Alaska, first reported the name Toklat but actually applied it to the river now known as the Kantishna River. A major tributary of the Kantishna now bears the name Toklat, which Allen spelled "Toclat" and said was a "Tanana Indian" word meaning "dish water." Earlier, during the census in 1880, Ivan Petroff called the same river the "Tutlut." Charles Sheldon said it was a "Toklat Indian" word meaning "head of the water."

In 1926, Julius Jette, a Jesuit missionary/anthropologist who spent thirty years with the Koyukons, wrote that Teklanika meant "headwaters creek," more accurately "glacier creek" or "stream issuing from a glacier." Jette offered that there was confusion between the names Totatlanika and Teklanika. According to researcher Dianne Gudgel-Holmes, local Indians do not use the name Teklanika. They use the name Middle River, or Old Middle River, for what we call the Teklanika. Jim Kari of the Alaska Native Language Center, University of Alaska, Fairbanks, told me that most Athabascan names as they appear on maps and in popular writings are vague renderings and corruptions, not to be considered anything other than approximations. Toklat, a corruption from the correct Athabascan *Tootl'ot Khuno'*, or *Tootl'ot no*, means "headwaters river." Teklanika, or more accurately *Toch'edka Neek'a*, means "upper *something* river." Usage of *ch'edka* is uncertain.

JUNE 9, 1986. I've made the turn off the Parks Highway onto the Park Road perhaps thousands of times. It's a simple turn across one lane of traffic. Nothing special, but a touch of excitement accompanies the action.

No huge monument, arch, or garish sign marks the turn onto the Park Road. A simple brown metal highway sign points the way. By Lower Forty-Eight standards, the Parks Highway (named after territorial Governor George Parks and not after the state and national parks along it) is a rather simple, two-lane road, but it is a major artery in Alaska. This admirably unpretentious junction marks the beginning of a truly magic road. Who would guess what treasures lie along it and the number of people who have shared in its magic?

In 1990 the Park Service constructed a new entrance sign at Mile .01 out of seven thousand dollars' worth of red cedar.

JUNE 10, 1989. Climbed a ridge near Sanctuary River to watch a band of lambs and ewes. Five of the six ewes were trailed by tiny lambs, all still with shriveled umbillici. At one point, two ewes assumed the alarm posture, alerted by the chirping of a ground squirrel. Although I received many long looks, an eagle presented the obvious danger. It swooped over the ridge but did not approach the lambs.

The lambs watched me with great interest but seemed reluctant to approach even when their mothers fed quite close. I remained motionless and silent, except for the occasional click of the camera. Most of the sheep in the park are very tolerant of humans. Some people label this habituation, or learned behavior, but there is evidence that sheep, when unhunted by man, are naturally very tolerant. When Alfred Hulse Brooks explored the region ninety years ago, he wrote of the gentle trusting natures of Dall sheep and caribou. Olaus Murie made the same observation while hunting east of the park in the 1930s. Workers blasting out the Park Road along the Polychrome Cliffs had to worry about keeping the sheep out of the way. I can't find fault with the way these sheep relate to people. They have not learned to fear us. Perhaps what some call habituation is actually a reacceptance by the sheep of a species that throughout history has been most untrustworthy.

JUNE 11, 1977. Much of the lowland tundra is greening up. Even the higher slopes are beginning to turn lime green. In a very short while, the long, sunny days will spark remarkable plant growth. Sometimes it seems the park turns green almost overnight. All winter and through the spring the grazers and browsers have lived off dried vegetation. Now, fresh salad.

From a pullout on the way up to Polychrome I saw several caribou cows with calves barely two weeks old fording the upper East Fork River not far from the wolf den. The river's in flood, and all of the calves, as well as some of the adults, were swept downstream. Through the spotting scope I couldn't tell whether the entire group made it safely across. No doubt wolves feeding hungry pups wouldn't pass up a gift meal deposited by the river at their door.

Caribou look ratty, almost moth-eaten, in their shedding winter pelage. Five small bulls on the Toklat, easily identified by their stubby, velvet antlers, were browsing willows; a sixth seemed to be selecting lichens. In fact, the ability to subsist in winter on lichens (an amalgam of fungus and algae) may be a caribou's most important adaptation to this harsh environment. Caribou paw through the snow to the lichens, which they locate by smell, thrusting their noses into the snow as they wander along. I'm somewhat surprised to see one eating lichens now that green plants are available.

A group of thirty caribou, including six calves, crossed the river gravels to the west side of the Toklat. I have no way of knowing whether they have calved on this side or the south side of the range. It is an arduous trek across the range for the calves. No doubt some already have been lost to wolves or bears, floods or storms, river crossings or late snows, infirmity or disease.

JUNE 12, 1986. Bank swallows are swarming around a mud puddle on the road near Eielson. They pick up mud by packing it on the surface of their beaks before flying back to the visitor center, where they are engaged in building nests under the eaves. Although six buses were parked at Eielson when I drove up, oddly there wasn't a person in sight. Just as I shut off the engine, a grizzly stepped off the porch and walked out into the parking lot. It rounded the building, walked down by the viewing platform, and began to graze on the lush grass growing over the leach field. Two trucks with four rangers soon arrived; two rangers entered the building. In time, the viewing platform was lined with visitors gaping down at the grazing bear as a naturalist gave a talk on bear behavior. When the bear looked up at the crowd on the walkway, dozens of cameras fired away. I wonder if anyone noticed that *they* were the ones behind bars?

After the bear finally sauntered away, I had a chance to visit with Ann. She's an interesting local who's built her own cabin, dogsled, and other large projects. She skis and drives dogs all winter. There are several single women of varying ages living in the park area. They represent a variety of skills, crafts, professions, and arts. They are nurses and teachers, mechanics and carpenters, artists and scientists, bus drivers and housekeepers. Many of them were born in the Lower Forty-Eight but succumbed to the hold the park exerts on certain men and women. Perhaps Outside (as Alaskans call the rest of the United States), they would be anomalous, but here they fit right in.

JUNE 13, 1986. Eight broken eggs are all that's left in the rock ptarmigan nest I've been watching. The chicks are hatched and gone. Nourished by yolk-sacs, ptarmigan chicks can toddle at birth. Within twenty-four hours of hatching, they abandon the nest, following the hen in search of food, usually flowers and insects. Perhaps the brood I encountered on the hike to the nest hatched here. They couldn't fly but instead did an admirable job of hiding among the lichens as the hen lured me away with typical ptarmigan histrionics. Within about ten days of hatching, the chicks will launch themselves downhill, but their attempts are more barely controlled glides than actual flight. Now they are able only to clamber over the tundra, relying on their coloration and the hen's broken-wing scam to protect them from predators.

JUNE 14, 1988. The Park Road, especially from Teklanika Flats up and over to Sanctuary, is in excellent condition. Tim Taylor sure knows how to run a grader. Smooth gravel and chuck holes at a minimum. The road wasn't always in such good condition.

In 1982 I was on a bus that went off the road on the flats near Teklanika Campground. We were going along at a slow speed when the bus suddenly swerved, went down a slight incline, and off onto the tundra. Since the embankment was slight and the tundra flat, the bus stayed upright and no one was injured. The driver was blameless; he'd lost all steering when both tie rods broke. It wasn't comforting to imagine what might have happened had we been on the narrow, downhill road into Igloo Creek from Sable Pass, a rock wall on one side, a shear drop on the other. Since 1972 two bus accidents have resulted in fatalities. In 1981 some people were killed and many injured when a bus went off the road near Eielson. Tour buses today go no farther than Stony Hill.

Since the 1981 disaster, a lot of work has gone into upgrading the road, with an emphasis on maintenance. A better-kept road spares not just the buses but the drivers as well. Bus safety standards and inspections also are more stringent. Any number of mechanical defects or shortcomings can ground a bus. Drivers, specifically since the 1981 accident, are given more and better training. The return rate for bus drivers, especially tour drivers, is high, another factor promoting increased safety.

JUNE 14, 1986. Long-tailed jaegers, although quite common, don't seem to nest along the road corridor in the numbers seen fifteen years ago. An observation like this is only subjective, however. Jaegers nest on the open tundra, sometimes on top of tussocks, and defend their nests with great vigor. They attack predators that pass nearby, even humans and large animals like caribou.

Perhaps there are too many hikers disturbing nests. Or maybe today they face multiple perils that take a cumulative effect: loss, through development, of safe havens during migration; diminished food sources due to high-seas fisheries; and destruction of wintering habitat. Then again, maybe I'm imagining things. I hope so. At least for some species, however, this park alone is not enough to ensure survival.

JUNE 15, 1976. Stony bear is dead, destroyed by rangers on the slopes of Stony Hill for which she was named. Since at least 1973, her home range has included the roadside areas from Grassy Pass to Stony Creek. She seemed to have no fear of the visitor center or humans and would approach hikers without hesitation. Last week she chased a squirrel under the door to the Eielson Visitor Center and remained on the porch, keeping everyone inside. Stony wasn't the first bear to frequent the visitor center; others have occasionally done minor damage there.

Officially, although she never hurt anyone, Stony was killed in the name of public safety. Recently she charged two maintenance men at Eielson. The incident with the squirrel unnerved some of the staff, especially since radio communication from Eielson is poor. Earlier this spring she was reportedly bred for the first time, so next year she would have had cubs, worsening an already volatile situation. Arriving at the decision to destroy Stony was not an easy one. Two years ago she was ear-tagged and transplanted to the south side of the Alaska Range. She promptly returned to her home range around Stony Hill. There seemed no other alternative. She was killed not for what she did but for what she might do. Those who actually killed her were greatly moved by her death. Ranger Steve Kaufman said that the biologist and the two backcountry rangers who administered the lethal overdose were in tears.

Most visitors today are unaware of the turmoil raging over this killing. Not only are heated words being exchanged by local residents, but the staffers themselves are sharply divided on the killing. An experienced seasonal naturalist, Rick McIntyre, said that although a human fatality would likely have a profound impact on the park, he strongly doubted Stony would have hurt anyone.

Current bear-management policy focuses on removal of "problem" bears by either relocation or destruction. Even though relocation has not always been successful, as in Stony's case, it is preferable to the ultimate sentence. In all cases the bear is given at least one chance, a far cry from the early days of the park, when death was the sole outcome of bear-human conflicts.

Two thoughts bother the critics: the assumption that all habituated bears (bears that tolerate close proximity to humans) are dangerous; and the conviction that with so few grizzlies protected in the world, the loss of even one, especially a female, is a tragedy. It is believed that a hundred thousand grizzlies or more once roamed the American West. Today fewer than one thousand are left.

Are all habituated bears dangerous? The answer is not clear-cut. Habituated bears have been implicated in attacks, usually because habituation results in bears' obtaining human food or garbage. On the other hand, some experts believe that habituation, as long as bears do not obtain human edibles, *reduces* the risk of human injury through a reduction in fear-induced aggression. A habituated bear may be less likely to respond aggressively when surprised by humans—and it is these surprise encounters that have often resulted in human injury.

Not surprisingly, females with cubs have been involved in a substantial percentage of the bear incidents in Denali. Two seasonal Park Service employees who ignored the standard caution and deliberately approached bears for photographs have been injured. A few visitors have also been injured in this same way.

Increased human use of bear country means an increased likelihood of encounters. Many midsummer encounters involve bears entering camps, perhaps out of curiosity. *Bear-resistant food containers have greatly reduced backcountry incidents by eliminating food rewards.*

McNeil River State Game Sanctuary on the Alaska Peninsula attracts large numbers of bears in densities far higher than Denali's one per thirty-one square kilometers. Since the mid-1950s humans have traveled there to photograph the bears. No one has ever been injured by a bear at McNeil. There, all visitors are accompanied by trained personnel, McNeil bears never obtain human food rewards, and all human behavior is conducted in specific places, in a predictable, reliable fashion. McNeil is the premier example that habituation does not necessarily make a bear dangerous.

Experience in Alaska and elsewhere indicates that a bear that regularly encounters people and obtains their food or garbage can offer an extreme threat. It is believed that even one incident in which a bear obtains a food reward can forever alter its behavior.

Rangers vigorously respond to people who try to feed bears, to protect both species.

Perhaps events in two other national parks may offer insight into the decision-making process that led to Stony's demise. The National Park Service lost a suit to a man who had been injured in Yellowstone by a tagged bear. And in Glacier National Park, two grizzlies, in two separate attacks, killed two young women. In the preceding weeks, one bear had destroyed private property to obtain food and garbage and menaced campers to get their supplies; the other had been regularly fed garbage. These two bears and others showed little fear of people or their habitations. Park service weathered a blistering assault for not doing something with the complaints received about the bears prior to the killings. Those incidents affected the bear-management policies in all national parks with indigenous bear populations. Our current chief ranger, Gary Brown, brings a unique perspective to his job. He had arrived in Glacier the day after the killings.

JUNE 16, 1972. This spring the new highway officially opened to through traffic. Fairbanks is now a little more than a three-hour drive away. Just last year, to get to the park we had to drive 180 miles from Fairbanks to Paxson, then the 160 miles of the dusty, potholed Denali Highway. It was a highway version of a torture test.

Now that the new road is open, however, public access into the park itself has been restricted to protect wildlife. The free shuttle bus system, instituted this year, is a bitter pill to swallow. I'm used to driving my own vehicle, enjoying unlimited access. I'm all for protecting the wildlife experience here, but the anticipated visitation levels seem rather exaggerated. One ranger predicted a million people a year in twenty years, a figure four times our current state population. This year visitation is expected to double over last year's record of forty-four thousand visitors. I hope he is wrong about the expected impact.

Denali recorded about seven hundred thousand visitors in 1990. At least some people had the foresight to plan for the future.

JUNE 16, 1986. Warm, partly cloudy, great for the mosquitoes. Fairly typical wildlife observations and numbers noted for this time of year and weather. Eighty caribou (two large groups), two moose, one plover, two golden eagles, and thirty sheep (lambs and ewes). Nine grizzlies, including two sets of females with three cubs each. (Seeing two sets of triplets is rather unusual.) Several beaver near Wonder Lake. Many passerines—warblers, white-crowned sparrows, robins, thrushes, and swallows. A fox with a squirrel in its mouth crossed the road near Primrose. Most of the animals, except for the fox and one bear, which crossed the road near the Toklat, were seen very early in the day and far from the road.

A week from the solstice, the park has greened up under the influence of the extended daylight. Each day summer strengthens its tenuous grasp on the land while bird song fills the brief northern twilight.

JUNE 17, 1980. Before catching a late morning bus, Mary Anne and I hiked to the goshawk nest. She hikes pretty well for an eight-year-old. Except for a few white feathers on their backs, both chicks have molted and are now brown. Through the spotting scope Mary Anne got a good look, but she lost interest when the birds didn't "do anything but sit there." Through the scope I noticed that the chicks have almost almond-colored eyes, a contrast to the adults' crimson ones. The fledglings appear almost full-grown. Perhaps soon they will take their first tentative flights.

On a ridge above Little Stony Creek, I ignored the mosquitoes and, on this warm afternoon, enjoyed the flowers—blackish oxytrope, mountain avens, bell heather, purple mountain saxifrage, and higher on the ridge, woolly lousewort. We found a breezy, exposed knob to picnic on while viewing the sunlight-dappled earth. Bird songs rolling across the tundra entertained us. "Such beauty," I said out loud, more to myself than to my daughter.

"Dad, you've seen this a million times," came the child's reply from behind a book.

"Yes," I thought, "I know."

JUNE 18, 1978. Arrived late at Teklanika Campground. Just as we finished dinner, the naturalist walked by with an invitation to the campfire talk. He seemed nervous, and in our chat he told me that he'd just arrived from Everglades National Park and had no first-hand knowledge about Alaska. He said he'd been studying and preparing for two months, but some of the experienced naturalists had warned him that most visitors to the park in the spring were Alaskans. He found that intimidating. A few, he'd been told, could be antagonistic, since the notion of "parks" seemed pretty radical to some Alaskans.

I wondered how he'd do. I wondered, also, whether he would be the kind to "do Alaska" and remain one summer or, like some others, come north with no real expectations of remaining but get hooked on the place and be unable to leave.

About two dozen people attended the campfire talk — a good turnout for such a cool, windy evening. The campfire put out more smoke than heat. (Some seasonals consider campfire building a greater challenge than speaking to the public.) Bird migration was the topic. The naturalist offered solid, new information. We heard of routes, navigation, and threats. It was one of the better campfire talks that I've attended, but then he called for questions. Someone asked directions to Mount McKinley. He hesitated, then pointed downriver. A few people snickered. Another person asked him about bear cubs. He said he honestly didn't know the answer. Nor did he know the answer to the next question. He took off his hat and scratched his head. "Does anyone want to know anything about alligators? I know all about alligators."

JUNE 19, 1988. Horseshoe Lake used to have such a peaceful backdrop before the Parks Highway was built and spurred the development across the river. At six-thirty this morning I tried to find a spot to make a picture as pleasing as that once afforded from the overlook. I found it impossible. Down by the lake itself, although it was calm with plentiful reflections, nothing seemed to work. (Later it was obvious that the problem was one of a failure to "see," an inability to take a fresh look and deal with reality.)

I berated myself as my frustrations mounted. Then, as I do nearly every time photography begins to go badly, I put my camera away and sat down.

For so early in the day, the sun *did* seem awfully warm. It was quiet and peaceful. A kingfisher called from a snag by the outlet. I saw fish jumping nearby, and a large fish swam close to the bank — a sucker-mouthed whitefish, feeding on the bottom. I decided to walk the shore and forget the photography. While looking for fish, I saw a railroad handcart submerged near the west shore. Some years ago it had either fallen or been pushed from the tracks above. I wondered what story remained untold.

A beaver surfaced nearby. Soon several beaver — judging by size, two adults and two yearlings — were working the bank. They've obviously seen plenty of people, for they swam close to me without alarm.

I followed one adult to the dam and watched it scuttle over the top and head downstream. The main dam evidenced little new work, but downstream, two small, new dams blocked the marsh. In the quiet water below them, a beaver towed a cottonwood limb in its teeth toward the lake. On its way to the lodge, it pulled the limb up and over all three dams.

Nine dams of varying designs and sizes slowed the outlet stream on its way to its confluence with the Nenana. One is four feet high and forty feet long. One is eight inches high and about one hundred eighty feet long. Located as it is in the narrows of the stream course, the tallest, about six feet high and twenty feet across, is an important element in the beavers' engineering. Not only does the dam flood the marsh, bringing new forage within reach of the beaver, it ensures an almost constant water level into which the beaver can escape. The dam is built with spruce cuttings. Beaver don't usually eat spruce bark but prefer the bark, twigs, and leaves of poplars, aspen, and birch, the gnawed remnants of which also go into dam building. Because of their own foraging, their preferred food types are scarce close to the lake.

Shorebirds, perhaps upland sandpipers, wandered the bank at the confluence. A robin sang from a perch above the dam. White-crowned sparrows called above bluebells flowering in the woods.

Back at the lake, I sat on the point by the outlet, watching beaver swim back and forth. One went ashore and took a full thirty minutes to return to the water with a poplar sapling. That's a long time to be away from safety but also an indication of how far the beaver must travel for food. It pulled the cutting across the lake to the lodge. The old lodge network on the peninsula is perhaps fifty to sixty feet long. In one shape or another, it has been there since my first visit, and like all good Alaskan homes, it has been added on to.

A muskrat swam by, grass trailing from its mouth. Though it looks somewhat like a small beaver, it is easily identified by its vertically flattened tail that both propels and directs it like a rudder. I got a close look when it scurried over the dam.

Sooner or later the water current carries all the lake's flotsam onto the dam, and no doubt the beavers make good use of what is caught there. Perhaps that explains how huge stumps too big for a beaver to move ended up in the dam.

About nine-thirty I heard the loud chatter of people coming down the trail. They didn't realize how far their voices carried, and perhaps if they knew they'd been overheard, their conversation would have embarrassed them. With a loud splash a cow moose entered the lake from the south shore and soon was knee–deep in search of aquatic vegetation. Loud oohs! and ahs! meant the hikers had made the discovery.

It was time to go. I made a wide detour to avoid the people and circled the south side of the lake, staying well back in the timber, walking amid thick growths of horsetail and occasional soapberry. Bears sometimes feed here in autumn when the berries hang heavy on the limbs; now they might be feeding on the horsetail. I moved with caution, keeping a sharp lookout, and sure enough, I found a grizzly track pressed into the soft mud.

JUNE 20, 1988. Over eight hours to and from Eielson and I saw only squirrels and ptarmigan, not one large mammal. Frustrating, not because "there ain't no animals" as one guy proclaimed, but precisely because they *are* there, and I didn't see any. The brush is thicker than people realize, effectively screening many animals from view. A single bush can hide a moose standing by the edge of the road.

JUNE 20, 1989. Eielson Visitor Center displayed the following information on wolf packs in Denali:

	Wolves	Collared
Chedotlothna	1	1
Highpower	7	1
Foraker	3	1
Birch Creek	13	4
McKinley River	7	0
Clearwater	6	2
Little Bear	7	2
Chitsia Mountain	4	3
Totek Hills	7	1
Stampede	7	2
Ewe Creek	3	3
Headquarters	7	3
Windy Creek	3	2
East Fork	17	2
McLeod Lake	8	3

Before December 2, 1980, many of the packs were outside the park and preserve. But with President Jimmy Carter's signature, Mount McKinley National Park became Denali National Park and

Preserve, in the process almost tripling in size from less than two million acres to over five and one-half million acres. Northern extensions to the park included vital wolf and caribou habitat and range.

The current wolf study, begun in spring 1986, is designed to identify and count wolf packs, map and locate pack territories, identify denning locations and rendezvous sites, and determine the packs' use of areas outside and adjacent to the park. A secondary objective of the study will test the hypothesis that wolf numbers each year are a function of the number of vulnerable prey.

Biologist Tom Meier and his partner, John Burch, have accomplished much in this fourth year of the study. For example, besides the census figures, which will change as pups are born and packs lose members, they have found that, of the suitable wolf habitat in the park and preserve, 36 percent is in the old park, 41 percent in the new park (which is open to subsistence hunting and trapping), and 23 percent in the preserve (open to sport hunting and trapping). Despite the wolves' vulnerability to humans, the main cause of wolf mortality is intraspecific strife. Radio-tracking also has demonstrated that Denali's wolves are at risk when they leave the park; several have been killed, some many miles away.

JUNE 21, 1980. Summer solstice. Today the sun's northward journey from the equator is over. Our longest day — twenty-two hours of daylight. At 63 degrees north latitude, there really is no darkness from late May until mid-July, only twilight. Tomorrow the northern hemisphere begins to tilt away from the sun; the imperceptible slide toward winter begins. Most year-round Alaskans celebrate this, some with parties that continue into the new day. Spurning one party invitation, I hiked up Bison Gulch instead, then onto the north side of Mount Healy to witness the brief night. A little over an hour after the sun dipped below the horizon in the northwest, at about eleven-fifteen, it rose again in the northeast, a little after one A.M. The northern sky remained a brilliant orange all night long. Bugs — always the damn bugs — kept me company. But who cares? A clear sky and the sun shining at one in the morning.

JUNE 21, 1989. High in the cliffs above Tattler Creek, I was surprised to see a ewe sheep with a tiny lamb at its side, born three weeks after the usual lambing peak. All lambing seems late this year, though spring has been mild and mellow with no unusual cold or snow to delay lambing. Perhaps last winter's extremely harsh weather delayed the rut. Will late lambs like this one be strong enough to survive when winter again descends on the mountains? Snow will fall again in just eighty or ninety days.

JUNE 22, 1980. This was my fourth early morning visit to the goshawk nest without seeing an adult. The limbs, bushes, and ground below the nest are strewn with white, downy feathers. The two chicks perch on the edge of the nest and flap their wings with varying power and speed; a wing stroke by one bird tumbles the other backward into the nest. Just when it looks as if flight might be imminent, the chick folds its wings and quiets. Soon, very soon, they both will take to wing. I know the adults are still providing food and will continue to do so as long as the fledglings stay near the nest. Neither adult arrives before I leave, blue skies beckoning me into the mountains.

Another clear morning, a week now of temperatures in the high seventies, low eighties. It is especially hot on the sheep ridges, but the breeze holds down the mosquitoes. The rams I've been following find shade in the cliffs, preferring the mosquitoes and cool air to the heat.

After the long winter months, this heat is outrageous, a ridiculous contrast. All life in the North swings on the cycle of the sun. Not only does the sun provide food and warmth, but it also controls the rhythm and pace of life. Ptarmigan, hares, ermines, and, farther north, collared lemmings and arctic foxes change from winter pelage, then back again, in a hormonal dance triggered by varying doses of sunlight. Migrations of both mammals and birds, breeding seasons, antler and horn growth, and hibernation patterns are partly stimulated by the sun. Birthing, too, must occur when sunlight is waxing, for when it wanes life falters, and soon a harsh icy grip will throttle the northern exuberance.

People are affected, too. The listlessness, depression, and occasional aggression of cabin fever have long been a factor of northern winters. Perhaps because we arrogantly believe humans are immune from nature, we have failed until recently to understand that the lack of sunlight, more than confinement, plays a significant role in the malady. Now we call it SAD, seasonal affective disorder. The cure? Travel to sunshine or receive therapy with full-spectrum lighting. Today my therapy for winter is to lie in the sun a few yards from a band of sheep and snore when they snore, move when they move.

JUNE 23, 1986. The fox den west of Eielson is active again this year. It has been used all but two of the last twelve years. It is an amazing site for a den, a dry ridge facing Denali and overlooking the McKinley River. Each morning and evening the fox family can view the alpenglow on the snowy ridges of the Alaska Range. Hunting is good nearby; the willow thicket larder is full of squirrels, voles, and ptarmigan.

But the fox family has neighbors. Grizzly tracks led me up the bluff above the den. From where I stopped, I could see the tracks leading from burrow to burrow, one of which was excavated like a bomb blast. Good thing the foxes have labyrinthine dens with multiple entrances. I assume all of the foxes escaped, but maybe the bear did get a pup or two.

It was fun to hide above the den and spy on the foxes as they awakened. Both adults were asleep in the sun when I arrived, but soon they were under assault from their pups. The three pups, though still rather tiny, were awkward and full of play, tussling and chasing one another around the den. They harried the red adult until it got up and moved away. They then fell upon the other adult, a cross fox, until she stood up and let the pups nurse. Two of the three pups were very dark, not the usual fuzzy gray. Perhaps in maturity they will be one of the color phases of red foxes — cross, silver, or black. A dark cross over the vixen's shoulders is very pronounced despite the summer pelage. In autumn and early winter, she will be very beautiful.

When the wind quits in early afternoon, the mosquitoes become worrisome to the foxes, and they disappear into their den. Even with layers of repellent, I, too, am happy to retire to my mobile "den" that will soon pass noisily on the road.

JUNE 24, 1989. A grizzly family, a female and two cubs, killed a moose on the trail from the hotel to the train depot yesterday. The trail has been closed, but an early riser this morning could stand on the hotel porch and see bears moving about in the timber.

A female wolf is regularly traveling the road through Igloo Canyon. Until the last five years or so, it was rather remarkable to see wolves close to the road. Now it is not uncommon. Some of the wolves from the East Fork pack, especially two females, display astonishingly little fear of people or vehicles. One often walks the road for twenty miles or more. Behavior that, except in the late 1930s and early 1940s, was observed maybe once or twice a year is now reported almost weekly. Denali may be the one place in North America where a person can reasonably expect to see a wolf.

As human visitation to the park has increased, so have interactions between humans and wildlife. Moose, at least in some parts of the park, tolerate people but to a much lesser degree than sheep. Moose can be dangerous and shouldn't be approached in the casual way some people approach sheep. Bull caribou, too, are often unafraid of people. Although I doubt caribou will become as tolerant as Dall sheep, today some bulls allow humans to approach without taking flight. Grizzlies, too, on occasion, have become habituated to people. But never, never, did I think that wolves would become this tolerant.

At least once before in the park's history, however, wolves may have been as bold as they are now. "Wolves here seem to follow the road from Mile 32 to Mile 55," Frank Glaser wrote in his government field diary on May 3, 1940, while on special assignment to census park wolves. "They do not seem to fear an auto, they just jump clear of the road and stand watching us after we get out of the car." (At that time, unlike now, wolves had reason to fear humans. Harold Herning, the ranger accompanying Glaser that day, shot and killed a "large, fat male" wolf they saw by the road — all a part of an official control program.)

Gordon Haber thinks that the habituation of wolves is bad and that the Park Service should institute an "aversive conditioning" program to discourage the wolves from approaching vehicles or people. His views seem radical to some people, but Haber's position springs from twenty-four years of observations and a pragmatism born of the knowledge that these wolves aren't always protected, even within the park. Four wolves were shot in 1968 along the north boundary between the Savage and the Sanctuary rivers. In 1969 a dead, skinned wolf was found in the Sanctuary River canyon with 00 buckshot in its skull. According to Haber, in the winter of 1982–83, the entire Savage River pack, ten to thirteen animals, was killed either in the park or just outside of it. In the winter of 1984–85, at least five wolves and a wolverine were poached within the park. Around 1981, the alpha male of the East Fork pack was trapped outside the park and escaped with a mangled paw. His pronounced limp made him recognizable until he disappeared in midsummer of 1987.

JUNE 25, 1978. The mew gulls on Sanctuary River are hatching.

Their nests, located on gravel bars in the river, are sanctuaries from foxes and other predators. I accidentally found one today while hiking. A few miles upstream from the campground, tired of fighting the thick willows, I decided to wade the river to the opposite bank. I aimed for a small island, but at midchannel I was dive-bombed by several gulls. On the island, I took a very brief look at the two eggs in the nest, each of which had a hole in it the size of a pencil eraser. Returning four hours later, I looked across the river with my binoculars and saw two chicks wobbling beneath an adult.

JUNE 26, 1986. A marmot lay sunning on "Marmot Hill" near Polychrome Summit. Through the binoculars, I could see it sprawled on its belly, legs outstretched, soaking up the afternoon sun. After this morning's rain, the clear sky and warmth receive just praise from humans and marmots alike. Soothed by the sun, the marmot hardly twitched a muscle in the hour or so I watched it.

It has been some time since I've seen marmots on Marmot Hill in the middle of the day. Perhaps the location is too close to the visitor rest stop for the marmots to find much peace here. Or perhaps they are here all the time, and I just don't notice them. Only a few of the several buses that have driven by have stopped to watch the marmot. They didn't stay long; it's just a marmot. I wonder if the passengers or drivers noticed the five sheep—two ewes, one young ram, and two lambs—bedded on the rocky slope just below the marmot.

All at once the marmot is gone. One minute there, the next down a hole like water down a drain. I caught a glimpse of an eagle soaring away on a thermal. Could the marmot have seen it or known it was coming? Could it have heard the wind over the wings? Or in a brief moment of alertness, was it lucky enough to see the eagle in its stoop?

JUNE 27, 1980. The goshawk nest is empty, the fledglings nowhere to be seen. Hiking in, I saw an adult twisting through the trees in an amazing aerobatic flight. Though I searched through the timber in the immediate vicinity of the nest, I saw no other adults or young. I walked back to the road, having gained minimal insight into the life history of goshawks.

Thwarted in my desire to watch the goshawks, I hiked instead to Triple Lakes, pretending to ignore the intermittent rain. From a slope above the lakes, I could look up and down the Nenana. The movement of weather here is sometimes stymied by the mountains. Today a high pressure area is to the north, a low to the south. From my vantage point I looked south to clouds and storm, north to clear skies.

Earlier this spring, a band of sheep fed on these slopes above the river. I thought it was their winter-spring habitat, so I was surprised today to find them on the highest point of the ridge bedded amid buttercups, windflowers, avens, and lupines. In sharp contrast to the sheep in Igloo and Tattler, these were alert and wary. They saw me at a considerable distance and moved closer to the cliffs. The ridge here is flat and gentle, ideal for predators, but the side is steep and rugged, good escape terrain for sheep. Later, following a trail along the ridgeline, I found wolf tracks and droppings full of sheep hair. At the north end of the ridge, just above the first lake, I discovered a pile of white hair and gnawed bones: the lower legs, hooves, and skull of an immature ewe. Perhaps the sheep have reason to be cautious.

JUNE 28, 1973. On a ridge not far from Eielson Visitor Center, I climbed to a rise to observe an eagle's nest through my spotting scope. For over an hour there was no movement in the nest and nothing much to see except for the startling sight of a ground squirrel moving around its burrow in a cliff below the nest. Suddenly the squirrel's mad dash for safety alerted me to the approach of an eagle—an eagle with a ground squirrel in its talons. It landed on the edge of the nest, settled its wings, and looked in all directions. Two eaglets, hidden until now, reared from the nest, begging with open mouths. The adult stepped gingerly forward, repositioned the squirrel in its talons, and began to tear at it with its hooked beak. It tore off hunks of flesh and passed them into the gaping mouths. As I'd seen with other birds of prey, the eaglets weren't always fed equally. Often the eaglet that fussed the most was fed the most. The squirrel did not last long, and when it was gone, one eaglet had gotten the lion's share. For a few minutes the eagle cleaned its beak on the nest and rested while scanning the immediate valley. Then it winged away, leaving the eaglets tussling with the squirrel tail.

In the high mountains, small rodents, squirrels, pikas, marmots, and rock ptarmigan sustain golden eagles. They also eat carrion, especially in spring when melting snows reveal winter's tally. Eagles rarely kill Dall sheep lambs and caribou calves, though once I saw an eagle dive repeatedly on a yearling sheep. The yearling leapt upward as if to show its vigor and strength, proof that it would be no easy victim. It seemed more play than a serious attempt at predation, but I was unsure. In the mountains, when a marmot whistles or a squirrel chirrs, not only do the little creatures look up or scurry for cover, but the sheep look up as well.

In 1990 an experimental satellite radio transmitter was attached to a juvenile golden eagle to gather information on autumnal migration. Winter movements in east central Idaho were also recorded. Some of Denali's golden eagles migrate as far south as northern Mexico before returning in the spring to nest. The park supports the largest known breeding concentration in Alaska.

JUNE 29, 1978. A large group of caribou, 200 or more animals, mostly cows and calves, have remained the last few days at the extreme west end of Polychrome Flats. Right after calving, caribou tend to bunch together in what biologists call "postcalving aggregations," possibly a defense against predation. Although in the past, 200 caribou might have been an unremarkable grouping, today it represents a substantial percentage of the Denali herd.

In the 1920s, Olaus Murie estimated the caribou in the McKinley region at 30,000 animals. "Although it is difficult to form even an approximate estimate . . . caribou of the Alaska Range probably total 25,000 to 30,000." In 1940–41, Adolph Murie counted 26,000 caribou; 7,000 caribou were counted in 1960; 2,000 in 1968. Will Troyer said yesterday that he estimates the population at less than 1,100.

The population decline is of serious concern. Troyer and others are looking for the cause—or causes. Emigration to other herds, severe winter weather, high calf mortality, poor range conditions, predation by wolves and bears, and hunting outside the park have all been offered as reasons for the decline. Also, the counts done in the early 1930s are somewhat suspect. Olaus Murie's oft-quoted 30,000 was offered as a *regional* estimate. At a time when individual herds were not so clearly delineated, he included animals from the Delta, Tonzona, Yanert, and Nelchina herds. Adolph Murie's road counts probably included some duplication and overlap. Nonetheless, there were substantially more caribou in the mid–1930s through the mid–1950s than now.

Ongoing research has offered further insight into population dynamics and predation. From the late 1970s until the present, the population has sustained a quality growth rate of about 9 percent per year. Through the use of aircraft and radiotelemetry devices, the caribou population was pegged in 1987 at 2,700; in 1988 at 2,900; in 1989 at 3,200; and in 1990 at 3,300. At the end of the harsh, deep-snow winter of 1989–90, biologists reported higher than usual predation on adult caribou and low calf survival, probably due to the poor condition of adults. The winter of 1990–91 was also harsh, with deep snow and crusting favoring predators. In a unique study of radio-collared calf caribou, biologist Layne Adams found that 40 percent of all caribou calves die within the first two weeks of life. Half are killed by grizzlies, one third by wolves. Although this data indicates a rather heavy toll, remember that the herd is increasing despite *predation. Calf losses this high are not unknown. Six out of ten caribou calves born on the McComb Plateau die within a few short days of birth. Since adult females have a very high survival rate—over 94 percent live from one year to the next—once a calf reaches five months of age, its chance for survival zooms upward to that nearly equal to adults.*

JUNE 30, 1986. Parks Highway, milepost 235. Driving toward the park, I saw what I at first thought were two wolves crossing the road, but they were coyotes. They hesitated in the brush at the edge of the road and stared back at me. This wasn't the first time I'd seen coyotes or heard reports of them in this stretch of road. They must den somewhere in the forest between McKinley Village and the railroad bridge. Although coyotes are rare in the park (quite likely because of wolves), this area seems to be coyote territory. Apparently they expanded into the region sometime between 1915 and 1920. Tom Klein photographed a very tolerant coyote not too far from here. Steve Jones has had them around his home, some-times even living in his abandoned dog houses. And on several nights, I've listened to their yodeling song.

It is hot and buggy today. I've spotted a number of caribou up high, either on ridge tops where the cool wind relieves them of the mosquito plague or lying on snow patches or icefields to find relief. I've also seen a number of red foxes walking the road, no doubt looking for road-killed squirrels. Spring is the best time of year to see foxes, especially in the early and late hours when they are out hunting to feed their hungry litters. I watched one fox dig out a ground squirrel next to the sign marking the turn into Eielson. The squirrel was pulled squirming from its den and quickly torn into huge chunks and swallowed, later to be regurgi-tated for the pups waiting at the den. Sometimes the prey is carried back in one piece. Bill Ruth took a picture of a fox with a hare, a red squirrel, and a red-backed vole clamped in its jaws.

JUNE 30, 1989. This evening's naturalist talk at the hotel was the best I've ever attended. A life history presented in an original way, complete with music and slides. Obviously, a lot of research and preparation went into tonight's talk. There was hearty applause.

It strikes me that Park Service owes a huge debt to its seasonal rangers and naturalists. As in all parks, these people make the place work during the peak season. They face the public, answer all the questions, and take care of the daily grind. The permanent, professional staff often stays in the background, putting in long hours, offering supervision, planning, doing the thankless and endless paperwork, and managing policy details.

Seasonals arrive by June and are gone in September. A small minority are college students; most are college graduates, a few with advanced degrees. Some work summers in Alaska and winters in national parks in the West and South that have high winter visitation. The seasonal shuffle between Everglades and Denali is common, as is that between Grand Canyon and other Southwest parks. Some seasonals have worked Denali for five or six years, one nearly sixteen. Seasonals have very little decision-making status, no career ladder, no transfer ability, and no benefits or retirement plan. Despite the high educational requirements, the pay is low, less than the local sanitation or maintenance people earn. Training requirements are often high, as are out-of-pocket expenses, like transportation and room and board. Even considering the low pay, long hours, and hard work, competition for Denali's relatively few jobs is intense. But, not surprisingly, many NPS seasonals abandon their Park Service careers after eight or nine years of service. It is not the love of the outdoors that grows old but rather the dead-end, second-class-citizen life-style that involves moving possessions one to four times per year and having no permanent home.

Put simply, the few permanent Park Service jobs can't accommodate everyone. Given the declining federal budget and the seasonal nature of park visitation, especially in Denali, the future holds little likelihood of change. Seasonal employees' expertise and experience should somehow be better integrated into the decision-making and planning processes. A lot of talent steps down from the train each spring.

In the past, when both the park staff and Park Service were smaller, new people were welcomed with open, almost greedy, arms. In February 1926, a relatively inexperienced young man arrived at the McKinley Depot, hired by telegram to work as a temporary park ranger at $140 per month, not including board. Grant Pearson quickly proved his mettle to his boss, Harry Karstens. He then went on to complete a thirty-year Park Service career in Alaska and a brief stint in Yosemite. He was part of the 1932 Lindley-Liek expedition, the first to climb both south and north summits of Mount McKinley. He became chief ranger, then acting superintendent of McKinley Park during World War II. In 1949 he became superintendent, retiring in 1956. In his retirement, he served as a state legislator and co-wrote with Philip Newell his autobiography, *My Life of High Adventure*.

Two former rangers have told me that Pearson was often difficult to work for. The same thing has been said of other superintendents. Karstens, Liek, and Pearson all had strong "sourdough credentials," an invaluable asset in Alaska prior to statehood. But the young seasonals stepping off the train these days may be just as talented. What may be lacking today, however, is the opportunity for such talent to be fully utilized.

Summer

*Cottongrass, living blizzards along the strand, always
the reminder of winter.*

JULY 1, 1988. Hiked into the backcountry near Moose Creek in a
pouring rain. Because of the deluge I quit early, setting up the tent
on a ridge overlooking Moose Creek drainage.

To warm up, I stripped off my wet clothing and crawled into
my bag. I fell asleep to rain hammering the nylon but awoke to
silence and clearing skies. I snored away both the storm and the
afternoon. By nine-thirty P.M. clouds had dissipated, revealing the
20,306-foot summit of Denali. (I prefer the mountain's Athabascan
name.) Taking advantage of my good fortune, I struggled into wet
clothes to go in search of a photographic location.

With a misty tundra pond as a foreground, I worked on a
composition of the mountain, anticipating the alpenglow about to
play on the summit. Although I've seen this show before, it still
affects me deeply. First there is a luminous mass of ice and snow
against a deepening blue sky. (Above 14,000 feet, fresh snow falls
year around.) The shear bulk of the mountain rising almost three
and a half vertical miles above the piedmont is dazzling. But as the
sun nears the horizon the shadows shift in color, and the cols,
couloirs, and vertical ice walls and hanging glaciers turn from blue
to magenta. What had earlier appeared to be a flat, featureless block
of ice becomes a multifaceted jewel in the late evening sidelight.
After sunset the massif is awash in amber, crimson, saffron, and
burgundy hues. Never are the colors or the intensity of light the
same two days in a row, in morning or evening. The magic always
surprises me. As midnight nears, the color line passes up the

mountain until only the summit blazes with the reflection of the sun's power.

When the last light finally winked out, I was left with an incredible sense of bewitchment. I had to struggle to tear my gaze from the mountain and head back. But as I stumbled a few steps in the right direction, I suddenly heard something that made me catch my breath. Off toward Wonder Lake, wolves sang a ballad to the sky. As it often does, the howling seemed near, then far, as if it were from one place, then from another. Although chilled by the cool evening and wet clothing, I stayed to listen to the wolves. When they stopped, I still couldn't step from the magic, though the eastern slopes of the summit were beginning to glow with the dawn of another day.

JULY 2, 1988. The flanks of the Alaska Range give one the impression of perpetual, unchanging design. But these glaciers and mountains do change. In the spring of 1986, observers noticed that seventeen-mile-long Peters Glacier was surging. A glacier that suddenly, dramatically advances has been dubbed a "galloping glacier" by the press, and Peters Glacier was definitely on the move. By the time the surge halted the following spring, it had advanced three and a half miles. Normal glacier movement is measured in daily increments of inches, but during this time Peters Glacier advanced 75 feet to 360 feet per day.

JULY 3, 1989. Some people think that Wonder Lake got its name because of its inspiring location. Grant Pearson wrote that it was named by prospectors who, after years of living and working in the area, supposedly blundered on the lake and exclaimed, "I wonder how we missed this before?" Pearson said the lake was known as "I Wonder Lake" until cartographers mistakenly left off the *I*.

This tale seems suspect. In the gold rush of 1905, almost every creek that drained the Kantishna Hills was staked from source to mouth. Moose Creek, the site of several gold strikes, drains Wonder Lake. Without doubt, it was discovered early. Charles Sheldon mentioned the lake in 1906. I have my own pet theory of how the lake was named: "I *wonder* where all of these mosquitoes came from?"

Spent most of the morning rummaging through the brush near the lake's outlet searching for the site of Polly's Roadhouse. Diligent searching revealed little, only a jumble of rusted cans and broken glass, perhaps not even from the long-removed roadhouse.

When the trail from McKinley Station to Kantishna was laid out in 1922, John and Paula Anderson staked a 160-acre homestead on this site and opened their inn. William Beach described the 1922 roadhouse as "a well-built log cabin . . . furnished with elaborate combinations of caribou horns . . . used for seats, candlesticks, shelves, and the like." For lunch, Beach and his companion George Godley were fed fresh trout, ptarmigan, vegetables, jams, a "mess" of blueberries, and chocolate cake and candy. Upon leaving, Beach presented Mrs. Anderson with a "bunch" of ptarmigan that he'd "knocked over," and she, in turn, presented each guest with a scarf pin made of gold nuggets from her diggings.

Beach's 1931 book, *In the Shadow of Mount McKinley*, highlights his many trips to Alaska. But the book fails to mention one curious incident: his prosecution for illegally killing a ram inside the park. Prior to his 1922 visit, Beach attempted to obtain permission to kill a sheep. Failing, he poached a ram near his Igloo Creek campsite. True to Alaskan standards in those days, a game warden who saw the sheep head in Beach's camp did nothing about it. But back home, Beach could not keep quiet, and word got out. In September 1923, he pled guilty in absentia, and was fined ten dollars plus court costs.

The Andersons staked their 160 acres in 1922, receiving patent in 1930. Their homestead and roadhouse became a park inholding in the 1932 park expansion. Not wanting an island of private property within the park, and since Mrs. Anderson had moved to California, Park Service initiated condemnation proceedings in 1939. In 1941, three court-appointed appraisers determined fair market value for the land, which was purchased by Park Service in 1942.

Historic remnants and relics interest me, even such mundane things as trash pits, which I find mostly by accident while hiking or photographing. Along Hines Creek is an old cache that only recently tumbled to the ground. The rotted logs and refuse on the south side of Riley Creek could have been part of the original park Headquarters or debris from the railroad construction camp or other private development. On the Savage River, near the original visitor camp, the willows are full of an amazing pile of litter, including an old wagon wheel. Upstream I've found what could be the remains of one of Harry Lucky's cabins and caches. Parts of a huge water pump can be found in the woods north of Igloo, as well as a few standing telephone poles, evidence of an old communications system. (Metallic telephone lines, strung first by Park Service, later extended forty miles by the Civilian Conservation Corps, connected parts of the park. I once saw a caribou skull whose antlers were tangled in fallen line.) Pieces of crumbling spruce tripods that marked the old winter trail are still on the tundra in Highway and Thorofare. Rusting powder cans below Polychrome attest to the original road construction. There are other finds. I wish more of Denali's history had been preserved.

Considerable effort has been spent this decade rehabilitating ranger patrol cabins and identifying and describing buildings at park Headquarters. The area has been designated the Mount Mc-Kinley Park Headquarters Historic District and placed on the National Register of Historic Places. The superintendent's office was originally a ranger's dormitory that has been remodeled several times. Officially, the oldest building in the district is a 1926 log office, recently used to house employees. According to William Nancarrow, however, the log structure now used to store signs is actually the oldest. It was built by the Alaska Engineering Commission in 1920 at Riley Creek and served as a horse barn before being donated to Park Service and moved to the current site. Historian William E. Brown confirms that since no blueprint or documentation exists in Park Service files, Nancarrow's evaluation is likely more accurate.

The 1926 log building underwent significant restoration and remodeling in 1990. The superintendent's building also underwent interior remodeling. The Wonder Lake ranger station, built in 1939, was declared uninhabitable in 1990 and will be rehabilitated.

JULY 4, 1969. Almost ten inches of snow has fallen since yesterday afternoon. It looked like midwinter in Sable Pass. A quarter mile west of the summit, a female grizzly and her two cubs dug through the snow for succulent plants, notably *Boykinia*, or bearflower. Later they bedded down by the edge of the road. In the falling snow, we sat in the truck watching them. All day small and large groups of caribou passed toward the west. The cloud cover fluctuated, the ceiling dropping to envelop the pass in near-whiteout, then lifting to a height of 1,500 feet or so. But the snow did not let up. We saw one other car, one ranger, and about four hundred animals, mostly sheep and caribou.

JULY 5, 1988. Big parties and holiday celebrations last night. The lodges were jumping and the rangers were busy. Lots of craziness. Times may change, but people really don't. "Exceedingly fine time at dance last evening," Harry Karstens wrote on July 4, 1924.

"Good time at Morino's Hotel somewhat marred by some of the men being full of moonshine."

Busiest weekend of the summer. Park and local campgrounds full to capacity. No room in the inn or on the buses either. Even the roadside gravel pits outside the park are full. Motor homes and campers park every place. Sunny holiday weather lured Alaskans from Anchorage and Fairbanks, but they are almost lost in the crowds of visitors from Outside and from foreign countries.

Going hiking today—anywhere but in the park. Well above timberline, small patches of fireweed bloom in fairly isolated patches. In late August when the air's full of wind-borne seed, I used to wonder why the fireweed didn't take over the entire slope. Many times here on the sheep summits and elsewhere I've seen clouds of seed floating by, but fireweed takes root only in disturbed soils. Fire, flood, human construction or damage, squirrel excavations, or other disturbances prepare the ground for colonization and revegetation. The isolated stands of fireweed I looked at today grew where ground squirrels have burrowed. A few sites were occupied, others were vacant.

JULY 6, 1989. "Hello. My name is Kathy Nava, I'm your driver. My job is to watch the road; your job is to watch for wildlife. Don't by shy—just shout out if you see something. Moose on the right. Caribou on the left. And I'll try to stop as smoothly as possible." And she did just as promised. We even stopped for a moose that she hadn't seen until a tour driver headed in the opposite direction gave her the moose hand signal: an open hand held next to the head. A thumb to the forehead, fingers extended upward, would have indicated a caribou; a raised clawlike hand, a bear.

"I love this job," Kathy said at one stop. "I've been at it six years now, and I'll keep coming back until they won't let me anymore." That's likely to be for as long as she wants. She knows the road, knows the trailheads, and doesn't play ranger. She pays attention to the road and to her driving, always erring on the side of safety. Staying constantly alert to her passengers' well-being is stressful. But she's determined not to be the cause of any accident. On her next day off she's going for a hike to look at wildflowers, "probably where I don't have to even *see* a bus."

JULY 7, 1989. Today I joined the crowd on the shuttle bus ride to Wonder—to get a feel for what the average visitor experiences. (Of course, I would pick what's probably the hottest, dustiest day of the year for this lark.) Usually I get off at one place or another along the road to hike all day or watch animals. So it was hard to accept an eleven-hour bus ride. The bus is hot, dusty, and noisy from the banging it takes from the washboard road. For a person as tall as I am, the seats are uncomfortable. These are school buses designed for transferring large groups short distances. However uncomfortable the shuttle bus trip, the unique wildlife sightings usually more than compensate for the discomfort.

For the first third of the trip, all the passengers are keen to spot wildlife, but many soon lose interest. When Dall sheep are spotted on a distant ridge, the bus stops and then lists as the passengers rush to one side to get a better look. The windows crash down amid shouts of "Where are they?" Soon we go on. Later the driver slams on the brakes. A grizzly crosses the road in front of us, and the excitement is intense. When the bear moves off into the brush, we start up again, and apathy seems to settle on the passengers. One person puts on a stereo headset; two others read books; several doze. Now that we've seen the bear, nothing we see later, neither the caribou nor the fox, inspires much interest. Denali's summit is covered in clouds, and Wonder Lake's mosquitoes are neither inspiring nor welcome.

Despite the terminology, this system is not a shuttle. No one gets on or off except at the rest stops and at Eielson. No one dares to get off—the buses are running so full it would be a long wait for another with a vacant seat. (Yesterday I waited three hours.) Considering the general overcrowding of visitor services and the ultimate closing of the road to all private vehicles, a shuttle ride is fast becoming a casual visitor's only option. In practice, these so-called shuttles are de facto tours, and as such are often a failure. Some drivers say little, if anything; others offer natural history anecdotes. (A few times in the past, shuttle drivers were told not to offer such information as it might be construed as competing with the tours, which were ironically filled months in advance with package tours.) Passengers are often on their own to see and learn what they can. The park is not "experienced," it is "viewed," sometimes with growing disinterest.

At its inception in the 1970s the shuttle was a unique, daring approach to park management and actually functioned as a shuttle. I support the shuttle system because I'm convinced no wildlife would be seen if the road were opened to private traffic. But we need a real *shuttle* system again. It seems a gross disservice to this marvelous reserve to limit human experience within it to mass transit.

July 8, 1972. Mosquitoes attacked Ron Lambert and me in ferocious assaults. The afternoon was as hot as I've ever seen it in ram country, perhaps more than ninety degrees. It had been a harsh winter with heavy snows, and the tundra was still spotted with patchy snow. Coupled with the heat, the excess moisture made conditions ideal for the mosquito hatch. I twitched constantly as the swarms bit through my repellent-soaked flannel shirt, but we were immeasurably better off than the rams we photographed. Insects ringed their eyes and nostrils and crawled over their soft undersides. Blood oozed through white hair.

In late evening, a strong breeze gave the mammals a respite. We followed the rams onto a spur of the ridge exposed to the wind. Around eleven o'clock, with the sun just down, we set up the tent. We'd been up since six following the rams, but we were not so much tired as glad the damn bugs were gone in the breeze. Once inside the tent, put up mostly to keep the bugs away, we lay on our bags watching the light thin out over the hills and the rams feed in the cooling air.

I awoke sometime after midnight to the sounds of the tent rattling in a stiff wind and of the distant roll of thunder. The night wasn't pitch black, and I could see heavy scud drifting over the valley. As the wind increased, the thunder crept closer, and flashes of lightning jabbed the Alaska Range. Ron, too, was awake and rolled over to watch the lightning edge across the valley. Soon the storm was directly over us, thunder loud enough to feel. We yelled with excitement as multiple bolts of lightning daggered the tundra and mountains.

I had a sudden thought. "Ron, do you know anything about lightning rods?" He grabbed the tent pole by the door, and just as quickly I pulled down the back pole. Lightning struck close by on our ridge. I can't speak for Ron, but I'll admit to fear. Our packs and tent poles were the only metal objects on this ridge, the highest one around. We gathered the flapping tent to us and watched the storm move east. As the wind died, huge splatters of rain began to fall. When the lightning receded, we replaced the tent poles and curled back into our bags. As the deluge began, the dry earth responded with the scents of soil, wildflowers, and mountain sheep.

Some hours later I awoke in sunlight to the hum of mosquitoes. A short distance away a ram stood staring out over the valley, his damp coat steaming in the golden light. Every now and then he'd stamp his hind leg in irritation over the mosquitoes biting his underbelly.

JULY 9, 1977. This week enjoying a tremendous profusion of wildflowers. While I was photographing some moss campion near the Stony Hill pullout, ranger supervisor Mike Tollefson stopped to ask if I'd seen any bears, specifically a subadult female. I hadn't, and I told him I didn't much care to while lying on my stomach, absorbed with flowers. We got to swapping bear tales, and he told me about the bear he was looking for. Apparently it frequented this area and had charged a hiker not long ago. More recently, some backcountry campers, upon arising in the morning, saw a bear approaching their tents. Without trees to climb in this tundra area and realizing they could not run safely, the group backed away as the bear closed in. Although the bear sniffed their packs and tents, it did no damage. The hikers had prudently sealed their food in plastic bags the night before and hidden them well away from camp.

Abandoning the tents, the bear turned toward the people, who continued to move away. One woman stopped, Tollefson said, and the bear walked right up to her. She said she just froze because there was nothing else to do. The bear smelled her shoes, then just like a dog, snuffled right up her leg to her crotch. There it stopped, looked up briefly into her eyes, then *gently touched her leg with its paw.* After what probably seemed a heart-stopping eternity but was only a split second of contact, the bear spun and walked away.

"Unusual behavior," Tollefson said in classic understatement. He and his staff planned to tranquilize the bear and relocate it to an outlying area.

This event occurred prior to development of bear-proof food containers. On August 14, 1977, a female thought to be the bear involved in this and other incidents was tranquilized, ear-tagged, and relocated from Little Stony Creek to a lake east of the Foraker River. On September 20, 1977, she was seen in the Toklat area but apparently caused no further problem.

JULY 10, 1989. A naturalist aboard the bus talked about wilderness and associated values. One passenger asked the naturalist whether he considered Denali a wilderness. The passenger didn't think so:

"It's got a well-traveled road running through it." There was a lot of discussion back and forth between the naturalist and several of the passengers. (I thought of Joe Van Horn's description: an "accessible wilderness.") Nothing much was agreed upon, including the old principle that wilderness begins where the road ends.

Under the terms of the 1980 legislation that enlarged the park, the pre-1980 portion (the old Mount McKinley National Park) officially became wilderness with prohibitions against certain kinds of incompatible activities, such as mining and off-road vehicle use. Some of the additions became park, and others were made a preserve. This new designation offered protection to the land and wildlife but allowed traditional uses, such as subsistence and sport hunting and trapping, thus preserving both nature and traditional Alaskan life-styles. The 1980 expansion, a piece of legislation perhaps unprecedented in modern world history, included a vast area of valuable, undeveloped wildlife habitat. (When asked in 1956 whether he had ever considered extending the northern boundary to preserve the only caribou herd in the national parks, Grant Pearson replied, "No, they wander over too large an area." Twenty-four years later, that large area became part of the park.) Most of the political heat during the Alaska lands debate flared over the discussion of wilderness, how much land would be "locked up— popular jargon for land to be removed from private ownership, resource extraction, and road building. The same public outrage and political rhetoric preceded the establishment of the park in 1917 and the 1932 expansion. All three pieces of legislation ultimately included similar compromises to placate specific interest groups.

Wilderness has become a buzzword, a rallying cry for a few people, a red flag for others. Personally, I'd like to see the word used less. *Wild* in one sense means "out of control." *Wilderness* has *wasteland* as a synonym. Our undisturbed and undeveloped lands are neither waste nor out of control. Another term seems more appropriate: *natural lands*. Perhaps it doesn't roll off the tongue, but it is both descriptive and accurate. *Wilderness* brings to mind savage beasts to be tamed and conquered—an anachronistic and dangerous concept in a time of shrinking worldwide natural lands. In modern America, *natural* is a word connoting wholesomeness, purity, and high quality. A natural land—Denali in its essence.

JULY 11, 1988. Bergh Lake is empty, nothing more than a wide spot in the creek bottom. I had to hike down and walk around the lake bed.

The lake was formed in 1953 when an earthquake triggered a tremendous landslide. Several days of torrential rains had not only destabilized the slope east of Stony Creek where the slide occurred but also claimed bridges and sections of the Park Road. "At twelve-fifteen P.M. on July 18, 1953," Dr. Bradford Washburn told me, "we felt the violent little shock halfway up Mount Brooks, as did Commander Howard Cole's Geodetic Survey team nearby. Others saw the lake forming shortly thereafter. . . . The lake overflowed its muddy earthquake dam in the midafternoon of August 12. We took a Camp Denali canoe out . . . and found it to be exactly seventy-five feet deep."

Bill Nancarrow, who became the park's first permanent ranger-naturalist in 1951, serving in that capacity until 1954, said that the new lake, which locals called Quake Lake, stretched all the way to the Park Road and threatened to flood it until the water breached the slide dam. Nancarrow said the lake was named for Knute Bergh, a Geodetic Survey pilot who was killed in a plane crash nearby on June 11, 1953. Scott Peak in the mountains just south of Mile 66 was named for Lieutenant Gordon D. Scott, another victim of the crash. These are not the only geologists who have lost their lives in the park. Mount Fellows, the prominent landmark to the east of the park entrance, is named in honor of Dr. Robert Fellows, a young geologist who died of a heart attack in 1949 while conducting geologic investigations in Windy Creek.

Above the dry lake bed I stopped to enjoy the flowers. Though they look delicate, wildflowers have unique strategies to survive this harsh latitude. Moss campion grows in dense mats to keep the inner plant warm. Tiny harebells thrive on thin soils that would not support larger plants such as the prickly rose. Labrador tea's thick leaves withstand the wind; alpine azaleas grow low and dense to minimize wind damage. Arnica's spoke-shaped petals maximize exposure to the sun. Louseworts are protected from the cold by a thick pubescence. Fireweed subspecies are adapted to varied conditions. The dwarf variety, only a few inches tall, grows on thin, arid soils; the six-foot-tall form thrives on the moist loam on the south side of the park.

In late afternoon at the fork in the road to the Wonder Lake campground, a grizzly bear cropped grass along the edge of the gravel pad where Berle Mercer used to keep his horses. Before the park expansion, Mercer's packhorses carried visitors into the park overland along the north boundary and ferried alpine trekkers to the foot of the range.

Somewhat surprisingly, the horses seemed to have little impact on wildlife. I once saw a bear grazing among them. Steve Kaufman, when he was a Wonder Lake ranger, said that a wolf had spent most of one day sleeping on the gravel pad near the horses. Berle told me that moose sometimes were a problem during the rut—bulls getting the wrong idea about a horse. Curious caribou also approached his pack strings. Mercer no longer operates in the park but still lives a few miles to the north, near Healy.

JULY 12, 1984. Along the Rock Creek Trail, the amber light of dawn on the treetops gives way by six A.M. to full daylight. Except for the gentle breeze that shakes the light from the leaves, it is quiet along what later in the day will become a busy trail. A moose forages through the spruce and aspen, its big hooves trampling the horsetail and dogwood. It stops near an aspen that bears the ragged gashes of a moose's teeth. In time the healing bark will enfold the wounds, but the scars of a moose's desperate winter hunger will remain as long as the tree.

Moose nuggets and hare pellets litter the thickets, one the miniature of the other and often the by-product of the same food sources. Hares seem numerous along this trail. Several bushes testify to their winter struggle. From about a foot above ground level, a point equal to last winter's snow depth, to about three feet high, many willows are debarked, some girdled. Many of the girdled plants, their vascular systems destroyed, will not survive; others less severely damaged will flourish despite their prunings. The smaller birch are untouched. Stems growing close to the ground are protected by numerous resin glands whose chemicals discourage hares from eating them. With the sun blazing over the peaks, I watch a hare nibbling flowers growing from the sphagnum, but I remain alert for other wildlife: on occasion lynx and grizzlies stalk through the bracken along this trail.

Near Rock Creek it is so quiet I can hear the dogs howling at the kennel beyond Headquarters. Winter transportation in the early days of the park was by foot, horse and sleigh, or dogsled. All freight and supplies, even the logs for some patrol cabins, were moved in winter by dog teams. Poaching patrols stayed afield sometimes for weeks at a time. Things began to change after the completion of the Park Road and the advent of the airplane. Dog-team patrols were no match for airborne poachers. Over the years, patrols have been slowly cut back. Today the principal use of the kennel is to provide daily demonstrations for summer visitors, though the dogs still go on a few winter patrols. Harry Karstens, famed for his dog-handling abilities, would surely cringe at the changes.

Sandy Kogl does an outstanding job supervising the kennel operation. Not only is she an excellent musher, patient and kind to the dogs, but she also knows how to train, feed, and care for them. She has built several high-quality hardwood sleds, and she trains seasonal naturalists to run a small team pulling a wheeled sled around a short demonstration trail loop. The dog feed cache and sled storage building where the demo begins has been in continuous use since its construction in 1929–30. In winter, Sandy often accompanies ranger patrols into the park.

When dogs sound off, I naturally think of wolves. Most huskies can howl somewhat like wolves, their close relatives. And in fact, hybrid wolves were once part of the park kennel. On May 15, 1940, in the process of excavating and examining the newly discovered East Fork wolf den, Adolph Murie took from it three pups—two grays and one black. He put two back and kept a female, which he named Wags, for further study. In 1943, a visitor described her as quite large for a female wolf and of gentle disposition. She had just recently been bred by one of the park's dogs.

Often this type of cross-breeding produced animals ill-suited for dog teams. In 1934, Frank Glaser gave the park his hybrid leader, Kenai, with the understanding that it would not be used in harness but only for breeding. Although high-strung and difficult to work with, the wolf-dog was said to be gentle and patient with children. Trouble arose when a ranger tried to use Kenai in harness and clubbed it to break up a fight. This was the only time the hybrid had ever been beaten. The next day the ranger made the mistake of turning his back on Kenai, who leaped and grabbed him by the neck, knocking him to the ground. Ranger Louis Corbley saved the man from severe injury, perhaps death. Kenai was destroyed.

In 1927, Harry Karstens' son Eugene, then ten, had another wolf hybrid, also named Kenai, as his constant companion. Eugene recalled that he and the dog were inseparable and that he loved to "rassle" with Kenai. Once when Kenai was asleep, young Karstens jumped on him and grabbed him around the neck. Kenai snapped at the boy, one big tooth just missing the boy's eye.

After World War II, Park Service got rid of its dogs, and their shelters stood empty. No wolf hybrids are part of the current kennel. Many of the park dogs are as gentle as household dogs and sometimes become pets. One loyal, hard-working team dog retired to a comfortable life on a farm in the gentle hills of New England.

The sound of the howling dogs fades as I head back down the trail. The morning is quiet again. Sunlight dapples the forest floor sprinkled with fallen dogwood flowers. The wind stirs the trees to gossip, and a robin sings somewhere to the north.

JULY 12, 1987. Denali *State* Park. In contrast to the frenzied activity now peaking at the national park up the road, the peaceful atmosphere here is stunning. On the hike up Kasugi Ridge, I've seen only two other hikers, yet the views west to Denali's summit and the sea of mountains surrounding it are without peer. Some people say that overcrowding at the national park could be relieved by developing this pristine state park. They propose building a hotel here with National Park Service funds and a visitor center staffed by both state and federal personnel. A cooperative agreement on this proposal was signed in 1985. Advocates say that their plan will offer tourists an alternative destination with views equal to those along the controlled-access Park Road. Opponents charge that development of the state park with roads and hotels will destroy an unblemished natural scene, impact resident wildlife, and in the end become just another destination, not a solution.

Denali National Park is a huge piece of real estate, as big as Massachusetts. Yet almost all of the visitation and impact occurs along the Park Road, partly because it provides the easiest access. But mostly it is the wildlife seen along that road that attracts so much interest. In contrast, the Denali Highway, to the east of the park, offers equally splendid vistas of tundra, taiga, and alpine. But few people travel there because most want to see Alaska's unique wildlife, not its scenery.

Sitting in the sunshine on a boulder overlooking the river valley and the refulgent mountains beyond, I ponder the park's overcrowding, an ironic situation considering its vastness. The northern third of the park is mostly rolling hills and taiga flats, the central mountain region is the section through which the Park Road wends, and the southern third includes the south slope of the range and its heavily forested foothills. Only the mountain region suffers from high impact. I hope that future development is prepared with clear vision.

Early in my hike I was lucky to see a grouse and also a black bear with glossy fur and rolling fat. I'll be lucky if I see a moose, too. Would visitors to a development here in the state park be content with such brief sightings, or would they expect more? Would the mountains be enough? A light breeze soughing through the alders and a warm sun on my back take me from my thoughts and back to the trail.

JULY 13, 1988. Last night I shared dinner and a drink in the hotel dining room with an old friend. Having spent so much time alone, I was distracted by the conversation and activity around us. My friend didn't seem to notice, but I overheard patter about motor homes, highway travel, ball games, ball players, TV. Saw drunks, flirtations, and the usual mix of people. The only clue that we were in a park, or even in Alaska for that matter, was the art prints and photographs of animals and mountains hanging on the walls. Finally, we adjourned for a walk through a different kind of thicket, a forest where thoughts seem clearer and simpler.

JULY 14, 1989. A wolverine has been seen several times recently near a drainage crossing open tundra. Although I've seen thirteen wolverines in varied Alaskan habitats, I know nothing firsthand about them. I packed my spotting scope but left my camera at home, thinking it would perhaps be enough to make a sighting.

My companion and I had difficulty procuring a ride and arrived late at our destination. Our hike had an air of excitement about it, though our chances for a sighting were low. Wolverines are never plentiful, and they roam over large territories. We would need great luck to sneak up on one, for they have keen senses of hearing and smell. More likely, we'd catch a glance of one in the distance or perhaps get to use the spotting scope for a prolonged observation of undisturbed behavior. But even that was a long shot. All of the wolverines I've seen were spotted accidentally while I was looking for, or at, other animals. Three times I've seen one approaching large animals—once sheep, twice caribou—but the wolverines didn't seem to be stalking. My only prolonged observation was when I watched a wolverine digging out ground squirrels. They are its primary prey, along with snowshoe hares, ptarmigan, grouse, and rodents.

From an observation point that commands the upper valley, we sat and looked. My companion, a park naturalist who had seen the wolverine the week before in this valley, used her binoculars as I searched with the spotting scope. We searched back and forth over the same bits of country, hoping to see a brown, golden-mantled form come bounding down a slope. I studied all the rocks that looked like sleeping wolverines, all the draws that could hide one. I jumped when a shape came over the ridge, relaxing when it focused as a mile-distant caribou. We scanned the creek bottom, slopes, and cirques for several hours, giving up only in time to reach the road at the appointed hour for our ride home.

The hours had passed like minutes. On the hike back, I felt a tension that meant that we'd have to return.

JULY 15, 1986. Throughout the forest along the Triple Lakes Trail, there are stumps, blowdowns, and standing dead timber from the 1924 wildfire. Many of the stumps—some of them fairly large-diameter spruce for this area—display the clean cut of handsaws or deep axe marks. This fire was fought with hand tools and back-breaking, life-risking labor. No chainsaws and air-dropped fire retardant were available in those days. It isn't difficult to imagine the danger of fighting this blaze and the desperate attempt to stop it before the flames reached nearby habitations and the wooden railroad trestle over Riley Creek. I can almost smell the smoke and feel the heat pushed along by the canyon winds. It is easy to picture the flight of animals, the frantic battle against the fire, and trees toppled to build fire lines.

July 1924 was very dry and hot, and as always under such conditions in Alaska, fires broke out all over the tinder-dry interior. Rangers fought fires from July 2 through July 26, when rain and cool weather put an end to the struggle. When it was over, an area of thirty square miles was burned—not a huge fire by Alaskan standards, but a dangerous, damaging one. "Morning of the 15th, a strong wind came up from the south again, bringing a raging furnace of flame and smoke to within a hundred feet of [park Headquarters]," Karstens reported to Washington. One ranger's home was close to the fire and in grave danger of burning, but everyone at McKinley Station pitched in to fight the fire. Eventually the flames jumped both Riley and Hines creeks. Karstens felt he could have checked the fire well to the south and outside the park if he'd had a portable pump and sufficient hose. Later, the area around the depot and park entrance was described as a burned wasteland.

Fires are still a summer threat. In 1982, lightning in a remote northern portion of the park started a fire that consumed more than seventy-five hundred acres.

JULY 16, 1989. Ominous lens-shaped clouds obscured Denali's summit this morning. These lenticulars, or "grindstone" clouds, have winds of a hundred miles an hour ripping through them. Often they signal a change in weather. To the north a high-pressure area is weakening, and to the south a low is moving in. Perhaps tomorrow will bring clouds and rain, ending this brief drought. Despite the bright sun, it is cold in the wind. I've been in a snowstorm every month of the year in these mountains. Sometimes I've seen a foot or more of snow in *summer*. Park Headquarters, elevation 2,055 feet, has recorded at least a trace of snow every month of the year. Yesterday it was in the high sixties; tomorrow it could be in the forties. Tomorrow night it could be snowing. Although that's probably not going to happen, winter is the reality of the subarctic, summer the illusion.

While I was visiting with interim park biologist Joe Van Horn, a report of a bear incident was phoned in; A yearling grizzly had torn up a tent in the backcountry near Cathedral Mountain. The bold two-and-a-half-year-old, trailed by its apprehensive mother, had entered the camp despite the shouting, arm-waving people. The adult seemed agitated and nervous as its cub played with the tent and its contents. Eventually the two bears moved off without getting any of the hikers' food, which was stored in one of the bear-resistant food containers provided to all backcountry users. Van Horn said that this was the first such incident in the backcountry in five or six years and that the situation would have to be closely monitored. A bear that has approached people once is likely to do it again.

According to Van Horn's records, there were only four bear-human incidents in the backcountry during the previous summer, one of which resulted in a minor injury to one person. No human food was obtained by bears and no property was damaged.

JULY 17, 1976. Hiked into ram country today via the trail from the Park Road. It wends through thickets, across two small muskegs, and up a narrow, brush-choked gully before heading straight up onto the ridge. Hiking through that gully always gives me the creeps, the same feeling I used to have as a youngster in California, leery of rattlesnakes. Here bears are the concern. Any encounter would be at close quarters. It took me an hour and five minutes to reach the top. I ended up following the ridge halfway to the summit of the tallest peak before finding a band of eleven rams. After a slow, in-the-open approach, I sat down within sixty feet of the sheep. They were soaking up the sun and enjoying the bug-free afternoon. (Where have the mosquitoes gone? A few days ago they were incredibly bad here.)

I didn't take more than a dozen photos all day—nothing spectacular. But it was still a marvelous experience sitting so close to the golden-horned, jewel-eyed rams that I could hear their ruminations.

A friend used to call my walks into the sheep summits "aimless wanderings." Maybe so, but I remain unrepentant.

On the hike back through the gully I was so uneasy—and the thick brush seemed so menacing—that I decided to count cadence in a loud voice. "Hup two, three, four. Hup two, three, four." In so doing, I hoped to avoid meeting a bear . . . or hikers. When at last the gully opened onto a grassy swale, I stopped and turned to look back. A grizzly was climbing the hillside behind me not fifty yards away. The day went silent and very cold. In that narrow canyon the bear had watched me, perhaps only ten feet away, as I shouted my fool head off.

When I reached the road, Chief Ranger Gary Brown and his wife, Pat, were parked on the bridge near the shuttle stop. When I told them of my encounter, they exchanged looks. "Humbling, isn't it?" Gary said.

JULY 18, 1989. Joe Van Horn showed me some of the bones of two caribou killed recently by wolves. One evidenced arthritis in its lower back, which Joe said was common. The other had heavy calcification along the upper spine, which he found unusual. He wondered what part these irregularities played in the demise of the two bull caribou.

JULY 19, 1986. Green is now the dominant park color, an unrelieved, unbroken green that makes me feel claustrophobic. In the thick taiga, the closed-in feeling is almost overpowering on a cloudy day. At least on the tundra, the rocky soils break the monotony and add contrast. Why do I feel this way at the peak of summer's puissance? Perhaps it's the lack of color variation that's depressing. Even during the monochrome of winter, the early morning and evening skies are often painted with pastel hues. Maybe tomorrow will bring color to the sunrise or sunset and into my mind.

While riding the bus, I am surprised to see a tent pitched in an alder patch above the Toklat River. I can't begin to count the number of bears I've seen there or nearby. All backcountry users are supposed to be a minimum of one-half mile from the road and out of sight, but these campers are neither. Judging by the location, they must have been seeking a windbreak when they pitched their tent. Only experience will tell them of the bears.

It takes experience to pick a campsite that's both comfortable and safe. Because firearms are not allowed in the park, campers must think in primitive terms—using terrain for protection and avoidance of conflict. Bears often feed and seek shelter and daybeds in brushy areas, so obviously places with restricted visibility should be avoided. My favorite campsite in the taiga is one that offers an uncompromised vista but is near, if not directly under, a large, climbable tree. On the open tundra I prefer an exposed knob or ridge with a wide view where a bear can be seen from a considerable distance. Often this site means camping in the wind. A prime location in the mountains would be just below a cliff, a place that commands a view but offers an escape route into the rocks in case a bear comes into camp. Always, always, I cook well away from the tent—fifty yards or more—and return to camp only to rest and sleep. I do not want cooking or food smells near my tent, even if I have to cook outside when it's rainy or cold.

JULY 20, 1989. There are eighteen adult wolves at the East Fork den and ten pups from two combined litters—an extraordinary total. Gordon Haber said that in his twenty-four years here, this is the second-largest pack that he's seen. This is also the largest pack Tom Meier has seen in his study. Just a few years ago the East Fork pack totaled only seven animals. It is impossible to say what has triggered this population boom. In May 1988, twelve pups were born; this May, ten more. Two double litters and twenty-two young wolves in two years. Meier suggests that perhaps a new, more vigorous alpha male has something to do with it. Two years ago the long-time dominant male disappeared. Prey availability or weather may have played a part, too.

JULY 21, 1976. Just one month past solstice, and daylight has noticeably diminished. Each day we lose almost eight minutes of light, nearly an hour each week. Dawn broke clear and sunny after a week of storms and rain. Looking across the slopes this morning, I felt a peculiar surge of excitement. The crisp morning air and something in the light—perhaps the way the shadows fell on the slopes or the angle of the light striking them—whispers that soon autumn will be here. Images dance behind my eyes: blueberries ripening on the hills, ice on the creeks and ponds, mist rising from the open water. And, oh, the autumn light! The long lambent light of fall. I'm thrilled by the memories. Animal battles, antler on antler. The smell of cranberry and the tartness of blueberries. A swallow of throat-numbing creek water. Frost on scarlet bearberry. Alpenglow on the serrated summits. Firestorm of light on Denali's crown. Cranes calling and passing in the windy afternoon. Even though winter would be that much closer, I wish today for the painted leaves of autumn.

JULY 22, 1989. The first day in the last ten that Denali has been visible—a wonderful, warm day with puffed cotton clouds floating about the summits of the Outer Range. The early demise of this year's mosquito horde makes the day even better, and the rain last night has put down the dust. All the shuttles are running full; it is the tail end of the peak of summer season. By the end of the second week in August, visitation should slacken.

Spent a pleasant few hours hiking the ridges above Eielson and watching a few sheep. Saw one grizzly at a distance; watched two eagles soaring on the thermals.

Near Sanctuary on the bus ride back, I was jarred from my reverie by a woman's quiet but angry complaint. "No place for a family," she was saying. "All I've done is tend to these kids while you gaped out the window. This park isn't for families." She was young, with two children. One, in diapers, squirmed on her lap while a preschooler leaned tight against her. The little remaining space on the bus seat overflowed with diaper and food bags. She was turned partway around, addressing the man behind her. Her hair was mussed, face flushed, eyes moist. The man sat with arms crossed, saying nothing. "Never again," she said, turning away.

Armed with statistics, surveys, and numbers, Park Service might disagree with her assertion that Denali is not a family park. Just last week I read a report that 48 percent of all visitors were in "family groups." But by its definition, a family could be two people, which was listed as the most common group size. According to the report, 53 percent of all visitors surveyed were over fifty-one years of age, 35 percent over sixty-two—not groups likely to be traveling with small children. This report also revealed that about half those surveyed stayed in the park only one night.

Perhaps the young mother was right. Day care is not offered anywhere in the area, and an eight- or nine-hour bus ride with small children over rough, jarring roads is not generally defined as "family fun." When the bus system was first established, Park Service offered three justifications for the access restrictions: the Park Road is not safe for unlimited traffic; controlled access would minimize wildlife impact; and buses would offer a "quality wilderness experience." When she got off the bus, the young mother had had all the quality wilderness experience she cared to have for one day.

JULY 23, 1989. Perhaps the most unique sighting of a wildlife struggle ever reported here at Denali occurred today.

This morning was cool with a high overcast. The convoy of tour buses headed out the road as usual. At eight-forty-five tour bus driver Alan Seegert spotted eleven wolves in the low saddle on the south side of the road near Mile 42, not too far from Murie's cabin on the East Fork. The pack was headed east, parallel to the road. In the creek bottom below them and upstream of the cabin were a female grizzly and three yearling cubs, also heading east. Seegert said the two groups appeared to be on an intersecting course, but the wind at this juncture (a crosswind to the bears) did not favor the wolves. Seegert theorized that when the angle to the wind became favorable, the wolves fell in behind the bears and followed them upstream.

At nine Ruth Colianni stopped her tour bus at Mile 41 when she saw six wolves 136 yards from the road. (The distances are fairly exact because the tour drivers were equipped with range-finding devices.) She said the wolves seemed casual—milling about, wagging tails, and touching muzzles. Then she saw two bears in an opening in the brush upwind and south of the wolves. Colianni soon recognized them as the family she had seen many times that summer, identifiable because the yearlings were smaller than normal, weighing perhaps only forty or fifty pounds. The wolves began to approach the bears. Within forty seconds the wolves were in full charge. The bears drew together in an agitated state. Dominic Canale, driving another tour bus, arrived in time to see the six wolves and several others pursuing the bears through the brush. In moments four bears — an adult and three small, dark yearlings — pursued by the wolves, flushed into the open, 246 yards from the road, first heading west then south away from the road.

The eleven wolves (a few passengers counted twelve) chased the bears upward along the west side of the gully. The female bear attempted to defend her young by placing herself between them and their attackers, and several times she feinted at individual wolves. Because the cubs would not stay together, she seemed distracted and confused. Intent on isolating the cubs and attacking on the female's blind side, the wolves easily went after the pair or the lone cub by turns. Much of the bear's energy, Canale said, was spent rushing from the single cub to the pair.

About 490 yards from the road, the wolves drove the bears out of sight into a forty-foot-wide gravel depression. I can imagine the tremendous growling and roaring amplified there as eleven wolves and four grizzlies fought for life. Within thirty seconds one cub bolted from the depression, followed seconds later by the female. The cub never hesitated but kept on running. The female stopped several times to look back at the two cubs left behind, but each time she followed her cub to the east. Eventually, wolves straggled from the defile and soon were lounging around the edge of the gully. Others followed in a leisurely fashion. A large white wolf trotted forth with a large portion of a cub in its mouth and lay down in the open to eat it. None of the other wolves approached it. (The alpha female at Each Fork den is a white wolf.)

The female bear and her surviving cub turned north and were last seen in the heavy brush near where they had first been surprised by the wolf pack.

According to the witnesses, the entire incident lasted twenty to thirty minutes. In their report Ruth Colianni and Dominic Canale wrote, "The whole process seemed damn easy for the wolves."

JULY 24, 1990. Although it is not the closest point on the road to the mountain, on a clear day Eielson Visitor Center offers an uncompromised vantage point. Just beyond the river and the near peaks, the mountain often seems close enough to touch. It is easy to understand why people want to climb to its summit. But that desire is what inadvertently triggered both the greatest threat to the region's wildlife and the movement for its protection.

In 1903, federal judge James Wickersham, presiding over the Third Judicial District, an area of 300,000 square miles, attempted to climb Mount McKinley from the north. The party turned around at 10,000 feet after encountering an enormous ice wall, now known as the Wickersham Wall. On the trip north the group prospected the Kantishna Hills. Back in the town of Rampart, Wickersham's party filed gold placer claims for Chitsia Creek, sparking interest in the area. In 1904, Joe Dalton, piqued by Wickersham's open promotion, found gold "in encouraging quantities" on the Toklat River. In the summer of 1905, prospectors Joe Quigley and Jack Horn found "paying quantities" of gold at Glacier Creek. Dalton and Stiles made further strikes on Moose, Friday, and Eureka Creeks. Thousands of gold seekers streamed into the Kantishna Hills during the fall and winter of 1905. Soon practically all the creeks that drained the Kantishna Hills, as well as the ridges in between, were staked from source to mouth.

Stampeders came up the Kantishna, a tributary of the Tanana, first by steamer, then by dog team. Glacier City, Diamond City, Roosevelt, Square Deal, and Eureka were built almost overnight. Hastily erected stores, roadhouses, saloons, and gambling spots sprang up. By late 1905 there were an estimated two thousand people in the hills. As was always the case, the few that staked the limited rich ground did well; the majority of the treasure-seekers went empty-handed. By February 1906, only about fifty people remained in the town of Eureka, later known as Kantishna. Charles Sheldon described it as consisting of twenty tents and a few cabins with fifteen men working Joe Dalton's claim at the confluence of Moose and Eureka creeks. Sheldon was not surprised that such a remote region had neither a gambling hall nor a saloon but did come complete with a lady of negotiable affection who absorbed "a large share of the miner's wages." (In 1910, Alaska had five men for every two women.)

In the Kantishna Hills, once accessible by a rough tractor route known as the Stampede Trail, are the remains of mining engineer Earl H. Pilgrim's Stampede Mine, once the nation's second largest producer of antimony. Pilgrim's involvement began in 1936 when he acquired existing claims and ended in 1978 with their transfer to others. In December 1979, the land was donated to the Park Service, and the mineral rights were given to the University of Alaska. The quitclaim deed charged the two entities to use the site as a study area for the development of efficient and environmentally sound mining techniques. To make the site a safe laboratory, an extensive store of explosives first had to be removed. They were scheduled for demolition by a U.S. Army explosives ordnance demolition team. On April 30, 1987, what was described as "procedural faults and miscommunication" between Park Service and the army team resulted in a huge explosion that severely damaged a mill and nearby structures. A great amount of property of historic value was lost; what remains has been weather-sealed.

Production from the Kantishna Hills from 1905 to 1985, when halted by a federal judge pending environmental assessments, included nearly 100,000 ounces of gold, 309,000 ounces of silver, 1,500,000 pounds of lead and zinc, and 5,000,000 pounds of antimony. The estimated nonadjusted value was twenty-four million dollars. In the early 1970s a ninety-two-ounce nugget was taken on a claim along Twenty-two Pup Creek, a tributary of Glacier Creek. Additional millions in gold, silver, and antimony may remain.

By looking through binoculars or a spotting scope, you can see a cabin at the base of the prominent mountain southeast of Eielson Visitor Center. The cabin was built with logs hauled twenty miles by dog teams. Near that site in 1920, Joe and Fannie Quigley discovered what appeared to be a rich deposit of lead, copper, and zinc. They named the mountain Copper Mountain; their discovery spawned the Copper Mountain stampede of 1921. In 1924, Carl Ben Eielson became the first pilot to fly into the park when he landed his World War I Jenny on a gravel bar of the Muldrow River. Eielson died in a crash in November 1929 while searching in whiteout conditions for the _Nanuk_, a fur ship locked in the ice off the Siberian coast. In 1930, by an act of Congress, Copper Mountain was officially renamed Mount Eielson. _The remains of Eielson's airplane, an all-metal Hamilton, came back to Alaska in 1991 in a Soviet cargo plane. Improved relations between the Soviet Union and the United States made the repatriation possible._

Miners, like market hunters, were a threat to the region's wildlife, prompting Charles Sheldon's successful crusade for establishment of the park. After the Kantishna Mining District was included in the 1980 park expansion, mining operations were shut down. The dozens of patented and unpatented claims in the area offer either opportunity or risk to the park, depending on one's point of view. Because landowners are guaranteed access by the 1980 legislation, large-scale development of Kantishna as a tourist resort or rekindled mining activity could gravely affect the Park Road and wildlife. Before mining was stopped, the use of the Park Road by large trucks was restricted to the hours of ten P.M. to six A.M. to prevent hazardous conflict with buses. Recently, daytime access to the four private resorts already operating in the Kantishna area has been a source of friction. [See August 16, 1990, entry.]

Roberta Wilson's Kantishna Roadhouse prospers near the original, which still stands. The old roadhouse was probably built in 1919 by C. Herbert Wilson, then U.S. commissioner to the mining district. As part of Roberta Wilson's laudable desire to perpetuate interest in the area's mining history, master craftsman Harold Eastwood restored the 1905 recorder's office after it was moved to Wilson's property. The roadhouse offers visitors a relaxed look at "real Alaskan life-styles," including the life-styles of miners.

Camp Denali, perhaps one of the premier natural history resorts in Alaska, is located between Kantishna and the old park boundary. It was founded in the early 1950s by Celia Hunter, Ginny Hill Wood, and Morton "Woody" Wood. The Hunter-Wood partnership, aided on occasion by friends, began the actual construction on Celia's trade and manufacturing site in 1952. Wildlife students Les Viereck, who later became the principal plant ecologist in Fairbanks for the U.S. Forest Service, and Ted Lachelt lent a hand. So did Jeanne and Dick Collins of Minchumina. Even paying guests, such as Walt Disney filmmakers Herb and Lois Crisler, pitched in. Wally and Jerri Cole, the current owners and operators, purchased Camp Denali in 1976. In addition, in 1987 they purchased North Face Lodge from Linda Crabb, who along with her late husband, Gary, had developed the lodge on land purchased from Grant Pearson.

Though one establishment emphasizes natural history and the other history and life-styles, the two resorts have similar roots. "Surely there were many visitors who were seeking experiences genuinely Alaskan," wrote Ginny Hill Wood in 1953, "who would like to go home feeling as though they'd gone a little sourdough." Visitors lived in tent frames and in the evenings heard stories of local sourdoughs, gold mining, and early history. Some of the area's incomparable pioneers had lived full lives of adventure, as well as of hardship.

Tales were told of Johnny Busia, a miner who came to America from Croatia in 1918 and was known for his colorful yarns and home-brewed "Kantishna Champagne." Another notable was Joe Quigley, who crossed Chilkoot Pass on May 9, 1891, his twenty-second birthday, and made one of the original Kantishna strikes. Joe met his wife-to-be, Fannie, in Fairbanks in 1903 when he was suffering from typhoid and she was his nurse. Fannie had left her home in a Bohemian settlement in Nebraska at age twenty-seven and had joined the Klondike stampede of 1898. She paid her way to other strikes by cooking and selling meals. She earned the sobriquet "Fannie the Hike" for her ability to reach early gold strikes on foot. Joe married the indomitable, independent Fannie in 1906. Their partnership dissolved in 1937 when Joe left for Seattle, where he resided until his death in 1958. Though a scant one hundred pounds, Annie at age fifty was said to be as tough as any man, able to mine, mush, and hunt with the "best of 'em." Fannie remained in Kantishna until her death in August 1944. She was seventy-three.

Grandiose schemes have been floated for the area. One man has proposed a rail spur along a route near the north park boundary linking Kantishna to the Alaska Railroad; a complex of world-class hotels would provide services. Fearing the impact of such development, Park Service hopes to purchase much of the private land. The estimated 5,800 acres of patented and unpatented mining claims are reported to be worth thirty-four million to forty million dollars. The environmental impact statement that dealt with mining in Alaska's parks recommended acquisition of all mining claims in Denali, as well as Yukon-Charley and Wrangell-St. Elias national parks and preserves. In 1989 Alaska's Senator Ted Stevens sponsored an appropriation to begin the multiyear process of buying the land. Both he and Senator Frank Murkowski, Alaska's junior senator, supported the appropriation "only on a willing seller basis."

Seventeen patented mining claims, representing 328 acres, passed into public ownership in 1991 with the 2.65-million-dollar purchase of the holdings of Kantishna Mines, Ltd. The transaction used part of a 6-million-dollar appropriation for purchase of Kantishna properties. The acreage was ranked by Park Service among its top priorities because of its potential for private development.

JULY 25, 1989. Early this morning, near Headquarters, I photographed a cow moose and two calves feeding on aquatic vegetation in a tiny, overgrown pond. Although twins are not uncommon, it was good to see that both had survived to midsummer. All three moose were watching me as I approached the pond, but they resumed feeding when I sat down. The cow looked sleek and curried in her short, thin summer coat. Her twins are losing their reddish color now. Soon they will be a rich brown. When the cow turned away from me, I glanced at her rump and did a double take, the Eden-like quality of the scene fading. On the back of each hind leg just above the cow's "knees," thick swarms of flies covered two large, open wounds where the flesh obviously had been bitten away. Either a leaping wolf or a grizzly had wounded the cow in a recent battle. Looking at the calves feeding in the pond, I could only wonder how she'd managed to protect them both.

This morning Ruth Colianni witnessed another wolf-grizzly battle. Just west of the East Fork bridge, she spotted a female grizzly and two spring cubs moving along a brushy river bar. When she stopped her bus in a pullout to alert her passengers, she noticed three wolves fast approaching the bears from behind a screen of brush. "All I could think was, *Not again,*" she said. "Although the white wolf was not with these three and I had no way of identifying them, it seemed likely they'd been in on the kill two days ago. I feared for the cubs." Breaking through the last bit of cover, the wolves charged the bears without hesitation. The tiny cubs ran to their mother, seeking safety beneath her. The female lunged at the attacking wolves, who circled and feinted to stay away from her.

"It looked like the wolves were trying to isolate the cubs, but the cubs stayed very close to their mother and ran under her whenever possible," Colianni said. The fight weaved through the brush, wolves circling and dodging in, the mother bear spinning and charging to meet each threat. "When the family finally was able to distance themselves from the wolves, the female seemed determined to escape across the river and bolted for the water," Colianni continued. But her cubs were unable to keep up. The wolves appeared and closed in on the cubs. The whole bus went wild with shouts of 'No! No! They're gonna get 'em. They're gonna get 'em.' It was pandemonium. Just as the female entered the river, she looked back over her shoulder and saw the attacking wolves. She raced back in time to intercept them, her cubs once again safely between her legs. The wolves backed off." The struggle continued upriver behind a low ridge. In a few minutes all three bears ran into sight and fled across the open tundra. The wolves were nowhere to be seen.

According to several biologists, today's bear-wolf interaction and that of July 23 seem consistent with observations of similar incidents. When threatened, say the biologists, spring cubs tend to stick closer to their mother than do yearlings. Also, older cubs often will either cower together near their mother or panic and run. In some situations, perhaps as exemplified by the incident two days ago, this panicked behavior seems maladaptive, since the female is unable to offer complete protection. On several occasions park researchers have seen large wolf packs approach and surround adult grizzlies, but each encounter ended without serious conflict. In 1940 six wolves were seen to "cut out" one of three yearling cubs who'd been feeding in a dump at Mile 49, but they did not kill it. In most cases involving bears, the wolves apparently were either testing a potential prey or approaching out of curiosity. Wolves are not seen as a threat to adult bears, but as recent events attest, they can be dangerous to cubs.

JULY 26, 1989. Wolves killed a caribou yesterday on the Toklat about one-quarter mile southeast of the bridge. I got up at three A.M., and despite the heavy, threatening overcast, I used one of my permit days to drive out and take a look. Two miles from the Toklat bridge, a gray wolf darted across the road and into the brush. One glimpse, no more.

At the Toklat, circling ravens pinpointed the kill. A bald eagle, only the second one that I have seen in this part of the park, was perched on a boulder near the carcass. Five ravens and a magpie squabbled over the remains. One raven sat on the antlers, haranguing its fellows pecking on the meat. Through the spotting scope, it appeared that half of the caribou had been consumed. I could see into the chest cavity; the white ribs stood out against the red meat. I poured some coffee and settled down to watch. My hope was that a wolf would visit the carcass.

When the tour buses began arriving at regular intervals, it was raining hard. Perhaps the soggy eagle was of interest to the visitors. I decided to head west and allow the morning rush to abate.

In Highway Pass the rain was negligible, but the west wind was fierce. In the canyon south of the road near Mile 57, I saw a herd of twenty-five caribou, only six of which were calves. Just as I was about to drive on, I spotted a wolf making a slow approach about three hundred yards from the caribou. Entirely in the open, the wolf maneuvered downwind of the herd to a gully that offered both concealment from and a direct approach to the caribou. One of the feeding caribou saw the wolf just as it reached defilade. The cow's head went up, her body stiffened. Another caribou noticed the alarm posture and looked up. But there was nothing to see, and after a bit both resumed feeding, unaware that the wolf, using the gully as cover, was drawing ever nearer.

The stalking wolf peeked out of the gully twice to check on the herd. Where the wash flattened into the open, the wolf ran unseen to another wash that was closer to the herd. Then the hidden wolf walked in a slow, almost disinterested manner. It sniffed the ground, pawed at a squirrel hole, stopped to scratch. Two hundred yards from the herd, where the defile opened onto the tundra, the wolf lay down to study the herd. Only six or seven caribou were still feeding; the rest had bedded down. After fifteen long minutes, the wolf was up, walking directly toward the herd. Almost at once one of the feeding caribou saw it. One by one they all took alarm. When the wolf broke into a run, the entire herd panicked uphill into the canyon, quite easily outrunning the wolf, which appeared to struggle uphill. Within a few hundred yards, the herd fractured, half continuing south, half up the mountain slope to the west. The wolf continued straight ahead, perhaps intent on running a portion of the herd into an unseen cul-de-sac. Where the drainage narrowed, the herd divided again, six continuing, the rest angling up the east slope. Pursued by the flagging wolf, the six caribou went from sight.

Soon three cows and one calf ran into view on the crest of the ridge to the east of the drainage. Once on top they turned to look back, but they had lost their pursuer. With increasing frustration I, too, searched for the wolf. Fifteen minutes later I finally saw it lying on a gravel bar near the original site where the caribou had been feeding. Sprawled on its side, the wolf appeared to sleep for twenty minutes before it got up, stretched, and headed west on the scent trail of the first herd fragment.

After another cup of coffee — I don't know why I thought more stimulus was needed — I drove back toward Toklat. Rounding the bend at Mile 54, I saw several buses parked on the Toklat bridge. Only a wolf or a bear would attract that kind of attention. And indeed, a wolf was feeding on the caribou carcass. It was a large gray and wore a radio-tracking collar. The carcass had been torn apart and much of it consumed. The wolf looked bloated, like an over-inflated balloon. Nearby the bald eagle sat in the rain, eyeing the wolf. Three ravens circled on the wind. Five minutes after my arrival, the wolf walked to the river to drink. Even through the rain, I could see that this wolf was not the same one that had been on the road, and it was not the one that had pursued the caribou, either.

After slaking its thirst, the wolf returned to the kill, sniffed and pawed it, but did not eat. Then it walked into the brush toward the southeast.

Less than twenty minutes later, the wolf padded into the open upstream from the kill, looking back over its shoulder at a grizzly that trailed twenty-five feet behind. Two steps into the open, the grizzly charged. The wolf bolted, then circled at half-speed. The bear, which was only half again as big as the wolf, slowed to match the wolf's pace. After a very short pursuit, the bear stopped; then the wolf stopped. The two were separated by only a dozen feet. Again the bear charged, provoking the wolf into a slow lope. The bear closed to within five or six feet before adjusting its speed to the wolf's. Suddenly the wolf halted, and the bear swerved to keep from running into it. Then, without looking back, the wolf lay down, tail to the bear. The bear stared at the wolf, which was literally just one jump away. Except for its ears, which were turned toward the bear, the wolf appeared to ignore it. After a long pause, the bear abandoned its game and headed across the river. Soon it had waded the river and was feeding in the soapberry thicket. When I left two hours later, the wolf was still sprawled asleep in the pouring rain.

Just before I drove away, a bus pulled up next to my truck, and the driver yelled the jaded statement of the century: "Forget about the bear and the wolf. There's a bald eagle by the bridge."

JULY 27, 1986. Between Grassy Pass and Wonder Lake it's hard to miss the beaver lodges, dams, and ponds, though it _is_ hard to tell in summer which ones are occupied and which are abandoned. One method biologists use to census beaver is to conduct a "cache count" just after freeze-up. Beaver collect food for winter by building a stockpile, or cache, of sticks in front of the lodge. Long cuttings of willow, aspen, birch, and poplar are hauled in and anchored in the muddy bottom in front of the lodge's underwater entry. Freeze-up securely anchors the feed pile in place and armors the beaver in their lodge. The water keeps the submerged cuttings fresh all winter. Before snowfall the tops of the plants show above the ice; an aerial survey reveals the active lodges. Then the question becomes, How many beaver live in an occupied house? An average will have to suffice because the number in each lodge varies. Winter lodges can shelter the breeding pair, their yearlings, their kits of the year, and often some older offspring. From just one lodge near Anchorage I once live-trapped and ear-tagged thirteen animals — not an uncommon family size.

Beaver do not hibernate, but the dark chamber built inside the lodge above water level and accessible only by underwater passages must indeed be a cozy winter home. Their combined body heat keeps the beavers' living chamber relatively warm, despite outside temperatures that drop to minus forty and colder. But seven to nine months in a den of stick and mud must grate even on the nerves of an animal as easygoing as a beaver.

Beaver often give birth before spring breakup. A female might endure up to sixty hours of labor before giving birth to four to eight young. The kits nurse for weeks, but they eat some solid food within a few days of birth. A beaver family without a well-stocked cache will not survive the winter.

Two-year-old beaver travel in summer in search of new territories and may move many miles, even overland far from the safety of water. In their peregrinations, these juveniles may inhabit abandoned lodges before moving on. Because they are safe havens for transient beaver, old lodges should not be disturbed.

A very active beaver colony near Wonder Lake has attracted a lot of visitors recently. The beaver have become so used to humans that they hardly seem to notice. They cut and haul branches, sit on the bank to groom or feed, repair the dam, or feed twigs to the kits, oblivious to the human gaggle.

Every active colony marks its territory with scent mounds, dark muddy patches on layers of grass or twigs. I've often seen beaver add mud to these mounds, then clamber up to mark them with the rich scent of their castor.

JULY 28, 1989. Wildflowers have such colorful common names: pixie eyes (for wedge-leafed primrose), ladies' tresses, king's crown, kitten tails, shooting stars, languid ladies, harebell, and the state flower, forget-me-not. I wonder why mammals, unlike some birds, do not carry more lyrical common names. Perhaps it's because of the European origin of many common names or because game birds and mammals are thought of as food or because settlers named them after similar-looking animals of the Old World. The name *sheep* surely does not do justice to the wild animal. Moose, which probably comes from the Algonquin Indian word *moosu*, meaning "he strips bare" or "he eats off," a reference to feeding habits, doesn't carry a very flattering connotation. In French, moose is *élan*. Ah, now there's an appropriate word.

The common name that most troubles me is *grizzly*. It even sounds fearsome — it rolls from the tongue like a growl. American aboriginals and early white settlers, armed as they were with primitive weapons, greatly feared this beast. Over the years grizzlies have acquired a reputation for ferocity far beyond their actual temperament. Now people are beginning to appreciate the bear for its beauty and marvelous nature. At one time grizzlies' scientific name was *Ursus horribilis*, "the bear that makes one's hair stand on end." Now they are classified *Ursus arctos* and more descriptively named the brown bear. *Brown bear* — same animal, different name, different effect. With fewer than one thousand big bears left in the United States, excluding Alaska, the time has come to modify the name as well as the attitude.

My introspection exploded when the bus driver slammed on the brakes. I was flung forward and back before tilting left as my fellow passengers charged to the windows. "Wolf! Wolf!" I joined the stampede. A wolf was pursuing a frantic ground squirrel in Highway Pass. The chase went left, then right, then crossed the road behind the bus. We charged to the right side of the bus. In a flash the squirrel doubled back across the road, the wolf in hot pursuit and gaining. We charged back to the left side of the bus. Fifteen yards away on the open tundra, the wolf closed on its prey with a quick pounce and a fatal snap of jaws. A roar went up from the bus, startling the wolf, as forty people watched the wolf gulp the squirrel in three bites.

This wolf was gray. In twenty years here, I've seen only one that wasn't. Reading field reports from the 1930s and 1940s, I've noted that a third to a half of the wolves seen then were black, the rest gray. I've wondered if legal aerial wolf hunting in the 1950s, coupled with poaching, has selected against black wolves, their color rendering them more vulnerable on the snowy terrain. *Of the eighty-two wolves that biologists Tom Meier and John Burch had radiocollared by spring 1990, only eleven were black. Meier estimated that only 10 percent of the park's wolf population was black. And most of them were not found on the open tundra but in the forested areas.*

JULY 29, 1976. I saw Bill Berry this morning sitting on a knob by Polychrome Pass sketching a caribou. Three hours later he was still there. No wonder his art borders on greatness. His illustrated book about Alaskan moose, *Deneki*, is richly detailed and accurate in both artistry and biology. Unlike many wildlife artists who draw from photographs or from imagination, Berry is a classic naturalist-artist. His drawings and his bronzes breathe life into animals. No detail seems too small to overlook. When I drove by on the return trip, I marveled at his concentration. In the calm, muggy weather, he must have been enveloped in mosquitoes. What truly amazed me was that he'd come here in the early 1950s, and after turning out an impressive body of work for nearly twenty years, he was still able to "see" in a fresh way a scene or an animal he had probably worked with dozens of times.

Before coming to Alaska, Berry had worked for Walt Disney Studios and on wildlife dioramas at Disneyland. From 1973 to 1975, he painted a diorama of Alaskan wildlife for the Denver Museum of Natural History. Through his dioramas, paintings, bronze sculptures, sketches, and books (*Deneki* and *Buffaloland*), he has achieved a reputation as a meticulous illustrator and chronicler of the natural world.

William D. Berry died in 1979. At the time of his death, he was working on a fantasy mural in the children's section of the Fairbanks North Star Borough Library. In 1989 The Alaskan Field Sketches of William D. Berry, 1954–1956 *was published by the University of Alaska Press, Fairbanks.*

JULY 30, 1987. Today a passenger became irate when the shuttle bus driver refused to allow him to get off the bus when it was near a caribou. Park regulations prohibit passengers from exiting the bus when it is within one-half mile of an animal. In the past I've seen people get off the bus and immediately begin running toward an animal to get a photo before it "gets away." Invariably, the animal flees.

At times wildlife harassment has been a problem in the park. Although there is no full agreement on what constitutes "harassment," it is generally regarded as anything that negatively affects wildlife behavior. Park Service asks people not to approach animals. Nesting or denning wildlife is specifically protected. Additionally, federal regulations prohibit the intentional disturbance, harassment, or feeding of wildlife. Wild animals in the Far North are waging a constant struggle for survival. They must obtain enough food, cover, and rest to cope with the unrelenting demands of weather and terrain.

One photographer, an off-duty park ranger who should have

known better, kept a golden plover off its nest so long that he endangered the chick. Instead of leaving the nest site so that the frantic adult could return, he picked up the chick to warm it in his hand. He did the birds no favor. On another occasion, photographers David Rhode and Michio Hoshino were photographing a cross fox that was hunting in the brush near the road. Every so often the fox would pounce on and eat what they assumed was a mouse. Hunting seemed extra good, but it wasn't until the fox came up with a hot dog in its mouth that the men realized someone had baited the hill.

Denali has developed an extensive photographers' code of ethics that must be signed by professionals seeking special travel permits. The code has undoubtedly prevented many problems, but it has been no panacea. Both amateur and professional photographers continue to violate ethics, and in response, each year the rules get tougher. As long as getting the shot is a person's sole motivation, violations of ethical standards will continue.

Some people, including some professionals, can't seem to stay away from bears. It is precisely this human-bear interaction that most concerns park managers. Bears and moose, especially cows with calves, can be dangerous. Park regulations read, "Grizzlies in the backcountry must not be deliberately approached any closer than one-quarter mile." The distance was selected because a person was once injured by a bear that charged from a quarter mile away. "Bears which are within one-half mile of the road must be observed and photographed from the road. Bears within one hundred yards of the road must be observed from, or immediately adjacent to, an accessible vehicle." Even one human-bear encounter, no matter how brief or innocent, can forever change bear behavior.

Another issue concerns the public enjoyment of the park. One of Park Service's chief management goals is to give visitors traveling by bus a chance to see wildlife. That's why other travel is restricted. But disturbing wildlife near the Park Road defeats this goal. So hikers and photographers should do nothing to interfere with animals in easy viewing distance of the road.

Denali National Park was set aside not as a photographer's playground but as a sanctuary for wildlife and natural country. All wildlife watchers and photographers should begin with the question, "Will my actions in any way harm or endanger my subject?"

JULY 31, 1985. Another fine day. This was one of the driest Julys in twenty-two years. The driest was in 1976, with only 1.11 inches of rain; the wettest was in 1967, the year of the big Fairbanks flood, when 7.39 inches fell. I savor this last day of July; few others have been so lovely.

JULY 31, 1988. The Park Road means different things to different people. It has private legends. Mine goes like this: "In that willow patch I once saw a wolf. There a fox. There a grizzly. And once, here at this milepost, a lynx crossed." Each mile holds stories and shadowed memories. Long stretches of road remain where I haven't seen animals, but the berries and fall colors in those places have been more than compensation. Not seeing a particular animal isn't the disappointment it once was. Now it's more fun to go afield without a specific subject in mind. Would anyone else find my road legend interesting? Would someone like to drive the road and hear the details? It would take a week to tell it all. My passenger would probably be bored to distraction. It is my legend, however, and every day I relive it in some small way.

Late Summer

Summer's puissance, shocking in its brevity, begins to fade.

AUGUST 1, 1988. Nothing fits more awkwardly in a backpack than one of the park's bear-resistant food containers, a hard plastic cylinder with a smooth surface. Despite the bulk, I'm more than happy to have one. Prior to the food container loan program, backcountry users in the park often had to cache their food on the ground, since there are no trees on the tundra. This practice was partly responsible for Denali's high level of backcountry human-bear incidents. A new bear-management plan implemented in 1982 has led to a ninety-two percent decrease in backcountry incidents. Education and use of the food containers have resulted in a substantial reduction in property loss and damage and a ninety-five percent decrease in bears obtaining human food or garbage in the backcountry. Today it would appear that fewer bears associate human campsites with food, making the backcountry a safer place to visit.

Denali's official "no established trails" policy, like the removal of the mileposts, is an attempt to preserve the park's wilderness aspect. Maintained trails, with predictable, oft-used campsites, would also result in increased bear-human incidents and encounters. Construction in the park of typical groomed trails would, in the end, negatively impact Denali's robust bear population.

To ensure a high-quality wilderness experience, as well as to minimize impact on sensitive wildlife, Denali's backcountry has been divided into forty-five units. A limited number of people are allowed overnight in each. Permits for some units are highly prized; a few go begging. Some units have been closed to both camping and day-hiking since 1978, a few since 1973. Others are closed temporarily because of problems with bears.

The policy's intent is to protect wolf dens and rendezvous sites, both active and inactive. Before whelping, wolves may prepare more than one den in their home territory, and throughout the summer, the pack may make complex, unpredictable moves, even using two or three sites simultaneously. Pups are often moved to secondary dens in early July. Wolves may relocate to combine litters, to avoid human disturbance, or to seek better hunting grounds. For all those reasons, it's difficult to say which dens will be active and which won't.

A study of the effects of human disturbance on wolves, conducted by Richard Chapman in the mid-1970s, found that the "mere presence of humans seems sufficient to disturb wolves at homesites." The most serious impact, he concluded, could be nutritional: if wolves move to secondary sites in search of prey but then must abandon the den because of human pressure, pups might not be ready by summer's end for the rigors of winter.

Chapman recommended closures around dens four to five weeks before whelping and until inactivity has been confirmed. The closed area, he wrote, would have to be large enough not just to keep people away, but also to prevent people from even pinpointing the dens and rendezvous sites, in accordance with Park Service policy forbidding the publicizing of wolf homesites. Gordon Haber, too, has called for closing a large area around each den so that the wolves can move into them undisturbed.

Just before the arrival of the new superintendent in 1989, the ban on hiking and backcountry camping in some units was lifted. The closures, rangers said, left too much of the park inaccessible. The new policy would protect only active dens and rendezvous sites, but Park Service said there was no change in its basic objective of protecting wolves.

Gordon Haber, who had been largely responsible for the old policy, protested the reopenings. Backcountry use, already at levels far higher than when the areas were first closed eighteen years before, would interfere with the wolves, he argued, and Park Service should close even areas of potential use.

For the new policy to succeed, one biologist said, Park Service would have to monitor sites and close areas quickly as needed. And on at least three occasions in 1990, areas into which wolves moved were promptly closed. "We cannot manipulate wolves into living where we want them," the biologist said, "Wolves, not biologists, should choose where they want to go."

Russell Berry, the park superintendent, has closed areas where pup survival could be at risk because of human intervention.

Today I was lucky to get a permit for one of my favorite backcountry areas. After a three-hour hike across the tundra, I pitched my tent on a little knoll above a beaver pond. Then I found a place to hide in the willows downstream from the beaver dam. I didn't wait long for action. Every beaver that came downstream stopped to work on the lower dam. It appeared that their work was not new construction but maintenance. Dam construction and repair are thought to be a response to the sound of running water. Just enough water was spilling over the dam to make an audible purling. Each beaver added twigs and mud where the water poured over the dam. The fourth beaver on the scene, the largest, pulled sticks across the pond from the far bank and worked them into the dam. The beaver swam with the cuttings grasped in its incisors, and I had a good chance to see how the skin flaps behind the teeth closed to prevent the intake of water. Once at the dam, the beaver aimed the stick with its front paws and, using its weight, forced the stick into the dam. Once, it dove to the bottom and shoved a large limb into the base of the dam. After adding wood to the dam, the beaver repeatedly dove, surfacing each time with mud held against its chest, which it then smeared with its nose and paws onto the dam. Satisfied with its handiwork, the beaver swam away, but it soon returned with a six-inch-diameter, twelve-foot-long tree. Battling the current, the beaver struggled to fit the sapling into the dam at its breach. After much splashing and shoving, the beaver succeeded only in pushing the stick over the dam and into the current on the opposite side. So much for nature's marvelous engineers.

AUGUST 2, 1980. Perhaps I'm being too romantic, but I cling desperately to the illusion of unexplored miles and unspoiled earth. I look away from the road. I go where my chances of seeing people are nil. I turn if a corner of the sky is marred by aircraft vapor trails. I don't like the sound of planes or vehicles passing in the distance. Each year the illusion of pristine nature is harder to achieve here.

Earlier today, while I was watching a moose near the road, a passing shuttle bus slammed to a halt. Windows clacked down. Faces obscured by cameras appeared behind them. Happy voices exclaimed at the size of the moose as it walked from the timber and into the open. There was the sound of motor drives, and I could almost smell the film as it burned through the cameras. Hidden behind a tree, I had to laugh. These aren't shuttle buses but *shutter* buses. They are even wrapped in Kodak yellow.

AUGUST 3, 1988. A man on the bus said he wanted to get a close-up of a bear just like "one of the photos in the hotel lobby." His companion cautioned him. "It probably took a lifetime of effort and risk to get it," she said, "and the guy probably knew what he was doing." Near the Toklat, he got off the bus; the woman stayed on. "Stupid," she said to no one.

Bears have hurt people here, and with few exceptions, the most severely injured have been those who willfully approached a bear. The man's comments made me think about the role and ethics of wildlife photography. Often pictures are published with no explanation of how they were taken. These pictures inspire others to duplicate them, and in the case of bear photos, the consequences can be serious. Most of the good bear photographs made here resulted from patience, not risk. The outstanding photo that inspired the man was taken from the Park Road by a photographer standing next to his vehicle. He used an extremely long telephoto that filled the frame without crowding the bear. The woman was right: The photographer who took the picture, Johnny Johnson, did know what he was doing. He was a park ranger from 1968 to 1977. He is patient, moves slowly around animals, uses all the best equipment, and knows animal behavior. He never approaches bears. No picture is worth a life — a human's or a bear's.

AUGUST 4, 1988. In Sable Pass the bus stopped for a bear. As always, there was lots of excitement. After a generous interval, we continued west. A man in front of me said to his seatmate, "Wake me when we come to the next attraction." *Attraction*? Since my first bus trip over this road in 1972, I've often been reminded of my childhood trips to Disneyland with its simulated rides through the Grand Canyon, beaver country, and the Painted Desert. Groups on a train peering out at fake bears, beaver, moose, and other animals hiding in the fake rocks or trees . . . nature study by mass transit . . . man apart . . . real world voyeurism. What a loss to experience Denali in this way. Just another attraction. Welcome to Denaliland.

AUGUST 5, 1977. On a long hike into the hills downstream from the East Fork bridge, I was dismayed to see a small aircraft rising above the canyon. A distant reverberating roar accompanied the takeoff. Knowing that aircraft landings in the park are illegal, I abandoned my photography and hurried to a prominence from which I had an uncompromised view of the river. The plane was too far away for me to get numbers even with the aid of binoculars, but I watched it head north until it was out of sight and out of the park. For over two hours I continued to study the slopes and river in the area where the plane had taken off, fully expecting to see hikers — most likely poachers — dropped off by the plane. Since the late 1960s an unscrupulous guide has had a camp on the Toklat River just outside the park. He brags that each of his "hunters" always kills a moose, caribou, grizzly, and Dall ram. Though there are moose and bear and occasionally caribou outside the park near his camp, there are never sheep. Sheep hunting season opens state-wide on August 10. A person not averse to hunting in the park probably wouldn't mind jumping the season by a few days. It was with great reluctance that I gave up my visual search and headed toward the road and the last bus out.

[I reported my observation to acting Chief Ranger Bob Gerhard. The ranger he dispatched to the East Fork the next day found aircraft tire tracks but no sign of any poaching activity. *In the 1980 expansion, the area surrounding the guide's camp was included in the park, but by then his operation was said to have moved to the Alaska Peninsula.]*

AUGUST 6, 1987. I was standing by the road glassing the Poly-chrome Flats when two women stopped their truck next to mine. "See anything?" they asked. They meant wildlife. "I see the moun-tains rising above the lime green tundra dappled with sunlight," I said. "I see the coruscating river channels and an eagle soaring on a thermal above the ridge behind us. I see shapes of animals and winged creatures in the clouds and their reflections on the glacial tarns by those huge erratics. I hear squirrels, ptarmigan, pikas, and marmots, and every now and again, the eagle . . . oh, and I see and hear you two." They looked at me as if I were a specimen from Mars and drove off. Their dust hadn't settled before I was anguish-ing over my flippancy. *What a jerk, Walker!* I had even used the biggest words I could dredge up. *Coruscating?*

I do believe, however, that people in their rush to see a bear or the mountain often miss what is really worth seeing. Whenever old Joe Hankins heard somebody complain about not seeing a bear, he'd cut them off with, "What d'ya expect? This ain't no zoo." True, it ain't, but next time I'll just say, "No. Haven't seen a thing."

The wholesale slaughter of caribou and other wildlife by market hunters caused many concerned citizens to call for the establishment of Mount McKinley National Park. (Courtesy of the Thomas Gibson Collection, Archives, Alaska and Polar Regions Department, University of Alaska, Fairbanks.)

The construction settlement of Riley Creek provided housing for railroad workers and, later, building materials for the original park headquarters. (Courtesy of the Alaska Railroad Collection, the Anchorage Museum of History and Art.)

Fannie Quigley journeyed to Alaska in 1898 as part of the Klondike gold stampede and remained there for the rest of her life. The independent "Fannie the Hike" was famous for her ability to reach even remote gold strikes on foot. (Courtesy of the Stephen R. Capps Collection, Archives, Alaska and Polar Regions Department, University of Alaska, Fairbanks.)

Maurice Morino's original Parkgate Roadhouse offered accommodations to visitors of the new park. (Courtesy of the Alaska Railroad Collection, the Anchorage Museum of History and Art.)

Morino's larger Mount McKinley Park Hotel was destroyed by fire in 1950. (Courtesy of the Anchorage Museum of History and Art.)

Horses pulled sleds loaded with seven thousand pounds of mail through the Nenana Canyon near the park. Large equipment, such as this railroad engine, called a dinky, could also be transported in this manner. (Courtesy of the Alaska Railroad Collection, the Anchorage Museum of History and Art.)

Top right: Harry Karstens was appointed the first superintendent of Mount McKinley National Park in 1921. (Courtesy of the National Archives.)

Bottom right: From 1922 to 1924 Karstens had his office in this log building on the banks of Riley Creek. (Courtesy of the National Archives.)

The buildings of the original park headquarters at Riley Creek were erected with materials salvaged from the nearby railroad construction camp and abandoned Lynch's Roadhouse. (Courtesy of the National Archives.)

Some sections of the Park Road were constructed by Alaska Road Commission laborers using hand tools. (Courtesy of the Alaska Road Commission Collection, Alaska State Library.)

Steam shovels and tractors were used to clear the route for the Park Road along the Polychrome Cliffs. (Courtesy of the Edmunds Collection, the Anchorage Museum of History and Art.)

The McKinley Park Post Office opened in the late 1920s. It was located in Maurice Morino's original Roadhouse. (Courtesy of the National Archives.)

The first car finally arrived at Mount Eielson in 1932. (Courtesy of the Alaska Road Commission Collection, Alaska State Library.)

A lot of snow fell in June 1932, but workers managed to keep open the section of the Park Road near Polychrome Summit. (Courtesy of the Alaska Road Commission Collection, Alaska State Library.)

Early visitors to the park were greeted by this large wooden gateway, just a few hundred feet behind the depot. (Courtesy of the Alaska Road Commission Collection, Alaska State Library.)

Frank Glaser came to the park in 1922 to help Olaus Murie capture caribou. He remained in the area, trapping on the Savage River until the late 1930s, conducting a census of park wolves and their dens in 1940, and working as a predator-control agent for the Fish and Wildlife Service until the mid-1950s. The sign by his side is grossly in error. (Courtesy of Jim Rearden.)

Frank Glaser's hybrid wolf-dog, Kenai, was given to Park Service for stud purposes in 1934. The high-strung animal was destroyed after attacking a ranger. (Courtesy of Jim Rearden.)

Bergh Lake, known to locals as Quake Lake, was formed in 1953 by an earthquake-triggered landslide that blocked off Stony Creek. The lake soon overflowed its earthen dam. (Courtesy of Bradford Washburn.)

Adolph Murie, shown in 1967 at the East Fork Cabin, travelled to Alaska in 1922 to assist his brother Olaus with a caribou-capturing operation for the U.S. Biological Survey. (Courtesy of Louise Murie-MacLeod.)

Joe Crosson (in the cockpit) made the first scientific flight over Mount McKinley and the second landing in the park. Carl Ben Eielson had made the historic first landing in the park in this same Curtis JN-4D, the first "Jenny" in Alaska. With Fairbanks proudly emblazoned on each side, the canvas-covered plane is now restored and on display at the Fairbanks International Airport. (Courtesy of the Alaska Aviation Heritage Museum.)

Proper handling of supplies and garbage will prevent the problems that can result when bears obtain human food. (Tom Walker)

From late August through much of September, bull moose battle for breeding dominance. (Tom Walker)

A Dall ram stands sentinel in front of Mount McKinley. Denali National Park is first and foremost a wildlife sanctuary. (Tom Walker)

Tour buses stop on Stony Hill for passengers to view the mountain. Increasing numbers of visitors threaten to overwhelm the park. (Tom Walker)

AUGUST 7, 1975. Best chance of seeing bears in the park is almost always west of Toklat River. Beyond Mile 54, brush is minimal and the open tundra and slopes afford excellent visibility.

One day in Highway Pass, I watched a bear digging out a squirrel on a steep, soft-soiled hillside a quarter mile from the road. Within just a few minutes the bear had excavated a hole large enough to crawl halfway into. In another ten minutes, only the bear's rump was visible, dirt flying from between its legs. An eruption of dirt and fur signaled a squirrel's break for safety as it darted from beneath the bear's hind legs. A veering chase, a burst of speed, a flash of paws, and—crunch!—the squirrel was lunch. It would hardly seem a meal worth the effort. Perhaps the female can be forgiven for not sharing it with her begging, two-year-old cubs.

The bear family moved downstream, going east along the creek parallel to the south side of the road. A caribou was headed west, going upstream. With almost perfect timing the bears reached one end of a thicket of willows just as the caribou arrived at the other. Heads down, the animals passed on opposite sides of the thicket at almost identical speeds, unaware that they were within ten yards of one another. The caribou walked on, while the bears stopped to graze the end of the willow bar. A cub stood on its hind legs, pulled down a branch, and teetering on one leg, tried to do the bear equivalent of chin-ups. With a sudden snap, the willow broke and the cub sprawled on its back. Frightened, it ran for its mother, spooking her.

AUGUST 8, 1989. Day after day, week in and week out, for almost four months bus drivers run the same route. They make ninety to a hundred trips a summer into the park. Perhaps no other park visitors have observed as much wildlife activity as the veteran tour and shuttle bus drivers. The opportunity to witness rare sights lures the same drivers back. Even so, the job can get monotonous with the same visitor questions, comments, and peeves repeated over and over. But a driver must have the wisdom and compassion to realize that each caribou, bear, or vista might be a first for this day's visitors. Perhaps for them the "same old thing" is a once-in-a-lifetime opportunity.

Today we spent fifteen minutes watching a bull moose in a roadside thicket. To me, he was unremarkable in behavior and conformation. Yet when we drove on, the smiles and thanks of two visitors from Sweden demonstrated what it's all about.

White gentians in bloom, about the last wildflowers in a succession of flowering, are a sign that summer is almost over. There are other signs, too: one yellow leaf here, another there. A few red leaves in the blueberry bushes already heavy with unripened fruit. Ripening berries. Stars visible in the brief, dark night. Northern lights. Bull moose antlers almost completely formed beneath their velvet covering. The brief boreal summer, so bittersweet in its intensity, is subtly fading.

AUGUST 9, 1975. Near the mineral lick west of Polychrome, seven ewes and four lambs waded into the muddy bog to eat the soil. Although the lambs seemed content to play, the adults ate the soil in earnest. Their tongues played in and out as each sheep cleaned its mouth after feeding. One ewe ate the mud and also drank the turbid water pooled in it.

There are at least seven mineral licks in the area from Igloo to Toklat. Sheep use two at high elevations; caribou use the one on Polychrome Flats; and moose, sheep, and caribou all like the four licks near Igloo Mountain and Big Creek. These sites used to be called salt licks, but apparently sodium isn't the ingredient the ungulates crave. It has been suggested that the ingestion of the magnesium- and calcium-rich soils balance the potassium from plants. Some of the ingested substances, especially calcium and phosphorus, help build strong horns and antlers. Perhaps the clay also rids the system of internal parasites.

A pika calling from the rocks drew me away from the sheep. It took a search to find the rock-colored pika, but then I found others as well. Two were collecting plants to dry for winter. In the Rockies, pikas are often called Haymakers, and on this warm, sunny day, they were living up the name. They scurried back and forth from pasture to rock pile, their mouths stuffed with greenery. To survive the winter, each pika stores a stack of dried plants in caves and tunnels.

A marmot's warning whistle as an eagle passed overhead sent pikas, marmots, and squirrels scurrying for safety. A covey of rock ptarmigan flushed as the eagle soared by. Soon the pikas were back at work. With snow not far away, they could not afford to procrastinate.

AUGUST 11, 1975. High sixty-six, low thirty-two. With the passage of a front, yesterday's rain turned to snow last night. This morning the mountains were white with the first snow of autumn.

Much of it has already melted in the warming, cloudy day. Many of the bus passengers buzz about the summer snow. Although that may be the season in the Lower Forty-Eight, here we are fast approaching autumn.

The bus stopped for a brood of willow ptarmigan on the road edge. Already the eight birds herald the impending season; their wings and legs are white. Before long their feet and toes will be fully feathered. All were picking gravel for their crops to help grind coarse food. With a sudden jab and snap of its beak, one bird plucked an insect out of the air. Over the last week, the mosquito squadrons have noticeably curtailed their sorties. And with twenty-five to forty species of mosquitos hereabouts, the daily flights were not minimal. As the season progresses, fewer insects will be available to ptarmigan, and once the berries are gone and the summer plants are dried up or covered with snow, their diet will shift to buds and twigs.

AUGUST 12, 1989. Ram country. Perhaps five or six years have passed since I last visited here. The hike in used to take me a little over an hour; today it's taking much longer. As late as 1982 this was one of the most popular hikes for visitors wanting to see Dall rams. But the trail has been only slightly used in the last few years, and it's being reclaimed by grasses and sedges. Bearberry nibbles at the bare margins of the rocky ground, and dwarf birch and willow crowd in elsewhere. At times I have to search through willow thickets to find the trail.

Joe Hankins, who spent summers at Igloo, spent many days with these particular rams. In 1967, in his midseventies, he made forty-three trips up this ridge. He first came to the park in 1956 and returned every summer until 1971. On good mornings, he'd get up at three and head for the high places. Or if the weather was bad, he'd wait until later to catch a ride on one of the park's three tour buses and share his knowledge of wildlife. He could talk about all the animals, large and small, but sheep were his favorite subject. When Joe died in 1975 at age eighty-two, he bequeathed $150,000 to the National Park Foundation, the largest sum ever donated to it.

After the long approach, I get excited in nearing the summit. These rams and this particular place used to mean so much to me. I'd come here several times each year just to be with the sheep. Once I camped three days on this ridge while waiting for a storm to pass. Today I feel the old magic and mystery — perhaps because of the overgrown trail, a trail through thick brush where I had to shout myself hoarse in case of bears. I know I'd feel differently if the trail had been covered with footprints. I promote the illusion of remote wilderness and imagine myself as the first person here. I tell my flagging body that a moment of sublime discovery is just over the summit. Or maybe the excitement is just the rewrite of past, satisfying adventures.

Sheep tracks are pressed into the soft soil near the top. Desiccated droppings mark a shallow bed. Though tired, I hurry to see what's on the opposite side. Ram country!

It's apparent at once that the rams are not on my side of the canyon. Scanning the gray scree slopes and lime pasturages, I spot eight rams on a pinnacle on the far side of the canyon, their curling headgear plainly visible. There are twenty-six more on an even more distant ridge. The slope below me is bereft of flowers, except for a few poppies, forget-me-nots, pink plumes, and harebells that persist in various wind shadows. Bare stalks of avens cover the slope. I'm stirred by memories of rams lying amid those beds of flowers. Heading up the ridge, I follow a sheep trail worn into the rock. Across the way, I see other trails in the slopes and cliffs. The thin, rocky soil is marked with many sheep tracks made when the ground was wet from rain. Now they are hardened engravings. Here, too, wolf tracks are imprinted over those of the sheep. The wind is fierce, and I seek shelter in a depression. Studying the high ridges with my binoculars, I wonder whether the wolf was the reason the sheep moved to the far side of the valley. Once I counted forty rams on the very site where I now rest. Today an eagle soars overhead, wheatears flit among the rocks in the wind shadow, a marmot whistles from the slope below, and tiny white spots negotiate a distant ledge. That is all, except for stillness and wind. Enough.

AUGUST 12, 1988. First frost. In the higher elevations, the leaves of aspen and birch are beginning to yellow. In summer, the plants' sun-energized chlorophyll turns carbon dioxide and water into carbohydrates. As the leaves die in autumn, the chlorophyll begins to break down, and other substances, such as xanthophyll and anthocyanin, show through as yellow and red. Those pigments were in the leaves all along, masked by the potent green. With the imminence of autumn, the colors in Highway, Thorofare, and Polychrome passes take on a pastel hue, a tantalizing promise of what's to follow.

Today I tried to follow part of the old wagon route that led twelve miles up Savage River from the site of Savage Camp, the first visitor facility established in the park. Most of the route has been naturally reclaimed through revegetation, erosion, landslides, and thawing and freezing. In a very few places the grade is still obvious, though the road was last used in 1941 and has been impassable since 1952.

Several miles upriver beyond the last timber, I climbed a slope to a prominence and sat down to study the canyons that flank Fang Mountain. This was where Adolph Murie worked in 1922. Murie, then a college undergraduate, traveled to Alaska to assist his older brother, Olaus, in a caribou-capturing operation for the U.S. Biological Survey. At the behest of survey chief Edward W. Nelson, Olaus Murie was instructed to live-capture bull caribou to interbreed with reindeer, which had been introduced to Alaska in 1891 from Siberia as a predictable food source for Alaskan Natives. Nelson hoped the cross-breeding would benefit the "inferior reindeer" by improving their meat yields and by transmitting hardiness and immunities.

That first summer, Olaus, who would become famous for his pioneering caribou studies and Alaskan travels, and his assistants built a corrallike trap with mile-long wings patterned after Alaskan Native designs. In 1923, with the new wagon road from the train depot to Savage River passable, the capturing proceeded. Men on foot drove the caribou into the trap, where the animals were roped and dehorned. In the same manner that horses are tethered, the captured bulls were haltered and staked out to graze. They were described as having an uncanny ability to avoid entanglement in their picket ropes. Later the caribou were crated, loaded into wagons, and eventually transported by train to the Biological Survey station in Fairbanks. The Murie brothers wryly nicknamed one captured bull "Harding."

One of Olaus's assistants was Frank Glaser, who had been recommended to Murie for his woods skills and wildlife knowledge. Glaser moved to the Savage River in 1924 and lived and trapped on the park boundary.

Adolph Murie kept a daily journal, which provides an extraordinary trove of insights and detailed observations. His days on the Savage River helping Olaus were happy ones. They ate wild meat—ptarmigan, sheep, and caribou—and "Ade" made pies and fudge. In midsummer 1923, they were joined by Ted and Jule Loftus, whose company they seemed to enjoy. In early July, on orders from Harry Karstens, they spent several days hunting sheep for an outdoor barbecue planned for the seventy-person Brooklyn _Daily Eagle_ newspaper contingent, which would soon officially dedicate the park. From July 5 through 8, Olaus, Ade, and Frank Glaser hunted Savage River and Jenny Creek near Harry Lucky's cache, and they killed five young sheep. The barbecue was held on July 8. The Muries and Glaser hiked down from Savage to McKinley Station in six hours; the "meat and outfit" had been sent ahead by wagon. Both the party and the dedication were proclaimed a great success. On July 17, young Ade went hunting again and shot a barren ewe in Savage River for another barbecue, this time in honor of President Harding, who was in Alaska to drive the railroad's golden spike. When the president's schedule changed, the train went through at two P.M. instead of five, so the presidential party lingered only twenty minutes at the park. Superintendent Karstens was invited to accompany the party for the railroad ceremony. He took advantage of the trip to lobby the president's powerful companions on the park's behalf.

On July 1, 1923, while driving a team of horses on the Savage River, the Muries accidentally discovered, near a wheel rut, the first documented nest of the wandering tattler. This is one small example of the influence the Muries were to have on Alaskan wildlife studies in general and Denali Park in particular. From 1929 to 1930, Ade studied moose on Isle Royale, where he advised the introduction of wolves to control the moose population. Just before being assigned to study wolves and sheep in Denali in 1939, he was in Yellowstone, observing coyotes and their impact on livestock and wildlife. He eventually became Denali's first resident biologist, spending parts of twenty-five years here. After World War II, Murie monitored wolves and studied bears in the park, with stints in the Tetons, where he investigated grizzly depredations on livestock. Even after his retirement in 1965, Murie was an important figure in the park not only because of his seminal wolf-sheep studies but because he lobbied hard for quality wildlife science and a moderation of postwar development schemes. Park service historian William Brown calls Adolph Murie "the single most influential person in shaping the geography and wildlife-wilderness policies of the modern park." Murie died in 1977.

AUGUST 13, 1988. This morning Helen Rhode's van was parked at the side of the road. Even after all these years, it's sad to see her without her late husband Cecil, a veteran wildlife cinematographer. He died in 1979 at age seventy-seven. Helen is sixty-nine now and still photographing wildlife for various publishers. The long days and hard work must be tough on her.

Cecil and Helen first came here in 1953, almost twenty years before the Parks Highway opened. They loaded their vehicle on a railroad flatcar for transport to the park. In 1956 they stayed about two months — until the snows closed the road. There were wood-heated shelters at Teklanika then, which offered a place to cook and stay warm. They were told by rangers that in late autumn they might get snowed in and be forced to leave their vehicle behind. The risk was theirs. Helen said the crew working on the Igloo Creek bridge told them not to worry, that when construction ended for the winter, they would be able to follow the heavy equipment as it cleared a path for the trip out of the park.

Cecil came to Alaska in 1936 and made his living as a film-maker and outdoorsman. In his closing days he continued doing what he enjoyed: working with animals. He never pushed his subjects, nor did he enjoy filming from the road or in groups, preferring instead to hike into the backcountry. He was a patient, hard worker. In 1979, just three months before he died, I saw the Rhodes in the hotel, arm-in-arm like newlyweds. "Cec's having trouble staying warm this fall," Helen whispered to me. The next day, however, I saw him climbing up Igloo to make sheep pictures. It was just after dawn, and he was nearly to the top.

AUGUST 14, 1989. Up at six-fifteen. Fine, clear morning. I begin to hike into my "new" sheep area around eight, reaching the top at nine-thirty. As soon as I gain the summit, I locate ten ewes and lambs. They are grazing in the saddle where the trail tops out. Shortly after noon, and after searching three big cirques, I find fourteen mature rams resting in the shadow of a slab-sided cliff. One is the huge "grandfather" I saw last year, but over the winter the tip of his right horn has broken off, perhaps in a dominance battle. No other ram in the band comes close in size or rank. Before he damaged his horn, I'd seen only one larger ram in my life.

I climb to the highest point on the escarpment above the sheep and sit down to eat my lunch. The rams are gathered where it is cool and windless. If they remain where they are, they will be in shadow when the sun sets. My intention is to photograph them in evening light, so this position does not look promising. I'll be patient in hopes that they will feed onto the top where the setting sun will strike them.

In early afternoon, a marmot whistles a warning. Soon the cirque is filled with marmot alarm calls. "Bear," I think at once, but that is not the threat. I glass the rams and see that they are all looking down into the center of the bowl. A wolverine is hunting through the rocks like a retriever at a field trial. Up, then down; back and forth, obviously following a scent trail. It leads to a covey of rock ptarmigan. They flush at close quarters, one here, two there, the wolverine dashing ahead to try and catch them. The wolverine is a deep chocolate color with a bright yellow flank marking. For so early in the season, its coat appears long and luxurious. It takes fifteen to twenty minutes for the wolverine to hunt the entire bowl; then it is gone, exiting through the narrow gap at the bottom where the creek's headwaters plunge over the lip of a precipice. Long after the passage of this extraordinary predator, the marmots call their warnings, and a few rams remain alert.

By eight P.M. the heat has gone from the day. Except for the largest ram, who heads downhill, one by one the rams feed uphill, staying in the light of the setting sun. They graze on the calm, cool summit as the dry autumn grass turns golden in the dying light. The rams feed close to me. Two even butt heads within a few feet of me. Around ten-thirty, minutes before sunset, I'm surrounded by rams burning red in the alpenglow, seemingly illuminated from fires within.

After sunset, to the south across the great glacial-carved valley, a full yellow moon rises above the crenellated summits. For a long moment, as the subarctic night settles on the ridge, a ram stands silhouetted against the moon.

AUGUST 15, 1988. Our bus rounds a bend and stops for a cow moose and two calves in the road. Our shuttle driver gives a good recitation on moose lore. When he finishes, a lady asks, "If a woman moose had two boy moose and they separated in the spring, as you say, if they met again in the future, would they recognize each other as brothers?"

"No."

"Oh. That's sad."

When the laughter fell away and the bus rolled on, I reflected that the answer to the woman's earnest enquiry becomes the question. Can anyone really know what an animal perceives? Perhaps when the moose calves meet as adults, they *will* recognize their relatedness, but we wouldn't know it. In our studies of animal behavior, we are cautioned to avoid making anthropomorphic connections, to avoid assigning human motives or characteristics to explain why animals do what they do. Perhaps we've heeded this admonition to a degree that has subtle, negative implications. In part, it is based on the premise of human superiority over "lesser" creatures. One study here at Denali, for example, concluded that the vast bulk of a grizzly's waking hours were spent feeding or searching for food. Could it be that when a bear smells a flower, it may not always be checking out a potential food source but simply enjoying the pleasant aroma? How can an observer really know what's going on in an animal's brain or judge its motivation?

My preference is to believe that the brother moose *will* recognize each other; that bears do things for the sheer fun of it; that Dall sheep enjoy vistas, sunsets, and rainbows; and that only human beings, in our arrogance, believe such things are impossible for other species.

AUGUST 16, 1987. In a pouring rain I climbed Igloo Mountain to watch the sheep. Soaking wet, I battled to keep my camera gear dry. Animals always seem so unaffected by these kinds of storms; their stoicism is bred of limited choice. They have nowhere to go. I, on the other hand, have a warm cabin. It was my choice to share what these animals experience.

It's been a long time since I've seen rams on Igloo at this time of year. They used to graze regularly here and also west of Polychrome, Toklat, and East Fork. This slope of Igloo has become almost exclusively ewe pasturage. The change appears to be a natural movement to other ranges; rams are now found where they weren't seen ten years ago. But why just the rams? Ewes and lambs still inhabit the same slopes. Perhaps the rams, because they are larger and use more forage, need to shift range more often.

I suffer from what biologist Steve Buskirk calls "a jockstrap mentality" of wildlife viewing. I like the big rams, bull moose, and caribou. Sitting here with the ewes, I realize how long it's been since I've done this, much preferring to watch rams. It takes real commitment (or something) to sit in the rain with these ewes. Despite the discomfort, I find it difficult to leave. The lambs' play isn't washed away by the rain, and their antics are a delight. One seems to think its mother is a trampoline.

Later, when I get on the bus, dripping water, I find being wet has an advantage. I get a seat all to myself.

AUGUST 16, 1990. Fairbanks Superior Court Judge Mary E. Greene today resolved what can only be called the Great 1990 Park Road Crisis, issuing a preliminary injunction closing a new campground-RV park in Kantishna.

Since 1972 traffic along the Park Road has been restricted to buses and a few private vehicles, many traveling to private land in Kantishna. In June, Superintendent Russell Berry lifted the eighteen-year ban on private vehicles after Kantishna landowner Dan Ashbrook and his fiancée, Valerie Mundt, announced their intention to open a two-hundred-unit RV park and campground and requested access. Three other Kantishna businesses, which do not cater to RVs, shuttle their guests in and out on their own private buses. A clause of the Alaska National Interest Lands Claims Act of 1980 mandated "adequate and feasible access for economic and other purposes." Federal attorneys advised Berry that Park Service had to open the road for those traveling to the new RV park. Access rights to Kantishna's private land, according to the lawyers, took precedence over the use of the road for other park visitation, research, and photography.

Headlines and television announcers trumpeted the news, especially after Berry announced that if traffic to Kantishna increased to a degree that made the road unsafe, both tour and shuttle buses would be banned beyond Mile 30. Buses would have to be restricted because, by law, private vehicle access to Kantishna could not be. In effect, one landowner could reduce public access along the entire Park Road. "We live in a society which operates under rule of law," Berry said. "I have to follow the law."

When the road opened, the traffic jam and RV stampede to Kantishna failed to materialize. Newspaper articles describing the new facility dissuaded many would-be customers. Pictures of the narrow, winding road and of an RV stuck in the sand on the bank of Moose Creek were discouraging. The first RVs to arrive found the road demanding and the RV "park" a heavily mined gravel riverbank without facilities of any kind. Others stayed home when they read that the proposed campground was on the far side of unbridged Moose Creek, crossable only by a hand-operated, one-person cable tram.

Ashbrook insisted that he and his partner had been "bushwhacked" by Park Service's premature announcement of their ongoing negotiations and that the campground-RV park wasn't ready for business. The partners said that full operation was planned for the following summer.

Just when the controversy seemed about to boil over, Roberta Wilson, owner of Kantishna Roadhouse and Ashbrook's former business partner, brought suit against him. She wanted to stop development of the campground-RV park on the grounds that it violated Ashbrook's agreement with her not to open any tourist business within thirty miles of the park. Ashbrook replied publicly that he was not in business but only owned the land that his partner Mundt was leasing.

Greene's injunction bars Ashbrook and Mundt from operating the campground-RV park, pending trial. Almost at once, Park Service reinstituted road access restrictions.

This is only one skirmish in a battle that could determine the character of the park. Nothing prevents another property owner from developing land and demanding similar access. Only an informal agreement, not a regulation, inspires existing resorts to provide bus access for their guests. A long-term solution is needed.

Kantishna became part of the park in the 1980 expansion. Historically, many Alaskans have not supported the concept of national parks. Others view the compromise language, including the special access guarantees that Ashbrook and Mundt cited, as flaws.

The 1980 act could be amended, or private conservation organizations could buy the private land, or Park Service could condemn the land (that has been done in the past), then pay fair market price as set by court-appointed appraisers. Federal law allows this action if private property is incompatible with park master plans, but Alaska's congressional delegation has consistently resisted this solution. Or Congress could purchase the inholdings. Some observers saw the road crisis as a political gambit to pressure Congress into passing the initial Kantishna land purchase appropriation. One reporter told me that he was convinced the superintendent "was trying to manipulate the situation for a buyout. One of the provisions of the access clause calls for reasonable regulations."

Given the park's single road access, any Kantishna development might degrade the wilderness and wildlife despite the vast buffers added in 1980. Unless the Kantishna problem is solved, writes William Brown in his park history, "the park road will become a stake in the park's heart."

Adolph Murie posed the question thirty years ago: Will this park be symbol and standard of our civilization's higher aspirations, or will it be sacrificed to the lowest common denominator of windshield tourism?

AUGUST 17, 1986. Visitation is rapidly declining; only half the buses are running full. After the hectic activity of July, it is nice to be able to get on and off the bus at will and to procure a campsite without a long wait. Already some concession employees and Park Service staff have gone south to winter jobs or school. People, like migratory birds, are heading south. Toward the end of the month, the pace will quicken, peaking on Labor Day in one last frenetic burst of human activity. And then comes the rutting moon.

AUGUST 18, 1982. In the last few days, summer hues have begun giving way to powerful crimson and gold. The ground cover is so beautiful that I fear crushing the plants underfoot. I find myself avoiding patches of tundra where crowberry, blueberry, and bearberry crowd amid the delicate white and yellow lichens.

This morning I watched a large bull moose feeding in a pond. Although it could be several days, perhaps two weeks, before the velvet is completely shed, its antlers were well palmated and fully developed. I'm always amazed at how quickly moose antlers grow. In early spring the antlers emerge, and by the first of June they have branched out. This year I saw a bull with six-inch-long beams on April 10; four months later his rack could be seventy inches wide and weigh as much as seventy pounds. Charles Sheldon killed a bull moose on July 29, 1906, whose antlers, although not fully developed, spanned sixty-seven inches. According to Victor VanBallenberghe, antlers are 20 to 25 percent developed by June 1. A month later they are 75 percent developed, and they are completely developed by August 15. VanBallenberghe found that 50 percent of total growth occured in June, coinciding with the vegetation spurt. The antlers shed in late November and December.

AUGUST 19, 1982. A ram grazing in the band that we are watching has only one functioning eye. An opaque white film covers its left eye. Perhaps this leucoma results from corneal abrasion or ulceration. It is the fourth ram I've seen with only one good eye. One ram, the largest I've ever seen in the park, had sustained an injury, and the eye itself was damaged and draining. In autumn

1974, it carried a heavy, symmetrical set of horns that tucked in at the chin before sweeping outward in a true curl and a half. The following spring, on Igloo Mountain, I saw that the ram had broken off fully half its right horn and had sustained serious injury to its left eye and left shoulder, perhaps the result of a rutting battle. (Rams collide head-on at an estimated sixty miles per hour.) In any case, the winter had not been kind to this aged ram. It walked with a limp, and by late autumn, when most of its fellows were approaching prime, its vigor seemed in decline. Though many people looked for it, the ram was not seen the following spring.

I also photographed a partially blind caribou three years in a row near Wonder Lake. I last saw him in 1985. His left eye was glazed over with a glaucous film, and each year he developed asymmetrical antlers, the left side somewhat misshapen and under-developed. It surprised me how successful some handicapped animals appear. One would expect the opposite, especially for animals that rely on their vision for protection from predators and for passage across rugged alplands. Yet all were mature and otherwise healthy individuals.

AUGUST 20, 1989. This morning I picked a quart of blueberries in fifteen minutes. They were plump, tart, and delicious. This autumn's bumper crop is the result of just the right mix of summer rain and warmth. We experienced no droughts, no summer floods. Today I woke intending to look for moose, not to pick berries. But while gorging myself and envisioning blueberry sourdough pancakes, I decided the moose could wait.

With an early start, I'd hoped to find a bull moose with its antlers free of velvet; it would have been the first this year. Last year by this date I had already seen one, but all four bull moose that I saw this morning between Mile 7 and Savage were still in velvet. I did see the first bull caribou with shed antlers. *The first shed caribou appeared in 1990 on this same date.*

Now that alder leaves have become a preferred food source for some moose, I find it easier to watch how a moose's lips grasp leaves and pull them into its mouth. The lips work with flexible, almost fingerlike mobility. The upper lip seems to ripple as it feels for the leaves, much the way fingers inside a mitten would feel for coins on a table. Lips and tongue move the branch back into the mouth. Then, when the branch is crosswise at the back of the mouth, a sideways movement of the head strips the leaves from the branch, accompanied by an audible, mushy *zip!* Each day it takes forty to sixty pounds of browse to feed a moose, so I have plenty of opportunity to study their amazing, almost prehensile, lips.

I had to struggle across considerable spongy ground to enter the forest where the bull was feeding. This kind of terrain is called muskeg bog or, as sourdoughs called it, moose bog. The muskeg has its own signature plant community. Cottongrass (a sedge), dwarf birch, sphagnum moss, and black spruce are the most obvious plants. These twisted, stunted spruce grow in poorly drained, acid soils where the permafrost—permanently frozen soil—often lies closest to the surface. Areas coarsely called "drunken forests" are black spruce thickets jumbled into disarray by the irregular thawing and heaving of frozen ground. Black spruce, even when only a few feet tall, can be decades old. Few are taller than forty-five feet, and they rarely exceed nine inches in diameter. Foresters classify them as *krummholz,* literally "crooked wood," a category of slow-growing trees gnarled and stunted by constant wind, permafrost, or poor nutrition. Early Russian arctic explorers called the northern forest the *taiga,* meaning "land of little sticks." Many black spruce possess a unique otherworldly look, especially in winter when covered with snow. Artists and poets have seen faces and gnomelike creatures in the odd shapes. For me, there is no more uniquely northern image than a raven calling from the top of a misshapen black spruce.

AUGUST 21, 1982. Many of the entries written into the guest log at the Eielson Visitor Center praise the beauty of the mountain (if indeed it's visible that day) and note observations of wildlife. But mixed with these comments are the usual complaints. "Put in a snack bar." "Pave the road." "When's the hotel at Wonder Lake going to be built?"

Since the very beginning of the park, controversy has swirled around the location of the park's visitor services and accommodations. An ongoing complaint has been that the mountain itself cannot be seen from the hotel area.

In 1906, Charles Sheldon envisioned a hotel near the terminus of Peters Glacier, almost ninety miles from the current facility. For at least the last thirty-five years, there have been calls for development of overnight visitor facilities in the park proper. Wonder Lake has often been proposed as the best site, but in 1931 there was talk of building an inn opposite Mount Eielson. In 1956, Park Service embarked on Mission 66, an ambitious plan to upgrade visitor facilities throughout the national parks for the service's fiftieth anniversary in 1966. Superintendent Grant Pearson proposed selling or removing the hotel and replacing it with accommodations within the park—"probably near Wonder Lake." Pearson also proposed a gas station, store, and boat launch for Wonder Lake. Work on the Eielson Visitor Center began in July 1958, and the finished concrete structure was dedicated on July 15, 1961. (Murie called it the "monstrosity"; employees referred to it as the "Dairy Queen.")

Many hotel schemes have been floated; most have sunk. Hotel construction in a remote area without easy access would be exceedingly expensive. And visitors arriving by rail would have to be transported to an in-park facility. But most important, few people seem to understand that the park is a wildlife sanctuary, not just a tourist attraction.

Lively, often heated, debate in the early 1960s centered on the park's future. Many of those involved had a strong desire to avoid the mistakes made in parks Outside. Yellowstone and Yosemite had developments within them that threatened wildlife, habitat, and natural features. Both had crowds, crime, jammed roads, and pollution. Most visitors would experience Denali only once in their lives; they deserved to find something unique and different.

Early Mission 66 proposals called for hotel construction, campground improvements, interpretive displays, and a bridge, shelters, and trail to McGonagall Pass. But it was the plan to pave the road that drew heated attention. State and national conservation organizations joined the battle. Adolph Murie called for minimal intrusion. His concerns ranged from the bigger issues, like road and hotel construction and air touring (which he thought should be banned) to the interpretive signboards. "The signs cheapen the park, they intrude, they vie with the arnica, the saxifrage, the yellow grass for one's attention," he wrote in his journal. "They intrude on the esthetics. Let us keep the landscape pure and unadulterated . . . they almost fence us from the wilderness."

People asked: If Alaska's wilderness cannot be protected at Denali, where will it be safe? In response, Park Service relented and canceled plans for road upgrades and interior park developments. It was a reaffirmation of the park concept: a wild land for wildlife, shared briefly by human visitors.

AUGUST 22, 1987. Today I spent twelve hours watching two bull moose near Sanctuary. The younger one, with a forked horn, was completely free of velvet, but the larger one was not. I guessed its antlers to span sixty inches. The youngster browsed alder while the mature bull ate willow. Much of the willow has changed color, but the big bull selected only green leaves. He is the only animal I've seen in the last two days still eating willow. The caribou, moose, and beaver were focusing on alder, the one plant still green.

Although these two moose traveled and fed together, there was very little interaction. On occasion, the younger bull "horned" the brush, but the other paid no attention. Perhaps when the youngster works his antlers through the brush, he is indeed polishing them to remove the last remnants of their velvet covering. Later, when mature bulls horn the brush, they will be doing more than cleaning them. Moose audio-locate one another. Vocalization and the thrashing of antlers can be heard at a considerable distance. One bull will thrash the brush in answer to another's distant challenge. He will follow the sound not only in anticipation of battle, but also in search of cows that may be consorting with his rival.

AUGUST 23, 1985. Five A.M. at Toklat River. Five wolves chased a bull caribou from the brush across from Divide Mountain and onto the gravel of the East Branch. Spread into a loose V, they quickly gained on him.

Just south of the bridge, two wolves caught the bull, slashing open his hams. He kept running, one wolf beside him and another close at heel. Before long, the pack closed in, panicking him into a series of futile leaps. Bleeding from his wounds, the bull lunged with his antlers, but the wolves dodged.

With lowered, velvet tines, the bull faced the wolves spread in a half-circle before him. Following a long pause, one by one, the wolves walked away. The damage had been done; now they would wait, risking nothing. After wading the shallow, turbid river channel, one wolf stretched, two others lay down, one sat and yawned, one licked its front legs and paws. But the pack's nonchalant air was compromised by long stares at the weakening caribou fifteen yards away.

Less than twenty minutes later, four of the wolves got up and headed southwest toward Divide Mountain, soon disappearing into the brush. Beyond them a female grizzly and her three cubs were heading downstream through the willows. Some distance ahead of them, a large, dark grizzly foraged in the brush.

The remaining wolf lay down, and with difficulty, so did the caribou. Just past full daylight, the wolf, apparently alarmed by the inbound Wonder Lake bus, got up and headed off after the pack. Soon he, too, was gone into the willows to the southwest.

The caribou stood staring after the retreating wolf. It tried to walk away but could only go a step or two before lying down. Twice more over the next half hour, the bull got to its feet but managed only a few faltering steps.

On the west side of East Branch, the grizzly family headed straight toward the lone bear feeding at the northern tip of the bar. The morning was exceptionally calm; not even a slight breeze ruffled the willows. At a half mile, with any wind at all, the bears could have smelled the bloody caribou.

The female saw or scented the lone bear. She half-stood to get a good look, her cubs quickly crowding about her. Recognizing the danger, she did not hesitate to hurry her cubs away. With many backward glances, she ran her family east into the river and toward the wounded caribou. The bears waded a channel of the river before turning upstream to the soapberry patch where they had been feeding for much of last week. As soon as the caribou saw the bears wading the river, it struggled to stand.

Just two hundred yards or less from the motionless caribou, one cub grubbed at the ground, while another cub and its mother cropped berries. The female fed into a clearing. Suddenly she swiveled toward the bull. The caribou's scent had reached her. She broke into a lope. Turning to flee, the caribou tried to run but faltered. The bear broke into an all-out charge. The bull ran into the river at the same place where the wolves had crossed. Just as he reached the far bank, the grizzly lunged into the river with a great splash. In a second she was leaping upward to grab the bull by the shoulders. The two plunged into the river, then out again, then back in again. The bull's abdomen, rent by the wolves, burst like a smashed watermelon, a flash of blood and guts spilling into the river.

For a full five minutes, the grizzly held the bull against the river current before finally pulling him down. In the water she tore at his neck and slashed at his abdomen. The splashing of his flailing hooves panicked the cubs on the bank into momentary flight.

It took a long time for the caribou to die. When the grizzly let go of the bull's neck and tore into its abdomen, it fought to escape, staining the gray water with its blood. At first the three cubs kept their distance, but once they'd snatched a taste of warm flesh, they were into the feast for good.

The attack came about nine-fifteen, and it was fully forty to forty-five minutes before the bull ceased to struggle. The bears fed and napped atop their kill all day. At dusk, a wolf came downriver and circled the bears, but none of the animals made any move. When darkness fell, the bears were asleep atop their partially covered treasure.

AUGUST 24, 1989. Two grizzlies, probably the same ones that played trampoline on a tent a few weeks ago, are in trouble again. Apparently the yearling cub has no fear of people and will approach a camp without hesitation. And this time the pair got ahold of human food by breaking into an improperly sealed food container. Park Service evacuated the backcountry area around Cathedral and Igloo mountains and closed it to entry. I met two people on their way out and gave them a ride to Igloo Campground.

"We'd just gotten our tent and camp in order, beautiful location, when here comes all these guys with guns, and they tell us to get out *now*," one said. "Bad bears. Then we're force-marched to the road, and that's it. Turned loose. Good-bye. All our planning down the tube. They say, 'Go to Igloo, stay there, catch a bus.' We wait by the road. Both buses that come by are full. Won't take us. So we walk down the road, which runs right through the closed area. Bears could be anywhere. We'd like to know why we were supposed to be safe on the road? Does the roadway ward off attack?"

They agreed that the evacuation of the backcountry was valid, but they felt that being left along the edge of the road displayed insensitivity — and a further risk to their safety because of the long wait for a bus.

AUGUST 25, 1989. These are the details, related by the Igloo ranger, of the backcountry incident that prompted yesterday's closing. A woman who was camping three-quarters of a mile up Tattler Creek awoke and saw a bear twenty feet from her tent. She yelled and made noise to scare the bear away, but the bear took no notice. Then she saw a smaller bear on the knob where she'd put her food container. The container was of an old design, with an unreliable seal. Soon both bears were eating her food. The woman got out of her tent and backed away. Spotting a hiker in the canyon bottom, she enlisted his help and together they went back and tried to scare off the bears. Again they were ignored. The two gathered what gear they could and departed.

This afternoon the two bears were just below the Park Road at a point about one-quarter mile from the sign marking the east end of the Sable Pass closed area. Joe Van Horn and the bear technicians ("bear techs") hurried to set up a tent in the direction in which the bears were traveling. After placing a backpack on a nearby knob, the techs got inside the tent. When the bears were within 250 feet of the tent, the techs crawled from it and hollered and made noise. The approaching bears were undeterred, so the techs then fired rubber bullets and noisemakers at them. The bears ran west, seeking safety atop a nearby knoll. The techs were attempting to condition the bears not to approach people.

This "aversive conditioning," an effort to alter a bear's behavior before relocation or destruction becomes necessary, has proven successful here in the past. Van Horn said that he hopes to apply this at least twice more before opening the area to overnight use.

In 1990 the smaller of these two bears, now a 175-pound, three-and-a-half-year-old, having separated from its mother earlier in the summer, was again in trouble. In Tattler Creek on July 26 at about nine A.M., the bear tore into two of three tents, awakening the four sleeping occupants. One man awoke to find the bear thirty inches from him, looking in through a torn opening in his North Face Tadpole tent. "When I yelled, the bear jumped back," the camper said, "but then only slowly, slowly moved away. It was not afraid." He said his tent had never been cooked in or used for food storage. He thought the bear was only curious. No one was injured in the incident, and the bear obtained no food from the bear-resistant containers. The bear examined everything at the camper's cooking area located a short distance from the tents. It bit into four water bottles and a plastic cup, and chewed up the stove windscreen, strongly scented with cooking odors. According to the camper, prior to slashing the tents, the bear also found and chewed up a toiletry bag that contained soap and toothpaste. While the bear remained in the vicinity grazing and eating berries, the hikers gathered their gear and left. A video tape of the incident, taken by one of the campers, revealed that they had seen the bear grazing in the vicinity of their camp the night before. By relocating at that time, perhaps the event could have been avoided.

The tundra knoll the hikers had chosen for their camp has been the site over the years of about a half-dozen human-bear incidents; perhaps a few bears expect to find humans—and human food—there. Immediately after the incident, the backcountry unit was closed again to entry. Soon the bear was located, sedated, and radio-collared for further monitoring and aversive conditioning.

AUGUST 26, 1982. Igloo Campground, six A.M. In the first campsite by the road, I was cooking hotcakes over the campstove on the picnic table when I was startled by my friend Libby's shout. She came running down the campground loop, shooing and clapping her hands like a farmer hazing chickens. Hearing heavy footfalls, I peered around the van and saw a blur of fur headed up the road, a grizzly dashing away. It ran up the access road, turned left on the Park Road, crossed the bridge, and disappeared into the brush on the far side of the creek. It was shaking its head and "blowing" in nervous excitement. On her return from the creek, Libby had seen the bear approaching the van, obviously homing in on the aroma of hotcakes. Her aggressive response — something she'd learned as a naturalist at Katmai — sent our unwanted guest packing and spared me a rude surprise.

AUGUST 27, 1989. Igloo Campground, about seven A.M. The first bus of the day brakes to a sudden stop just before the bridge. Windows slam down, a sure sign that an animal has been sighted. The bus driver dashes into the campground and runs from tent to tent, crying "A bear! A bear just upstream from the bridge. Keep all food away from the tents." Only one camper is awake. After the driver runs back to the bus, murmured voices become audible above the wind. I look up at the low, scudding clouds and sip my tea.

Soon, disheveled campers parade by my tent to gather on the bridge and watch the bear. I doubt the bus driver meant to *summon* them. Later, as the campers straggle back, I overhear them say the bear has fed in the willows opposite camp. The bus drives on, the campers return to their tents, and by seven-forty it is quiet again. I boil up more tea and wait.

Last night a bear was digging roots and eating berries across the creek from the campground but it was not seen by the buses, campers, or the rangers, so its presence did not become a problem.

A fast-moving vehicle approaches from the east and turns into the campground: two rangers in a truck. In a moment, I hear footfalls on the campground road. I see a male grizzly (dribbling urine as he walks) hurrying toward the Park Road. He's yawning, an indication of nervousness, and when he reaches the road, he turns and runs across the bridge into the brush on the upstream side of it. He's left wet tracks in the dust, and later on I backtrail him to where he crossed the creek to enter the campground. I inform the rangers of his passage before returning to my tea. Soon one walks through the campground, hand on holstered pistol.

At about five-thirty A.M. *on August 3, 1990, a lone camper in Igloo Campground was awakened by noises outside his tent; then for a moment the tent shook. He yelled and sat up: he heard nothing. After waiting thirty seconds, he unzipped the tent to look out, but he saw no bears or other animals. A twenty-inch rip had been torn at the bottom of the tent, and the sleeping bag had been pulled a short way out. Garbage cans nearby had the exposed plastic liners shredded and ripped off. Later the camper told me that his tent had never been used as a cooking shelter and that he did not have edibles in it. He thought that his tent had been damaged out of curiosity, because "it was closest to the metal food locker" and garbage cans. A ranger searched the area but saw no bears. An hour and a half later, less than a mile west of the campground, collared bear number 102 and her two cubs were seen on the road. They were presumed to be the culprits, because the previous evening they had been seen in the vicinity of the campground and they had been subjects of aversive conditioning, for frequenting the road and climbing on vehicles. The campground was closed, as well as the surrounding backcountry unit, for the remainder of the season. A week later, bear number 102 was recollared; her male cub also received a collar.*

AUGUST 28, 1985. Colors brightening each day, the tundra most vibrant at Sanctuary and Primrose. Gold, crimson, and green rivers of living plants. Today the bloodstained antlers of moose and caribou add to the autumnal palette. Four bull moose that I saw yesterday were out of the velvet, shed clean overnight.

All that remains of the caribou kill on the Toklat is gnawed bone, broken antler, and a few small scraps of hide. The day after the kill, two wolves circled the grizzly family atop the buried remains, then moved on, without their share.

Later that same day a lone bear, homing in on the scent trail, came running from half a mile downstream. The female stood her ground, and the intimidated smaller bear ran off without a fight.

What a boon this caribou has been to the bears. Each autumn, they must gorge themselves and build up a thick layer of fat prior to hibernation. Biologists call the autumnal binge *hyperphagia*. These particular bears, nourished by this abundance of protein, should overwinter well.

AUGUST 28, 1988. Up at five A.M. High of forty-one. Cloudy and calm with some sunny periods. Accompanied by biologist Derek Stonorov, I found the bull moose I've been watching the last few days. Here's a behavioral chronology:

7:30 A.M. Moose bedded in timber near lakeshore.

8:05 A.M. Up and feeding.

8:15 A.M. Runs to lakeshore to drink.

8:20 A.M. Back in thicket, browsing.

10:00 A.M. Lies down in heavy timber after feeding. Ruminating.

12:15 P.M. Up and browsing. Alder about 80 percent of intake.

2:00 P.M. Lies down in same timber shelter as before.

4:15 P.M. Up and browsing alder again.

6:30 P.M. Circles back to water hole. Drinks. Leaves pond and rakes antlers through brush.

6:45 P.M. Lies down in the open next to water hole.

7:10 P.M. Another bull can be heard calling from hillside behind us. A deep grunt, uttered in cadence, tells us — and our moose — that the bull approaches.

7:15 P.M. Bedded moose looks up but does not move. Approaching bull "horns" brush. We can't see bull, but can hear him and see willow tops waving.

8:00 P.M. Newcomer in the open. Bedded bull up. Equal in size, they spar and display. Much testing, little real fighting.

8:35 P.M. Bulls feeding quietly in willows.

9:05 P.M. Observations end.

AUGUST 29, 1988. Up early. Clear and windy. Moose observations continue. Chronology:

6:45 A.M. Original subject found feeding less than one hundred yards from where last seen. Second bull not in sight.

7:20 A.M. Drinks from small pond in thicket.

8:05 A.M. Lies down in timber after audio-locating bull from last night.

8:20 A.M. Bull II moves toward bedded bull. Once in sight, lies down seventy yards from Bull I.

10:00 A.M. Bull I up. Light browsing on willow, small amount of alder. Moves three hundred yards uphill.

10:45 A.M. Lies down.

12.35 P.M. Up to eat. Selects alder. Moves uphill five hundred yards.

1:10 P.M.   Lies back down.

3:00 P.M.   Up. Light browsing on willow and alder.

3:15 P.M.   Begins to move deliberately uphill, calling as it travels. Circles downhill toward road. Moves in large circle back to same water hole as this morning.

3:45 P.M.   Drinks.

3:55 P.M.   Lies down by water hole. From opposite direction, Bull II can be heard calling and horning brush as it approaches.

4:05 P.M.   Bull II shows up. Displays antlers, thrashes brush, circles Bull I. Bull I does not get up, despite Bull II's display. Low moans from bedded bull. Bull II moves to water hole and drinks. Straddles water hole and stares at other bull twenty-five feet away.

4:30 P.M.   Bull II lies down twenty feet from Bull I.

6:05 P.M.   Bull I up to drink.

6:08 P.M.   Bull I displays, thrashes brush, and moves toward Bull II, which rises. A face-to-face display begins. Much moaning. Bull II backs off without making contact. Bull I follows and jabs it lightly in the rear. Bull II whirls, and the two meet in a hard antler clash. Heads down, the two push and shove, their bodies leaning into each another. A more violent conflict than last night's interaction.

6:25 P.M.   Bulls stop sparring. Stand close together, facing away. They begin to browse. Both feed uphill into thicket and eventually separate.

6:40 P.M.   Heavy willow browsing.

6:45 P.M.   No rut smell from either moose.

7:00 P.M.   Grizzly in vicinity. Observations end.

AUGUST 29, 1988. Teklanika Campground. The midsummer rush is over. Only the best sites are occupied, and the campground is less than half-full. License plates: Holland, New Zealand, United Kingdom, Japan, West Germany, Switzerland, and Iowa.

This evening I was photographing a large bull moose feeding in a meadow when we both had our attention diverted by the sound of antlers raking the brush atop a nearby knoll. Although I couldn't see the moose, I could see a tall willow waving above the concealing brush. My subject started at once to work his way up the knob to investigate the challenger. I followed at a discreet distance.

The bulls met on a gravel clearing on the knob — almost exactly where Bill Ruth's ashes are buried. A park ranger from 1966 to 1977, Bill was killed in a car wreck in 1983 at Mile 232 on the Parks Highway. Because of his love for the park, where he'd lived since 1963, and acknowledging his special interest in moose, this spot was chosen as his last resting place.

Now the two moose faced each other in threat display. The bulls thrust and parried for advantage. Soon the battle moved downhill into the brush.

Returning from the park in late evening, I found this month's issue of *Alaska Magazine* in the mail. Inside was a portfolio of Bill Ruth's moose photographs entitled "The Rites of Autumn."

AUGUST 30, 1988. Two buses move slowly up the curving approach to Highway Pass as a wolf walks down the road ahead of them, not veering off the road. The wolf, with a black-tipped tail, is one of two females that have taken to walking the road. As she often does, she is hunting squirrels along the edge of this huge "trail." But like the foxes that also trot the road, she will eat any squirrels she finds run over by passing vehicles.

Near Mile 56 she comes to a halt at the edge of the road and peers into a gully. I look, too, but I don't see anything. She crouches and stalks like a cat. A few steps, then a pause; a few more steps, another pause. She crouches lower, moving forward with steps placed as gently as if she were testing thin ice. Suddenly she charges, and with dazzling speed, she rockets down the tundra slope. I see that her prey is a squirrel almost two hundred yards away. It soon sees her and scrambles for a burrow some distance away. The wolf reaches the burrow just a second or two after the squirrel. She digs at the opening like a dog caching a bone. She stops, thrusts her muzzle into the opening, retracts it, then digs faster. Again she stops to smell at the opening; she shivers, then dives and backs away with the squirrel kicking in her jaws. A few steps from the burrow, she stops to crush the squirrel's skull. Then she pulls it apart head first and swallows it in eight or ten bites.

As the wolf licks her muzzle, she looks up at the line of parked buses filled with passengers watching her. Back on the road, she hunts each gully and rise, stopping to look and listen for prey. Once she spooks a covey of ptarmigan but pays little attention. Followed by her entourage of motor vehicles, she falls into an easy walk. She finds a dead squirrel and stops in the middle of the road to eat it. A westbound shuttle bus spooks her.

The wolf follows the road west another four miles, eating two road-killed squirrels and catching four others. Not once does she chase a squirrel without catching it. Her technique is always the same. She chooses a squirrel far from its burrow, and she can dig out squirrels quicker than the grizzlies I've watched.

After a twenty-minute nap on the tundra near Mile 61, the now-sated wolf heads back. The day has cooled; her pace has quickened. Near Mile 54, where she had first come onto the road, she leaves it and heads for the drainage leading down to the Toklat.

AUGUST 30, 1978. Large groups of sheep are massed on the flanks of Double Mountain. Yesterday a large herd of lambs and ewes was grazing on the flats below Polychrome Pass. Obviously, the autumnal migration to winter range is under way. Soon the herds on Double Mountain will make their move toward the Outer Range, retracing the path they took in early June. I've wondered if these groupings and migrations aren't set off by weather, perhaps a first snow or the approach of a low-pressure front. Yet even in years when the weather remains mild and storms are rare, the sheep migrate. Perhaps like many other phenomena, the migration is triggered by the changing length of daylight.

An oddity of the physical world: Sometimes by observing and reporting a phenomenon, we alter it. I hesitate, then, to even write of this afternoon's experience.

Five rams fed as I sat facing them behind my tripod. One walked toward me. He was soon so close that I could not focus the lens, so I leaned away from the camera to see what he would do. He stopped five feet in front of me. With cocked head, he eyed me with the look that rams reserve for curiosities. I'd seen the look before, but this time I saw a peculiar intensity and intelligence. A vivid image, almost a dreamscape, snapped to mind: I saw the ram's broken bones and skull scattered in the dust. What looked to be a grizzly track branded the soil near the skull. And as quickly as it had come, the scene evaporated into the gaze of those golden eyes. The ram turned and walked away, and as he went, I realized that what I'd envisioned was not a grizzly track but the print of a human hand.

AUGUST 31, 1989. Big Creek. A bull moose bedded down in the timber around nine-thirty A.M. He was carrying well-palmated, velvet-covered antlers. When my morning photo session ended, I headed back toward the road, but from a high saddle I spotted a white wolf moving in the brush above a mineral lick. In a crouch, I hurried downhill to the concealment of a thicket of stunted, wind-twisted spruce. Through my binoculars I picked out the white wolf and a second wolf, dark gray with a black back, hiding near it. It seemed likely that the white wolf was the alpha female from East Fork. She gave the gray a tail-wagging, almost fawning greeting when he rose and approached her.

Together the two stalked through the brush above the lick before lying down in positions overlooking it. After fifteen minutes, I shifted my binoculars from them and was startled to see another wolf, a gray, wearing a radio-collar, hiding in the brush near where I'd first spotted the two. Then I saw two more, a large gray and a smaller one also wearing a collar. Besides its collar, the smaller wolf was distinguished by a scraggly, almost bare, tail. These two lay down in the brush alongside the third.

Looking back downhill, I saw that the first pair had descended to the flat and were crossing above the mineral lick. They jumped the small creek that feeds it, separated, and began to hunt the spruce thicket opposite the lick. For a few moments they were out of sight, giving me a chance to look back at the other wolves. All three were sitting on their haunches watching the two work the woods. After a few moments, the white and the gray appeared in the clearing just a hundred yards below me. After scenting the breeze, they moved downwind of the lick into the large timber thicket that leads eventually toward the wide pass into Big Creek. Once the two wolves were in the timber, the other three broke from hiding and raced downhill after them. Soon all five were across the marsh below the lick and into the spruce. Through an opening, I saw the five wolves pass in single file, ten to fifteen yards apart, with the white wolf in the lead. I knew that at least one bull moose was bedded in that thicket.

Half an hour later, I saw the white wolf, closely followed by the black-backed gray, passing the upper lake and heading into the pass to Big Creek. The other three soon followed. Yesterday I saw two hundred sheep, mostly lambs and ewes, on the ridges above the creek.

Autumn

*The bittersweet season of painted leaves heralding the
return of frost and darkness.*

SEPTEMBER 1, 1988. Sable Pass. It's only human nature, I suppose, that when visitors see the Sable Pass sign, they expect to see a bear, as if this were an amusement park or a zoo that offers animals on display. Park Service used to bill the area from Mile 37 to Mile 42 as "the ancestral home of the grizzly bear," an area closed to human entry in order to give the bears space and to avoid human-bear interactions. But bears are not seen here on every trip.

Fred Dean, who has studied park bears since 1957, thinks the best time of year to see bears in Sable Pass is late June to early July. Then, bear families can be seen grazing on grasses and succulent plants in damp swales. Sightings are also common in late autumn when blueberries ripen and leaves begin to drop. But even when several bears are in the pass, they can be hidden by brush. Those bushes that follow the watercourses are often taller than a human.

But today expectations are met. Near Sable summit, a bear crops blueberries close to the south side of the road. Buses jam up for a close look at the unfazed bear, one of about 350 in the park.

Over the years, photographers have congregated along this section of road in hopes of photographing bears, at times creating "bear jams" or "camera wars." Some of these people are almost more interesting than the bears. One person, a priest of some unidentified religion, used to get off the bus and make huge signs of the cross to bless the mountains, buses, people, and animals. When he took to walking out on the tundra to bless the bears, he was invited to desist. One year, a German could not be dissuaded from marching out on the tundra and right up to bears, photographing them from a military posture of attention. He, too, heard from the rangers.

Another photographer said he'd been charged by bears thirty-seven times. You'd think he would have learned something the first time or two. Someone else took more than four hundred rolls of film in his ten days in the park — a record, perhaps, but one of dubious merit. Another man showed up two autumns in a row to drive his rental car back and forth between Igloo and East Fork, trying to photograph bears. He obtained some excellent wildlife pictures, but when he left he said, "I won't be back. You can't do wildlife photography here." He has published several wildlife books, mostly using images of captive and tame wildlife "models."

Although bears are interesting creatures, their reputation is built more on fable than fact. Most people would like to see a bear; a few others seem genuinely willing to risk life and limb to get a picture of a bear. Some of the interactions I've heard about are tales of lunacy. Since bears are unable to judge intent, they may view any close approach by a human as a threat. Perhaps everyone has the right to assume personal risk, but no one has the right to risk other people's lives — or the life of the bear.

SEPTEMBER 2, 1981. What a wonderful year for cranberries and blueberries! This afternoon, while waiting for two bull caribou to finish their rest, I sat amid scarlet bearberry plants and munched both the blueberries and tart crowberries within arm's reach. There were enough left over to fill a plastic bag for tomorrow's breakfast.

Although the caribou did little more than ruminate, I enjoyed watching them. Like moose and sheep, caribou graze or browse for an hour or so, then lie down to chew their cuds. Their ruminations are often punctuated by naps — but they allow their alertness to flag only for short periods. These two caribou, for instance, took turns dozing. While one stayed awake, the other would lay its head on the ground and sleep for five or ten minutes, then jolt awake with a quick look about. They seemed incapable of what humans call relaxation. Justifiably so. If an animal were to sprawl on the tundra and fall fast asleep for an hour or two, it might waken to the bite of a mortal enemy.

Despite threatening morning skies and a blustery wind, I spent the entire day on the slope with the caribou, hiking back to the road in bright, late-afternoon sun. When I got off the bus at

Igloo Campground at eight-forty-five, an amber light was sneaking onto the peaks and shoulders of Cathedral Mountain, while the wind shook the last daylight from the treetops. By nine-fifteen I was the only one still cooking dinner in the quiet campground. A few people sat by warming fires; one stood watching the alpenglow. While eating, I heard the murmur of voices from within small tents. A pleasant serenity settled on the dusky scene. Life without TV.

SEPTEMBER 3, 1988. A man walked the tundra today, following a wolf that was hunting ground squirrels. Unlike the photographers, he had no desire to get close to the wolf; he stayed at a distance to watch through binoculars. Late in the day I spoke with him. He is a Japanese wildlife biologist, and he'd come to Alaska to attend a symposium on wolves. He has spent the last three days observing this wolf. He told me that wolves became extinct in Japan in 1927 because of loss of habitat. He was interested in the enhancement program going on in the southern states for the endangered red wolf and in the return of wolves to Yellowstone. He spoke of his desire to translate into Japanese some of the classic American books on wolves. He hoped one day to return wolves to one of his country's isolated islands.

"It will take time, of course," he said, "but I hope to help bring this about within the next hundred years."

SEPTEMBER 3, 1989. Plover Ponds. A hard rain keeps me in the tent all day. In late afternoon the cacophony of passing cranes rouses me from a nap. The flights continue into the early evening, when the rain finally quits and the clouds part. Taking the cue, I load my pack to go in search of photographic subjects. I spot a bull caribou feeding on a nearby ridge. He ignores me. Soon I'm watching through my camera. Behind him the western horizon turns crimson. He continues to feed without raising his head. I grow impatient. The sunset colors won't last long, and I want the perfect silhouette. Cranes, chorusing behind me, approach low and fast. Their calling grows louder, but I can't tear myself from the viewfinder for fear of missing my one chance for the photo. Then the cranes are over me, and I hear the *whump, whump* of their wingbeats mixed with their shrill cries. They startle the bull; he prances a few steps. I can see the birds in the viewfinder! They are just ten feet above the ground as they pass over the bull. I photograph until the sunset fades to ebony.

SEPTEMBER 4, 1982. A cold, windy, overcast afternoon. On the east side of Stony Hill, I stopped to glass for sheep and caribou. It took determination (and a heavy parka) to sit in the wind with a spotting scope. In the alplands above Bergh Lake, I saw what at first appeared to be a sheep, but the scope revealed a light gray wolf. A moment later, a darker wolf trotted into view. The first wolf lay down while the other examined the parka squirrel dens that pocked the slope. Soon both headed downhill, but before going very far they paused and, after a long stare, raced back uphill, spooked by a group from Camp Denali hiking near the lake.

Ascending the slope, the wolves went behind the summit ridge. Yesterday I saw a band of ewes and lambs in that very spot, but today there are none. In thirty minutes the wolves crested the summit and headed down into Highway Pass. After driving to a pullout that offered a good view, I spotted them angling down into the valley.

Below the talus slopes they stopped on a grassy prominence that dominated the pass. Both appeared to study the tundra sprawling below them. They split up, one staying on the point, the other hunting a nearby willow thicket for squirrels and ptarmigan. Then, favoring its left front leg, the hunter loped from the willows and headed east. Its companion ran to catch up. Against the rocky hillside, the wolves' coloration blended in, but on the green slopes they were conspicuous.

Two bull caribou, one of which had unusual palmated antlers, were grazing in a gully half a mile east of the wolves. Although feeding in the open, they were hidden from the wolves, which were coming straight toward them.

A quickened pace soon brought the wolves to the edge of the gully in which the caribou fed. Just two hundred yards from the caribou, the wolves drew together, flanks touching. After a short pause, the lame wolf crept forward catlike, its companion trailing behind. Ten . . . twenty . . . thirty yards closer. Then the wolves charged. Almost immediately the smaller bull saw them and raced away to the east. The wolves veered toward the gully in which the larger bull had been feeding out of sight. In moments the wolves, too, were hidden from view. Long seconds ticked by.

Suddenly the bull dashed over the ridge and plunged straight down the rocky slope with the wolves just twenty to thirty feet behind. One faltering step and he would feel their bite. Going downhill, he picked up speed and widened the gap. Once he reached level ground, the wolves stopped and watched him race away.

After a brief pause, the wolves ran back uphill. As soon as they regained the ridgeline, the second caribou, which had stopped to watch from a few hundred yards away, saw them and bolted. With no trace of a limp, the light-colored wolf put on an incredible burst of speed, leaving its partner lagging. On the sidehill the gap between hunter and prey narrowed. With the wolves only a hundred and fifty yards behind, the bull ran out of sight behind a hill.

When all three animals came into view again, the wolves had closed the gap to fifteen to twenty yards. The bull turned toward the road, then swerved west, heading downstream toward Bergh Lake. Here one wolf slowed to a stop, but the light gray leader continued.

To keep the chase in sight, I had to drive to a different vantage point, and I missed part of the action. But from the flanks of Stony Hill I soon spotted the bull on the shore of the lake. Both wolves were again closing in. Without hesitation the bull raced into the wind-swept lake. A wolf jumped in behind it. Very quickly the whitecaps proved too much for the wolf, and it returned to shore. The caribou easily breasted the waves and swam to the east side of the lake. Once out of the water, it stopped to look back at the wolves. After a long look across the lake, the wolves gave up and trotted out of sight to the north.

For over an hour the bull watched the far shore, content to stay in the same place, conserving energy for the next encounter.

In a little under two hours the wolves had covered over five miles of rugged country, ascending and descending a thousand-foot ridge. I wondered how they had chosen their prey. Although they had been closest to the big bull, they had given up on him to chase another that was over a quarter mile away. And why, with all the possibilities, did the caribou run toward Bergh Lake? Was it because of the downward slant of the route or because the lake offered safety?

SEPTEMBER 5, 1981. Biologists Jim Taggart and Cindy Zabel accompanied me on a hike to a rugged mountain slope. It was their first close look at Dall sheep. The rams dancing across the cliffs seemed to awe them.

Just as we were leaving, we saw several ewes and lambs ascending from the heavy alders below. One lamb had bloody legs from the knees down. We got a close look at the tardive lamb when the band filed by us. Its legs were bloody from open sores and its mouth and nostrils were covered with black lesions. We guessed it suffered from contagious ecthyma, a disease thought to be transmitted to wildlife from domestic livestock. An outbreak of the disease a few years ago in Fairbanks killed a captive herd of musk-ox and sheep. I took pictures and made notes of the lamb's condition.

While watching the diseased lamb, we heard noises in the brush behind us and turned, expecting to see more sheep. Instead, a grizzly, its nose to the ground like a hunting dog, hurried out of the alders below us. We hollered and backed away, but the bear had picked up the blood scent and would not be deterred. We watched as the bear charged toward the blood trail. To our relief, when the grizzly reached it, instead of continuing uphill toward the lamb and us, it turned downhill and raced off on the backtrail. We hurried the other way.

Investigators later found that the lamb did indeed have contagious ecthyma, as did others in Igloo and Savage. Additional research revealed that the disease was common to some wild populations in Alaska and not the danger previously believed.

Strange things happen around the park this time of year. Today, while we were on the slope with the rams, two rare "tundra pigs" were observed by several shuttle busloads of tourists. A ranger, dispatched to Savage River to investigate, found nothing, but moments after he left, the tundra pigs were again seen dancing on a rock not far from the road. No one knows exactly what these strange, bipedal, pink creatures were doing, but perhaps the dance was courtship. The male displayed a huge phallus.

SEPTEMBER 6, 1990. Today I saw three radio-collared animals — a wolf, a moose, and a bear. Seeing the tracking devices bothered me greatly. These collars ruin photographic opportunities, but I also do not like them for personal aesthetic reasons. Adolph Murie concluded his book *The Grizzlies of Mount McKinley* with some strong thoughts:

> *I shy away from the word 'management' because it has been mis-used and the less we have of it in national parks, the better. Wildlife managers want to manage everything*

> *. . . the observation of tassels in the ears and the knowledge*
> *that the bears have been manhandled systematically de-*
> *stroy for many people the wilderness ethic . . . We might*
> *imagine a situation so critical that intrusive, harmful tech-*
> *niques would be necessary. But . . . in Mount McKinley*
> *National Park the added information obtained does not*
> *merit the sacrifice of the intangible values for which parks*
> *are cherished. In wilderness parks, research techniques*
> *should be in harmony with the spirit of wilderness, even*
> *though efficiency and convenience may at times be dimin-*
> *ished.*

One biologist suggests that Murie's comments, written at the end of his career just when radio-telemetry was coming into wide use, are "sour grapes." He said that if Murie were alive today, he'd be using radio-telemetry techniques. I'm not convinced. Maybe Murie's view was ahead of its time. Ethics always seem to be a few steps behind scientific advances.

Research is a valid activity at Denali, but like all other activities, it should be as nonintrusive as possible. Before permits are granted to researchers, all aspects of the proposed study, including conflict with other visitors, should be carefully weighed by Park Service. Often the park is the only place where some kinds of studies can be conducted. Many research proposals have been rejected because the work could be done elsewhere. Currently, researchers have voluntarily modified their studies to minimize conflict with visitors. Two wolves that regularly patrol the road have not been collared precisely because of their habits and high visibility. Moose collars are now made of narrow, brown leather — inconspicuous at a distance. And I realize that because the bear I saw today interacted with humans this summer, its radio-collar may help rangers save it from being destroyed.

We'll probably never return to the policy of the late 1960s, when no collars were allowed on animals at all. But I hope Park Service will continue to weigh all research proposals carefully and consider the animals' rights.

SEPTEMBER 6, 1979. After a long day's travel, I arrived at the park after midnight last night and camped at Morino. I slept late and was awakened by footsteps approaching my tent. Someone bent down and started the zipper. When I sat up, the noise sent the person running. I struggled out of the bag and the tent, but the campground looked empty. Forgoing breakfast, I struck camp and caught a ride into the park, hoping to get away from would-be thieves.

In midmorning after setting up camp, I located a large bull moose and four cows. When they bedded, I sat down to eat my breakfast, a frozen peanut-butter sandwich. The howl of a wolf drifted over the forest. One by one the moose stood up and moved to the edge of the timber. From there they could see both the willow flats and the knoll where the howl had originated. They stood motionless, watching. I abandoned my sandwich and crept closer. Impressed by the bull's bulk and polished antlers, I could not imagine a wolf challenging him, or even one of the cows.

The howling died away but the moose remained alert. Minutes later, another wolf howled from the river behind us. Immediately there came an answer from the knoll. The moose did not look behind them; all five looked to their right. About two hundred yards away, a gray wolf emerged from the timber and headed across the flat toward the knoll. The willows were thick, and the wolf jumped, much like a rabbit in high brush, from one clearing to another.

Soon the wolf disappeared onto the slopes of the brushy knoll. Only the far cry of a raven rent the silence. After a few minutes the moose began to move away. They continued across the Park Road and the creek to the timber on the east side of the valley, putting space between themselves and the wolves.

SEPTEMBER 7, 1989. I have camped out near Moose Creek the last four days, hoping to photograph caribou and alpenglow on the mountain. Near-constant rain kept me close to camp, however, and I never saw the mountain. In mid-August the caribou moved fairly rapidly west. By the beginning of this month, the only places to find them along the road were at either end of it, Savage River, or Wonder Lake. From the tent, I saw caribou on almost every ridge. The rain was frustrating.

When my backcountry permit expired, I had to head in. I caught the eight-twenty A.M. eastbound shuttle from Wonder Lake and arrived at Eielson at nine-thirty. A man boarded the bus wearing just one shoe and carrying the other.

"My shoe blew up." He lifted it, showing a massive seam failure from heel to toe. "Hard walking," he said.

He told me that late last night while hiking beyond Grassy Pass, he missed the last bus and ended up walking to Eielson. The intermittent rain had become a downpour. He wore only a denim jacket; he had no raincoat, hat, or food. He reached Eielson after eleven. "It was dark. Only the bathroom was open. It was heated, and I slept in it," he said. "This is my first time in America. I'm on my way to university in Chicago. My home is in China."

SEPTEMBER 8, 1974. Everyone looks for bears, moose, or caribou. The more common animals don't get much notice. For example, the ubiquitous marsh hawk, now called the northern harrier, seldom attracts attention. Gray jays flit from tree to tree. Arctic ground squirrels, called parka squirrels by Alaskans, sit beside the road or on open slopes. Red squirrels chirr from forest limbs, and at this time of year spruce grouse often sit along the road edge. Coveys of ptarmigan are also common. Sharp-eyed folks can often see soaring golden eagles. The few times a bus does stop for a look at a ptarmigan or a squirrel, there's always the voice in the back of the bus: "What is it? What do you see? Is it a bear? No? Let's go."

On the return bus trip, someone comments that animals are cruel. A fox had killed a squirrel right by the bus; we watched as the fox tore the squirrel apart and ate it. Someone else said that animals have harsh existences and die terrible deaths. I suspect that these interesting opinions are commonly held and that behind them is a belief that humans are neither cruel nor susceptible to terrible deaths. But I wonder which is worse, to be a squirrel torn limb from limb by a fox and die within two or three minutes, or to be a human fighting cancer for months or even years, undergoing all sorts of horrific treatments before succumbing? Ironically, as more people come to appreciate nature, they are often horrified by its reality. It's hard for me to think of natural predation or natural animal mortality as *cruel* because the term implies *intent*. I've never seen animals inflict pain for pleasure. On the other hand, torturous human deaths and deprivations have stemmed from prejudice, religion, and politics. I'm sure Holocaust survivors could tell us much about cruelty, but could a ground squirrel?

SEPTEMBER 9, 1984. More sheep are crossing the high brushy ridge above the Sanctuary River; they are heading from Double Mountain to the flanks of Mount Wright. They face grave danger. Head-high brush impedes their travel and offers concealment to bears and wolves. A few predators are likely to know of this autumnal migration route to winter range. Indeed, I once found the remains of a ram on the bluff overlooking the river. Ahead of them, too, is the road crossing. As absurd as it seems, sheep have been struck and killed by passing vehicles. Once across the road, the sheep must still fight heavy brush on the long upward climb to the safety of alpine crags and summits.

In midmorning I slowed my car to a stop near a car parked at the edge of the road in Highway Pass and joined the visitors glassing the distant band of ewes and lambs. Just as I started up again, I glimpsed a wolverine running through the brush uphill from where we were parked. I scrambled for my camera. An eagle flew low overhead, and I heard the people call out to one another. As they looked at the eagle, they missed the wolverine.

In the time that it took to put down my binoculars and pick up my camera, the wolverine was gone. I had a fleeting glimpse of it as it darted through the willows. A few minutes later it hurried west across the open tundra. I drove half a mile west and stopped. Almost at once I saw movement on the ridge above, but there was more than one animal. The wolverine was chasing a small grizzly cub. They ran some thirty yards up the open ridge before the female bear, trailed by another cub, charged over the ridge in pursuit of its cub and the wolverine. With help in sight, the fleeing cub turned and appeared to charge its pursuer, which was only a few feet away. The wolverine braced itself for battle. The cub dodged to the side and ran by to the safety of its family. Only twenty yards separated the bears and the wolverine. Although I was too far away for any sound to reach me, I could see the bear's jaws opening and closing as if she were under stress or vocalizing. Soon both parties were going in opposite directions.

SEPTEMBER 10, 1978. Clear and windy at Igloo. Thirty-four degrees. A few short miles away at Teklanika this morning it was eighteen degrees with a heavy frost. If June 15 is roughly the average date for the last spring freeze, then the growing season here is only a little more than seventy to eighty days.

Autumnal colors have peaked and faded in the park's higher elevations. This year the peak was about September 3. Some years it's as late as the second week of September or as early as the fourth week of August. How long the colors persist depends partly on precipitation, wind, and frost. Wind and heavy rain or snow pull the leaves from the plants. Sometimes the tundra and taiga seem ablaze one day, drab the next. Other years, the colors linger and fade as the leaves drop one by one.

SEPTEMBER 11, 1982. It was cold and clear this morning after three inches of snow last night. I was prepared: insulated boots, long johns, winter woolies. A golden sunrise found me watching a bull and cow moose bedded in the willows along the creek. Sunlight reflecting off the frost on their backs sparkled like faceted jewels. Just after sunrise, the cow got up and began to feed. The bull stood and approached her with a moan. She moved quickly away. I examined their beds, burned through the snow to bare ground. One is thawed to gravel; the other to lichen and moss. Melt-water seeped into both. The shape of the moose's hip and spine was pressed into the snowbank. Long brown and white hairs littered the snow. Standing in the bull's bed, the pungent rut smell assaulted my senses; I could almost feel the bull's energy burning my feet.

I've seen quite a few snowshoe hares in Igloo forest but no sign of lynx yet. I wonder when sightings of lynx will again become common in prime habitat. Of course, "common" is relative when referring to such a retiring, nocturnal animal. Perhaps the seeming resurgence of the hare population will bring about a concomitant increase in lynx. Without hares, the few lynx that haunt the woods know hunger. In the winter of 1955 or 1956, when hares were nearly nonexistent, Bill Nancarrow saw a lynx waiting motionless in the snow for almost seven hours before finally catching a squirrel. "The hares had crashed," Bill said, "and there was nothing else to eat."

In March 1973, driving from his cabin to the park post office, Johnny Johnson saw two lynx wrestling in the snow in the ditch along the Parks Highway. He watched them for twenty minutes before they moved off into the brush.

That same year, Bill Ruth told me of a lynx den he'd seen in this forest. It wasn't a burrow or cave, really, but merely a protected spot under a deadfall. After the site was located, the three kittens were moved away by their mother. With abundant prey, lynx have three to four kittens per litter. On the downswing of their cycle, when prey is scarce, yearlings do not mate, and adult females have only one kitten. Lynx are resourceful scavengers and capable predators (in Newfoundland they are the principal predator of caribou calves), but without hares, they starve.

Because hare and lynx cycles span decades, there is no accurate record of their population fluctuations in the park. In 1926, Joseph Dixon of the U.S. Biological Survey offered some early insight into how quickly hare populations can crash. According to Dixon, hares peaked in the winter of 1925, and were still abundant the following May. But just two months later, on July 25, 1926, Dixon couldn't find any hares, even in prime habitat. Hares were said to be nonexistent in 1932. (The theory then was that hare populations crashed because of disease, some sort of "plague.") Lynx also disappeared after being very numerous in former years. Bill Nancarrow witnessed another sharp crash in hare populations in the early 1950s. Apparently, hares peaked again in the early 1960s and 1970s. Each time, lynx population highs were reached a year or two after the hare peaks.

Just as hares have their mortal foes, lynx are preyed upon by wolves and coyotes. Charlie Ott reported seeing coyotes tree lynx on two occasions in the early 1950s.

A great silver, ear-tufted lynx, padding silently over the snow, is my fantasy animal. I have seen very few free-roaming lynx in the wild (surprisingly, I've seen three times as many wolverines). Yet I can easily envision their yellow eyes burning in venatic zeal. Just now the woods are silent, waiting for the gray shadows that, perhaps, will stalk here again.

Although hares were somewhat common in the early 1980s, their populations did not reach the previous level. Lynx never became obvious or commonplace either. Robin O'Connor-Beasley, a state biologist, once released a young radio-collared lynx in the park to monitor its movements and behavior. But in early winter, as soon as the Nenana River froze, the lynx crossed the ice and was trapped and killed outside the park.

SEPTEMBER 12, 1981. I wonder how many people on the bus see the distant caribou or sheep on the ridges.

Picking out wildlife takes training, knowing what to look for. A tour driver told me, "With ninety-six eyes on board, I still make seventy percent of the observations." I wonder how many passengers see more than I do but do not speak up. And what of the people who see a harrier or a golden eagle or a grouse but, recognizing the chauvinism of the mammal lovers, keep quiet? In spring the song of white-crowned sparrows can be heard even through the open windows of a bus, but I can't imagine a bus stopping for people to listen to them.

If a large mammal is close to the road, there'll be shouts, and the bus will come to a halt. We will spend a few minutes watching. But so much more is missed. Once I saw a bear at a distance and called out. The bus stopped, but passengers couldn't pick it out. Their skepticism was palpable.

SEPTEMBER 13, 1979. This afternoon, right behind the Wonder Lake ranger station, I watched a grizzly swim to the beaver lodge in the middle of the pond. After shaking itself, the bear sniffed at the lodge, then tore into it, flinging sticks left and right as if digging out a squirrel. It dug and pulled at the sticks and mud until it had torn an opening big enough to gain access to the beaver's sleeping chamber. Although I haven't seen a beaver in this pond for a while, no doubt the lingering aroma of castor excited the bear.

Its rump wiggling at the sky, the grizzly delved into the mysteries of the lodge's interior for quite some time. Then it backed out of the hole and stood blinking in the bright sun. A twenty- to fifty-pound beaver would make a good meal, but there were none to be taken from this lodge. After a few more desultory explorations, the bear belly-flopped into the pond and swam west toward the road. A passing road-grader spooked the bear as it emerged from the water. It bolted across the road, over the tundra, and disappeared into the timber along the lakeshore.

In early evening near Wonder Lake's outlet, I watched the same bear as it fed on blueberries. Since the bear had been soaking wet earlier, its color indeterminate, I based my judgment on size and general appearance. It was a prime, mature animal with jet black legs, a golden head, and a fully furred body that all but glowed in the afternoon backlight. A bear of this color is often referred to here as a Toklat grizzly, as if it were a distinct species. Neither Adolph Murie nor Charles Sheldon ever wrote about Toklat grizzlies, although each made note of the great color variation of Denali bears. But Dr. C. Hart Merriam, a taxonomist, concluded from one of the specimens provided by Sheldon that indeed the region's bears were a distinct species. Merriam labeled them *Ursus toklat*. Early taxonomists tended to identify dozens of bear species and subspecies based on minor variations in skull and bone measurements, hair color, and body size. Modern taxonomists tend to lump animals together, recognizing fewer species and subspecies. Grizzlies do vary in color from black to almost white. This bear's entire hindquarters are stained with crushed blueberries. Using the fruit bush's botanical name, would the early scientists have classified it as *Ursus vaccinius*?

SEPTEMBER 14, 1988. I saw familiar vehicles on the side of the road; Johnny Johnson was visiting with Charlie Ott. Compared with Charlie, Johnny and I are greenhorns here. Charlie came to the area in 1950 and has headquartered in his cabin at Deneki Lakes ever since. Through the 1950s and 1960s, when he wasn't pursuing the duties of his park maintenance job, Charlie photographed the park more completely than anyone before him, documenting everything from lichens to wolves. He retired from Park Service in 1974. His outspoken activism and staunch support of conservation rank him as a truly zealous protector of the natural world.

Charlie was raging to Johnny about the park's "ruination." He has been critical of park development as early as 1964. "It should remain a primitive park," he was quoted as saying in a magazine article. "Inconvenience should be part of it. Anything too easy becomes cheap."

The road access restrictions have been especially difficult for Charlie. Even with his seniority, each year he is allowed only a two-week special travel permit into the park. True, he could get on the shuttle. But at his age, with a bad back and loaded down with all the paraphernalia of a photographer, the suggestion is ludicrous. Park Service should make an exemption and let Charlie come and go as he pleases. He's given more to the park than he's ever taken from it.

Charlie believes that in wildlife photography patience is the key virtue, coupled with "a feeling for the rights and feelings of the wildfolk." He once said, "I can tell if [the animals] don't want their picture taken, and I won't."

On May 7, 1989, when Charlie was over eighty, the University of Alaska, Fairbanks, bestowed on him an honorary Doctorate of Letters. "He has personally taught scores of scientists and professional photographers about 'his' park, giving lessons about nature and technique that no textbook could begin to explore," read the citation accompanying the presentation. "Through his donations of time, photography, and funds, he seeks to ensure that what he has enjoyed will continue to exist for the enlightenment and appreciation of future generations." That same year, Charlie sold his cabin to Mike Speaks, donated his books and papers to the university, and moved to Oregon.

SEPTEMBER 15, 1985. Caribou bulls are sparring on the ridges above Wonder Lake and in the Kantishna Hills. Often these jousts turn serious; minor injuries are common. I watched two bulls lock antlers and test each other by pushing, shoving, and circling. Unlike the powerful, inexorable thrusting of bull moose, caribou bulls spar with their lowered, rapierlike tines driven by dancing legs. Their battles are more like a fencing match than a sabre duel: thrust met with parry, speed as important as power, grace enamored of violence.

Since many bulls have already begun to join the bands of cows and calves, these sparring battles are ever more earnest affairs. The mature, experienced bulls seem the least willing to put up with a young bull's approach, threat display, or encroachment on the herd. Soon young bulls will dodge about the perimeter of the bands, avoiding the assaults of the herd masters. Although the peak of the rutting season occurs in mid to late October, the bigger bulls already have some of the mixed groups in turmoil. Where just a few days ago the small herds were easy to approach, many are now flighty. Even the habituated bulls, when they are with a group of cows, are intolerant of humans. Except to watch and photograph from a distance, it is time to leave the caribou alone.

In late afternoon I was surprised to see a solitary, familiar bull grazing on a ridge above a tundra pond. Even at a distance I recognized the one-eyed caribou by its misshapen left antler. I approached from upwind so that the animal could get my scent. After verifying my scent with a glance of its good eye, it went back to feeding. The bull seemed at first to be pawing and eating lichens, but soon I saw that it was uncovering and chewing bones — caribou bones. Portions of femurs and tibias, ribs and vertebrae. Aided by heavy salivation, the bones were being ground up and swallowed. The bull continued to paw up a circle of plant cover two feet in diameter until all of the dark moldering bones were eaten.

SEPTEMBER 16, 1985. Today's planned hike with Jane didn't get very far. Just after negotiating the thickest brush on the route, we started up an open slope covered with fresh snow. We walked with heads down, watching our icy, treacherous footing. Where the slope flattened out, I came to a fresh grizzly track in the snow. I looked up. The bear was about two hundred feet away. Swiveling around, I took Jane by the arm and propelled her back the way we had come. She gave a quizzical look but kept going without a word. I looked back at the bear, still unaware of our presence, then hurried after Jane. With many backward glances, we retraced our steps the way we had come.

We spent the remainder of the morning in the timber, watching a flock of spruce grouse peck gravel along the edge of a stream. A cock grouse swaggered in the top of a small spruce above the flock. With fanned tail and extended wings, he attempted to strut but could not keep his balance in the treetop. He'd manage a few steps, then start to fall. To save himself, he'd grab awkwardly at the tiny boughs growing at the top of the tree, all semblance of dignity lost in a ruffle of feathers. Once restored to his perch, he'd jerk and bob his head in an apparent effort to regain composure. After a moment, the flock below would rouse him to display again, with the same checkered results. He was doing such a poor job of impressing the hen and her almost fully grown brood that they never even looked up from pecking gravel, except, of course, when his fluttering missteps drew their attention. Jane wondered aloud whether he knew the season.

Grouse seem so unwary as to provoke wonder about the number that survive to maturity. They must have defensive strategies I know nothing about. They are strong fliers and can elude many predators, but watching these unwary birds, I know that owls, lynx, sharp-shinned hawks, and goshawks must take a toll, especially when they are collecting gravel in the open. This time of year I commonly find groups of grouse or individual birds any place where gravel is easily collected. All summer they have had easy foraging on the plants of the forest understory: cranberries, blueberries, crowberries, flowers, leaves, and plants. In winter their diet will be almost exclusively spruce needles. The grit they collect will be needed in their craws to grind the fibrous needles into digestible pieces.

Just before we left, the cock finally abandoned the tree and fluttered down to the hens. We left him strutting before the unimpressed flock.

SEPTEMBER 16, 1990. Last week I photographed five fine bull caribou at Caribou Creek. Today, after a long hike, I could find only four of them, and they were skittish. On the hike back, I saw a velvet-free, bright red antler sticking up out of the willows. It would be the fifth bull at rest. I made noise so that the bull would not be startled by my approach, but it did not arise—and never would. The stripped skeleton of the fifth bull lay where it fell. The bull was probably killed and eaten by wolves. A cursory look revealed no abnormality or imperfection in the remaining bones. Perhaps mature bulls succumb to predators in autumn because they are fattened for the rut and are slower, or perhaps the extra weight causes them to overheat in a chase. I do not know the reason for the bull's demise, but I now have pictures of him taken five days apart, each roll showing him in startlingly different form.

SEPTEMBER 17, 1989. Today, at last count, six hundred private vehicles have passed through the Savage River check station. The single-day record was set yesterday, the day the road opened to the public, when about fifteen hundred private vehicles entered the park. It was bumper-to-bumper traffic almost the length of the road. Two vehicles went off the road and rolled over. Several others went into the ditch and needed towing. (Because wreckers must travel from either Cantwell or Healy, a simple tow may cost three hundred dollars.)

This end-of-the-season road opening occurs each year, usually the day after the shuttle buses stop running. In the 1970s the road opened immediately following Labor Day weekend and remained opened until closed by weather. One dry year the road was open to Wonder Lake well into the end of October, but there was little traffic. Another year the road was closed by weather in the middle of September. By the mid-1980s the autumn road opening had become an anticipated annual rite for some Alaskans, and monumental bumper-to-bumper traffic jams ensued. With so much traffic on the road, inevitably there are accidents, violations, wildlife-vehicle collisions, and monumental "bear jams."

In response to the late-season visitor crush, Park Service contracted for the shuttles to run later into the autumn, which controlled access for a longer period. Part of the General Management Plan's mandate is to cut traffic. So instead of waiting for weather to close the road, Park Service established a scheduled, incremental road closing after the initial opening to private vehicles. The road would be open to Wonder Lake for a brief period, followed by a closure at Toklat. A few days later, the road beyond Teklanika would close. Weather conditions would then determine the final road closure beyond headquarters at Mile 3. But just as the road was being closed, a growing number of visitors began arriving, having timed their vacations to coincide with the opening of the road to unlimited public access. Yesterday's accident was the predictable consequence of the converging trends.

The Park Road justifiably remains a narrow, gravel, mountainous route, not suited to unlimited, high-speed traffic. Surely wildlife would not venture so close to the road if it were more intrusive.

In 1915, as part of the park proposal process, a wagon route was drawn from the Alaska Railroad right-of-way to a point on the McKinley River near Muldrow Glacier. In 1920 an Alaska Road Commission engineer, Hawley Sterling, explored the area and proposed two routes. The high mountain option was chosen over a lowland, muskeg route. (Hawley warned that the lowland route would be expensive and difficult because of its soils, stream crossings, and water tables. And in fact, the mid-1960s construction of the Stampede Trail, which followed this lower route, was a fiasco and was quickly abandoned.) Work on the Park Road began in 1922.

Harry Karstens pioneered the initial twelve-mile route from McKinley Station to Savage River. The trail to Mount Eielson, then called Copper Mountain, and on to Wonder Lake was roughly flagged by Sam Sanderson's ARC crew. The trail crossed bog, tundra, forest, and mountain pass. Every ten to fifteen miles, travelers used nine-foot-by-ten-foot shelter tents equipped with wood stoves.

The Park Road was paid for by Park Service but built by the Alaska Road Commission, which also built all the roads in the Territory of Alaska. Colonel James G. Steese, chairman of the commission from 1920 to 1927, oversaw much of the early construction. The road was approved for both visitor and commercial access. Steese supported extending it to the Kuskokwim River and beyond to the Bering Sea.

William N. Beach and Charles Godley, perhaps the first two actual tourists (as well as photographers) to visit the park, reported in 1922 that the trail was only roughly flagged to Savage and was indistinct beyond. They met Woodbury "Wood" Abbey, in his second year of a survey of the park and boundaries. Abbey's crew was short of provisions and laboring under primitive wilderness conditions.

By 1923, the road was passable by wagon to Savage River, where a tourist camp had been established. Only thirty-four people made the trip to Savage Camp; in 1924 a round trip cost sixteen dollars. Packhorse hire was eight dollars per day, and saddle horse hire was ten dollars per day. By 1925, the route to Savage was being traveled by auto, but all travel beyond was described as "pick your way."

By 1928, forty miles of road had been completed. Although only six hundred people visited the park in 1937, work proceeded until the road reached Wonder Lake in 1938. In 1940, four and a half miles of road connected the Park Road to the Kantishna Mining District, opening a "new tourist attraction." On August 4, 1957, the Denali Highway opened, linking the park with Alaska's road system. The opening of the Denali route brought a 560 percent increase in Park Road traffic that month.

Road improvement commenced in 1957–58 as part of Mission 66 under the supervision of the Bureau of Public Roads. To meet anticipated traffic loads, the bureau planned to pave the first thirty miles; to realign, upgrade, and oil the middle forty miles, possibly paving that section later; and to leave the remaining miles beyond Eielson primitive. Construction and realignment continued through 1967 before mounting public pressure halted the work.

"Recreational development is a job not of building roads into the lovely country but of building receptivity into the still un-lovely human mind," Aldo Leopold wrote.

Many took a similar view, including the Murie brothers, who led the fight against the road building. "It seems ironic that the service personnel who should champion simplicity and preserva-tion of esthetic values," Adolph Murie wrote, "have, for the most part, defended construction of an unsightly road. A complete change of attitude is needed."

Although the 1965 master plan stated that "improvement of Park Road will be accomplished with the least possible intrusion and scars caused by construction will be eliminated when possible," what the opponents wanted was elimination of the project, not its scars.

By 1969, the battle was over, but not before the road had been paved as far as Savage River and a total of thirty miles realigned and upgraded. "No further paving projects . . . anticipated in the near future," Park Service informed prospective contractors.

The road's condition has long been a subject of commentary. Newspaper editorial cartoons have skewered the Park Service over it. In 1983 one cartoon showed a tourist lost in the bottom of a pothole; another had an auto disappearing into one. On July 25, 1985, heavy rains washed out sections of the road, stranding hun-dreds of visitors for a brief time. Equipment operator Tim Taylor recalls that the roadbed itself was a danger. When he drove a bull-dozer onto one section, it "quivered like jelly."

The road was closed from August 26 to September 3, Labor Day, 1990, by landslides brought on by heavy rains. The road bed remained stable, the problem was mud and debris coming down onto it. Some visitors were stranded for a night, many others inconvenienced, or their trips dis-rupted. Again voices were calling for a road "upgrade," but it must be pointed out that the same foul weather also shut down the Alaska Railroad and closed the Parks Highway, repairs to both lasting well into late October.

On September 14, 1990, the road was opened to Wonder Lake for four days, traffic limited to 300 private vehicles per day, entry by prior permit only. Permits were awarded by lottery; four out of five applicants received permits, an 80 percent chance of winning. Only about 200 vehicles entered the park on the peak day, poor weather a factor in limiting turnout. Superintendent Berry called the new system both "fair and successful" and indicated it would be continued.

Whenever the question of paving the road comes up, it revives the entire debate. Perhaps the issue can be boiled down to unlimited access on a paved route offering minimal wildlife observations versus a rugged road with unique wildlife sightings.

"I do hope the road stays narrow and winding," the writer Sigurd F. Olson said in a letter to Adolph Murie. "I [also] oppose any tourist facilities [in the park]. Here then is a great opportunity to do the very thing that should have been done in other parks, keeping all development outside. The reason McKinley is such a wonderful sanctuary is because there are no interior developments beyond headquarters."

Perhaps none have spoken out against road improvements more bluntly than Charlie Ott. In 1964 he called the old road a speedway. He favored a twenty-five-mile-an-hour speed limit (it is currently thirty-five with some slower zones) and said, "You don't go tearing to beat hell through a museum."

SEPTEMBER 18, 1985. With notebook in hand, I sit on a tundra ridge overlooking a valley dotted with small caribou herds, and I compare these scenes with those of my youth. Southern California was not a joyful place for me to grow up. The landscape was often achingly beautiful, but the things being done to the land, air, water, and wildlife hurt me. In the evening I'd look over the valley and chaparral and try to imagine how it must have appeared when the first Spaniards filtered out of the south. I'd look beyond the housing tracts creeping inexorably over the land, and I'd try to ignore the brown haze blotting the horizon and searing my lungs with each breath. In Denali I don't need imagination to see the primal creation. Streams do not flow with chemical poisons. A deep breath is often like a swallow of pure, icy water. And one youthful fantasy is easily nurtured: when I meet them with genuine humility, the animals often accept me without fear.

Just after dark, driving east, I slam on the brakes to avoid something crossing the road. Eyes blaze in the headlamps. Wolves in the road! Two. Three. Four. Tiny bonfires wink out as the shadows move and meld into the dusky brush thickets.

SEPTEMBER 18, 1990. A band of sheep crossing the high plateau between Divide Mountain and Mount Wright drew my friend and me onto the flats to look for a vantage point from which to watch the action. We hiked from Teklanika to a knob that overlooks the route. In the distance to the north, two bands of sheep worked their way up Mount Wright's slopes. We surmised that one of them was the group we'd seen earlier from the road. Another group, six sheep in all, were bunched on the slope to the south of the plateau. Soon they would begin what could be a perilous crossing.

We had just sat down to watch when a bull moose appeared in a willow thicket below the sheep. It was moving steadily north. Although the moose looked out of place on the open tundra, the wanderings of rutting bulls often take them out of their usual habitat. In twenty minutes, the bull had crossed the plateau and disappeared into the thickets along the Sanctuary.

We also saw a lone bull caribou grazing near the moose's route. After the moose passed by, the caribou fed undisturbed for ten minutes before its head jerked up as it stared south toward the sheep on the ridge. Because of the high wind, we had almost missed what the caribou had not, the howling of a lone wolf. It took a while to pinpoint the spot from which the repeated howling emanated, a low saddle above the sheep. We moved to the north side of the hill to escape the wind and to watch for the wolf. There the howling was louder and clearer. We marveled that the sheep seemed undisturbed. Perhaps they couldn't hear the wolf because of the lay of the land and the wind.

One sheep separated from the band and started downhill. Another ewe led her lamb the opposite way, uphill toward the saddle. Upon rounding the brow of the hill, the two stopped to stare. After long moments of immobility, the ewe turned to look back at the rest of the band, which was following the first ewe down onto the flats. Both animals rushed off after their departing companions. Soon the reunited band, all ewes and lambs, was running onto the plateau and pushing through the dwarf birch. They were not pursued. The howling continued.

We expected the wolf, or wolves, to appear soon, but we saw none. Finally another wolf howled just once, close to the first, and that was the end of their song.

It took the sheep band forty-five minutes to make the crossing and reach the road. Just as they went out of sight, off to the east five bull caribou raced onto the plateau in panicked flight. We saw nothing behind them, but they never stopped running until they had gone into the Sanctuary.

When we eventually abandoned our lookout, the valley was empty. No sheep, no moose, no caribou. Yet the air was full with the memory of wolf song.

SEPTEMBER 19, 1979. On a slope above Jenny Creek, I watched a fox catch and eat a squirrel. The fox appeared on the hillside above a thicket where I saw a flock of half-white ptarmigan land. Its pursuit of the squirrel ended in the quick snap of jaws. After eating half its catch, the fox carried the remnant uphill a short distance, laid it down, and with its forepaws began to dig a hole. As it dug, I crept within good binocular range. The fox was ebony except for a faint brown cross over its shoulders, white-tipped guard hairs, and a white-tipped tail. It was nearly a silver. Its coat was already long and thick, in sharp contrast to the scruffy, thin summer suit it wore only a few weeks ago.

After the fox dropped the carcass into the shallow hole, it pushed dirt over it with its nose to bury it. Satisfied with the cache, holding its fluffy tail straight out behind, the fox trotted up and over the ridge.

In many parts of the North, red foxes occupy relatively small home territories. Fox populations on isolated, prey-rich islands share less space; foxes inhabiting poor-quality habitat require more. Earlier this year, I watched a red fox mark its territory by urinating on plants and rocks, building what biologists would call an olfactory fence. Scent posts not only delineate territories but also identify sex, breeding status, and other bits of information.

Foxes have been known to make incredible long-distance journeys. One marked fox traveled a straight-line distance of 245 miles. Many such dispersals occur in early autumn and winter when first-year pups wander in search of their own territories. A predator's life is not an easy one. The majority of the foxes born in the spring will not survive the first winter. Perhaps the adult I saw today will not live through the coming months of darkness and cold.

SEPTEMBER 20, 1985. A white bull moose was reported last week by a pilot flying over the Kantishna Hills. This would be the first white bull seen in the park area since the mid-1970s, when a mature bull was seen several years in a row in the Kantishna-

Stampede area. Its existence was well known, even by trophy hunters in the Lower Forty-Eight. In fact, one taxidermist allegedly offered ten thousand dollars for the hide and antlers if they were suitable for life-size mounting. One fall the white bull disappeared. After spotting it from his own plane, a local pilot had had a friend fly him out in a different plane and drop him off at a nearby landing strip. The season was open and the bull was outside the park; he shot the bull legally. To avoid criticism, the pilot conducted himself like a poacher and never mentioned the hunt openly. He confided to two people that he wanted to keep the moose from going to an outsider. The bull was killed to be safe from being killed? The mounted head now hangs in a private home.

SEPTEMBER 20, 1990. This morning, just inside the park's south entrance, not far from Triple Lakes, eight Canada geese and seven trumpeter swans fed and rested on a small pond, taking a break in their southward migration. These are not the only migrants visible just now. Numerous sharp-shinned hawks, as well as other sky hunters, are common on the ridges above the Nenana. Cranes can still be heard morning and evening. Wings dust the treetops and peaks as the birds move south. Some years, especially when early snow mantles the summits, I, too, wish I could take wing and join the clamorous flights on their journey toward the sun.

SEPTEMBER 21, 1987. Very quiet along the road today. Just one car is parked at the Teklanika barricade, the farthest point west still open to traffic. I park next to the car and trudge up the road; footprints in the damp earth indicate that the driver has gone ahead of me. Bear tracks cross and recross the road near the Teklanika bridge. While bending over them, I hear a faint howling from the west, over the forest, over the purling river—a faint chorus of several wolves, rising from somewhere near my destination. Excited, I hurry on.

Hours later I sit on a knob overlooking a spruce thicket where it fades into a willow flat. Numerous moose tracks and trails lace the frosted brush; the aroma of rutting moose perfumes the air. Despite having seen a bull moose and two cows in the snowy forest, I've yet to take a picture. The rutting bull is intemperate, and it would be unsafe and disruptive to linger near him. Through binoculars, I scan for other moose, the wolves all but forgotten.

Their song could have come from anywhere. There are no tracks.

Because of the cold wind, I cannot sit in the open. I am dressed for hiking, not sitting. I move down onto the flats, and almost at once I find a set of wolf tracks. I touch one; it is frozen hard, perhaps made last night. I begin tracking. Another set of tracks joins the first. A short distance beyond, there is another, then another. Some distance ahead, a magpie noisily flies from the brush. At once I abandon the trail and walk wide of the site. There's a strong chance the brush conceals a kill. I must be very careful. I circle the place warily. I cut across another wolf track. Then many tracks both to and from the site. Wolf tracks radiate from the spot like the spokes from a wheel. There are no bear tracks in the light snow. I walk in.

The remains of a bull moose are at the center of a circle of bloody, hair-strewn, trampled bog. The neck vertebrae are exposed, the hindquarters gone, the viscera stripped away. White bones speckled with tiny bits of raw flesh lie in the grass. Although forelegs and ribs are still covered with hide, the chest cavity is hollow. The antlers, now stained with bird excrement, are those of a large, mature bull.

The skull offers one tantalizing clue to the cause of death. The wolves have gnawed away the fleshy part of the nose and tongue, but there's a large puncture wound between the eye sockets that the wolves could not have made. Not long ago Michio Hoshino saw a bull near here with a shard of antler protruding from what had been its eye. Maybe the bull died in a rutting battle and is being scavenged. If not already dead, perhaps it was weakened by injury when the wolves came coursing through the woods. Whatever the cause of death, the moose's flesh now energizes these wolves. I am tempted to linger but do not, nor can I return another day. Such a kill will likely attract a bear.

SEPTEMBER 21, 1990. When the owl first flew, I thought it was a great gray owl, but I wasn't sure. Once, earlier this summer, I thought I'd seen three great gray owl fledglings, and with excitement I'd taken their pictures. But when the photos came back, the birds obviously were great horned owls. There was no mistaking this owl, however, when it landed barely six feet above the ground in a black spruce. Chill yellow eyes set in huge facial disks watched my careful approach. Through the binoculars I could see the black triangle under the beak and the white stripes on either side. This was a mature great gray. As I watched, it regurgitated a pellet, or casting. In time it flew off, dodging and weaving its way through the thick timber. I retrieved the pellet, a wad of fur enclosing rodent bones and the skull of a shrew — a full story of night hunts on silent wings.

SEPTEMBER 22, 1977. Autumnal equinox, the day the sun crosses the equatorial plane, the day when night and day are of equal length all over the earth.

Another warm, overcast morning, temperatures in the forties. The northern weather pattern takes some getting used to. In autumn and winter, clear skies bring cold weather; cloudy skies bring warm weather. (Where I grew up, the opposite was true. In winter, we longed for the clouds to part and for the sun to warm us.) In the Far North, from mid-September until April, winter nights are so much longer than winter days that the heat lost on a clear night exceeds any warmth that may be gained during a short sunny day. Clouds, however, form an insulating blanket that holds in the heat, moderating the extreme winter cold. The near-zero mornings we've had recently are no fluke. In less than a month, on clear mornings the temperature will perhaps drop to minus twenty and in another month to minus forty or colder.

Since early September we've been experiencing typical autumn weather for the park. Precious intervals of clear, cool weather alternating with periods of thick overcast and rain. Often, as the cloudy weather dissipates in front of a high-pressure front, snow falls at higher levels, leaving behind glistening peaks rising against azure skies. With each passing front, the snowline descends the mountains until finally snow falls throughout the park. The sun still commands enough power now to melt the snow from the lower elevations, but the thaw begins later each day. Soon the sun will be too far south to vanquish the cold.

SEPTEMBER 22, 1990. All this week I've been observing a group of cow moose and two bulls in the timber a few miles west of park Headquarters. Each day, Monday through Wednesday, I could find them in one copse or another in the same little drainage. Yesterday I could find only one moose, the smaller bull, a forked horn.

Today the other bull may be dead. Late in the afternoon, a large gray wolf emerged from the drainage. He was rather slow and lethargic, unconcerned with the two cars that stopped to watch him. His stomach was distended. After a bit he went back into the brush.

An hour later the wind shifted and carried the smell of death to the road. The twilight timber was calm and still. I cupped my hands and howled once. A moment passed. Then from the ridge across the creek, one, two, perhaps three, adults answered. The yapping of pups joined in. Then silence. By the kill, a deep howl lifted through the trees. The pack answered. The song went back and forth before a final silence. Soon shapes ghosted through the timber. An adult, then three pups, stopped to stare toward the road. Then they were gone, and ebon night enfolded the silent forest.

SEPTEMBER 23, 1977. Despite temperatures that zoomed into the forties by early afternoon, several inches of snow remained on the ground at Sable and Polychrome. Near the Toklat roadblock, Mike and I watched a grizzly wander through the brush by the road. It ignored the soapberries, which Murie called buffalo berries, and instead dug roots. Later we watched it swim the river channels and cross to the west side of the Toklat.

In midday we spotted a bear on the slope of Divide Mountain, high above the east branch of the Toklat. Against the snow the bear was obvious; otherwise we'd never have seen it so far away. We were unable to identify it as the one seen earlier or even to judge its color. The bear was merely a black shape on the snow. At first the bear looked as if it were digging out a squirrel, but then it enlarged the excavation until it was nearly hidden inside. We wondered whether it was digging a den. It seemed early. Murie wrote of a bear that dug its den on October 11 and didn't emerge until April—a hibernation period of almost seven months. A study of radio-collared bears in an area adjacent to the park found that most bears denned in mid-October and exited in the first week in May, spending in the mean around two hundred days in hibernation.

Of course, just because the bear was digging a huge hole didn't mean that it was a den or that the bear would hibernate any time soon. But whatever it was doing, the bear spent hours at the task. By late afternoon, it was asleep atop an enormous mound of dirt.

SEPTEMBER 24, 1981. Zero this morning. Clear and calm. I was not prepared for this. It took more than an hour to get my vehicle started. Because of my late start, I missed a chance to photograph moose in the first light. The day was slow to warm. Even after sunrise, handling the camera, lenses, and tripod bare-handed was almost painful. My tolerance for working with chilled metal was exhausted while fooling with the vehicle. They say Alaska has two seasons: nine months of winter and three months of damn late fall. Today I'm in agreement.

In early evening on the flats southwest of Savage River, I saw a cow and calf moose running in full flight toward the west. They crossed the mile-wide flat at a steady pace, never slowing to look back. Just as they ran from sight into a brush-choked ravine, a grizzly broke from cover in the east, loping along on their trail like a dog on a scent. The bear seemed undeterred by the mile lead of the moose. It traced their route precisely as would a hound, entering the ravine fifteen minutes later in the same place as had the moose.

I burned to know what had previously transpired. Had there been a struggle, or had a close sudden meeting in the timber provoked the chase? I wondered if the bear would be distracted by hunger or fatigue, or if it would close in and force the cow to make her stand? I would never know.

Most calf loss occurs primarily in the first two months of life. According to recent research, bear predation on moose calves has increased from 1974 to 1984, even though bear densities probably did not increase. Of every hundred calves, perhaps only ten to fifteen survive until fall. Victor VanBallenberghe suggests that the higher mortality is attributable either to a learning process in bears, or to a higher bear-to-moose ratio.

SEPTEMBER 25, 1985. A cross fox was sitting by the entrance to Savage Campground when I drove by. When I stopped, it trotted up to the vehicle and sat down a few feet from the door. Other than being skinny and unkempt, the fox was unremarkable. On a hunch, I pretended to throw something out the window. The fox responded as would a dog chasing a treat. Obviously, it had been begging and obtaining food from summer campers. Probably the "hunting" was easier here than on the tundra. I wondered how it would do when the campers had all gone home and there were no more crackers and hotdogs to hunt.

When I rolled up my window, the fox trotted to the passenger's side. I drove on, hoping the fox would survive the coming cold and snow. Quite likely, in a month or so it will be dead of starvation, a victim of human kindness.

SEPTEMBER 27, 1976. Plus eighteen and clear. A heavy fog rises from the Nenana River and from the partially frozen lakes and ponds nearby. Farther into the park, fog also obscures the Savage, Sanctuary, and Teklanika drainages. Driving the fog-bound road requires caution and a slow speed. I would prefer not to meet a moose head-on. Gnarled black spruce loom through the fog like gnomes in a dream. Some are startling. I stop often. Was that a moose, a person beckoning, or only a tree? Today the drive has more than the usual touch of mystery.

It is good to rise with the glitter of stars and frost, to wander the thickets in search of moose. The sound of frozen plants and fallen leaves crunching underfoot and the swish of nylon against grasping branches seem blasphemous in the silent, fog-shrouded woods. The birds of summer are gone now, and only the gray jays' gossip is a distraction in the silence. This dawn hike is not like the quiet stalk after patient glassing. It is at best a blundering search. Finding a moose in the fog often comes down to a chance discovery of tracks and trails, of hoof prints in the frost or snow. More than once I've located moose by the soft moaning of a cow or the traveling call of a bull. It can be but a faint sound through the trees. *There! Hear it?* Or sometimes the discovery is a hammer's strike to the senses. Suddenly, through the opaque mist obscuring the forest, comes a harsh bellow, the crackling of brush, and the rattle of antler against antler as aroused bulls lock in combat. Each time, unbidden, I step closer to the magic.

After a warm, sunny afternoon spent lounging in the forest near a group of twelve moose—one herd bull, two immature bulls, and nine cows—I pitch my tent in Savage Campground. It is quiet; I am the only camper. Gone are the sounds of people and bus traffic. And gone, too, are the sounds of the river. After setting up the tent, I walk to the river's edge, where thin shelf ice already reaches toward midchannel. A reduced water volume flows gently over the gravel. Water as clear as any I've ever seen makes me thirsty just looking at it. I work down the bank and balance on a rock. I reach beyond the ice to fill my cup and sip the throat-numbing water.

Just after dark an awakening breeze stirs the trees to life. As night creeps over the land, I sit by my warming fire enjoying the wind song and the air perfumed by wood smoke. Sparks blaze into the inky night and become glittering stars. I am tired and ready for sleep by nine o'clock, but it is not to be. To the northeast, flashes of light arc above the crags, a tease of what is yet to come. Soon the aurora hides belts of stars and backlights the summits. I put the coffee on to boil.

SEPTEMBER 28, 1985. Rising early this morning, I went in search of the moose herd I photographed five days ago. They were about one mile from where I last saw them, and instead of nine, there were nineteen. A radio-collared bull, with outsized antlers, had assumed preeminence. Two cows, each with a calf, also had joined the group. (Cows with calves rarely mix in rutting groups until the cow is near estrus.) Two small bulls hesitating at the edge were largely ignored by the dominant bull except when one approached a cow.

Twice while hiking up I saw subordinate bulls driven from the group. The cows, however, wandered at will. Unlike bull elk, which assemble and control "harems," bull moose do not control their cow groups; instead, the cows' feeding pattern sets the pace of movement and direction.

The group consisted of three bulls and sixteen cows, not an unusual combination. Even though both males and females are protected from hunting, the park moose population is about 70 percent female. Winter and predators take a disproportionate toll on the weakened bulls. After fasting through most of the month, the dominant bull is just now beginning to feed again. Once the rut is over, if the snow and cold hold off, he'll have a chance to regain some of his strength. Even so, winter will be a severe test.

With all the turmoil in the group—the bulls racing about, the cows intemperate even with one another—I never strayed far from a good-sized spruce at the edge of the timber. Engrossed in watching the activity, I was startled by the sound of a bull thrashing the brush to my left. Most of the cows and all three bulls looked in that direction. Pausing only briefly and vocalizing his own challenge, the dominant bull at once walked toward the sound. A large bull emerged from the timber.

With little posturing, the herd bull charged in a violent clash of antlers. Momentum and size favored him, and his challenger folded under the tremendous force of the initial blow. Unable to gain purchase with his hind legs, the newcomer was forced to the side, his antlers slipping off those of his attacker. The herd bull drove his antlers hard into his opponent's neck and shoulder, routing him.

The two bulls crashed off into the timber. Before long the herd bull rushed back into the open, his tines marked with blood. He charged straight toward one of the small bulls, now close to his favored consort. The entire group was soon in turmoil as the big bull chased the two younger ones away. I moved closer to my tree until the group settled down.

As the morning wore on and the sun came out, the moose fed down off the willow flat and into the heavy timber. A few cows soon bedded down, but five or six others and the three bulls remained active. I could hear the plaintive moaning of the cows as one or another of the bulls approached.

While watching one of the young bulls, I almost missed the moment I'd hoped to witness. Looking back at the dominant bull, then partially hidden in the timber, I saw that he was resting his head and neck on a cow's rump. I kept still. Staying in contact with the cow, the bull reared into copulatory position. In just seconds, the cow struggled from his embrace. All the fighting, the bloodletting, the stress, the weeks of turmoil were reduced to this brief climax. It seemed, in fact, anticlimactic.

SEPTEMBER 28, 1990. Naming animals is something I rarely do. It humanizes them, perhaps diminishes them in some way. But the moose I call Big Daddy has earned his name. His antlers span seventy inches or more, and he carries his fourteen hundred pounds lightly. Monday afternoon his antlers were perfect, the long fighting tines unmarred. He had sixteen points on the left antler, eighteen on the right. By Tuesday morning, three tines were broken off and another was fractured and loose. There were two long bloody gashes in his shoulder.

In the last few days he has gathered twelve cows and run himself ragged defending them from four small bulls. Today the herd fed in thick timber, and only two or three cows were in sight at any one time. A loud moan from one side or another of the thicket would be a cow announcing the unwelcome advance of a bull. Big Daddy would charge off to protect that cow, when a moan in another direction would make him race the other way. Once, the next-biggest bull came racing down the middle of the thicket with Big Daddy in vigorous pursuit. No saddle horse has galloped faster, and when Big Daddy came to a three-foot-tall deadfall, he leaped it with amazing agility. Both bulls disappeared into the timber, the smaller jabbed on by a violent antler thrust to the rump.

One cow was in estrus. Big Daddy copulated twice with her. He stayed close by her when not defending the other cows. Often she followed him as he moved through the timber. Conventional theory is that in most species the largest males do the bulk of the breeding. These dominant males guard the females and chase off the subordinate males. A new theory, developed from work with baboons, postulates that young males who stay quietly at the edge of the group often do more breeding than previously believed; they are able to take judicious advantage of the turmoil created by the large males. For example, while Big Daddy was raging against another bull on the far side of the thicket, the estrus female accepted the bull that Big Daddy had earlier chased through the herd. They, too, copulated twice. I have seen this same thing happen with Dall sheep. If these events read like a TV soap opera, then perhaps I can be forgiven for anthropomorphizing and naming Big Daddy.

SEPTEMBER 29, 1985. Heavy, wet snow has closed the road at Headquarters, Mile 3. A ranger says that if the sun comes out, the road will reopen later in the day. Disinclined to miss the morning activity, I shoulder my pack and hike up the road. I know there are moose five miles ahead, but I hope to find closer subjects. Government vehicles have been on the road beyond the barricade, and I walk where they have broken the snow. I am so used to driving the road, it seems strange to walk it.

As the sun emerges from behind the clouds, the snow begins to melt, and I hike in shirtsleeves. Walking the silent road turns out to be a great idea, much better than waiting for the road to open.

At nine-thirty, near Mile 7, three cows are being courted by a smallish bull at the edge of the road. Just as I sit down and set up my camera, a car comes splashing up the road. It slows and stops nearby, and two people get out and begin taking pictures. The moose move into the timber.

"Nice morning, isn't it?" the woman says. "We thought we were the first ones up the road after it opened. Where did you park?"

SEPTEMBER 30, 1985. The road is closed again in early morning because of ice, then is reopened by midday. In the afternoon, a grizzly with a heavy, silver-tipped coat wanders across the road near Sanctuary. His thick pelage creates the illusion of great size. I watch him meander up the snowy slope and through the brush flanking Mount Wright. He wanders slowly, pausing to dig some berries from beneath the snow and once to tear open a rotten log. Then he rears to his hind legs and scratches his back against a dead spruce. His facial expression is almost human. *Ah! What a relief.*

Soon only the old males will be active; the females and cubs will be in their dens. Within two weeks, even the males will be in hibernation. This sighting makes an exciting end to this year's stay in Denali.

Before the bear moves out of sight, he looks back at me . . . and yawns.

Into Winter

On into winter; frost and darkness.

OCTOBER 2, 1981. Bleached bones are scattered along a rocky ridge: ribs, femurs, vertebrae, and the jewel of the discovery, a skull grinning in the cool, gray afternoon light. As if fearing a bite, I gently pick it up and cradle it in my hands.

Somehow the mandible has survived the scavengers and is still attached to the skull. The half of the skull that has been hidden from the sun is brown, the remainder ivory. Viewed from the top, the skull is shaped like a spear point. A long snout widens at the eye sockets; the zygomatic arches curve out, then back, to reattach below the rather small braincase. Dark suture lines outline the segments of bone.

The highly diversified teeth, each with its function, identify this as a carnivore's skull. From front to back, the teeth include the following: small gripping incisors, long stabbing canines, crushing premolars, cutting carnassials, and bone-cracking molars. For a skull only six inches long, the canines seem oversized. I open and close the jaws, marveling at the tight interlocking fit of the teeth. I imagine the canines stabbing into a vole, squirrel, or ptarmigan. By the lack of wear and the clean, polished look of the teeth, I know that this red fox died young.

I put the skull back just so, fitting it into the depression that it made in the dryas mat. Most of the ribs are cracked and broken, the vertebrae separated, but that tells me nothing. I wonder whether the fox died in this open, windswept place or whether some larger animal carried it here.

OCTOBER 3, 1990. Low, plus six. A light dusting of snow reveals tracks, evidence of animals passing in the night. I walked a trail this morning that I've walked half a dozen times in the past two weeks without once seeing a large mammal. Squirrel, hare, and ptarmigan tracks patterned the powder. Tracks of two moose crossed the trail. Then, a mile farther, four wolves joined the path, heading west, their big prints adding special interest. It was a thrill to follow them, knowing their passage had knocked the snow off the crowding brush. In the trail was a dark mound, a dropping full of hair and bone fragments, a clue to yet another drama.

Voles and shrews have lately appeared numerous — I have seen several scurrying from one covert to another — and now, with the snow on the ground, I see their tracks everywhere. The next few years should be banner ones for foxes, lynx, owls, weasels, and even wolves. Reading sign in the snow is often more intriguing than reading a whodunit: there is no author to plant clues or give evidence. I must unravel the mystery myself.

OCTOBER 7, 1990. Not far from the banks of the Nenana, in a dense spruce thicket, there is a one-acre clearing crowded with young spruce, dwarf birch, and willow. I found it today by following lynx tracks. No wonder the lynx went there: I have never seen so many hares in one small place. I saw the first as soon as I entered the thicket. Within a thirty-foot radius of where I stood, no fewer than seven hares were visible, and others had already hopped away. Most were crouched in willow or birch thickets or beneath the thick branches of spruce.

There were brown ones, white ones, and in-between ones. Patchy snow covered the ground, but the hares were out of sync; the white ones were on the bare ground, the brown ones on the snow. In wonder, I moved about the clearing, spotting perhaps twenty-five hares. But the total may have been higher, all varying from summer brown to winter white, most closer to white than brown. They have gathered here for the browse. Every plant shows damage and girdling, even the dwarf birch. If the hare cycle hasn't peaked, it will soon. The habitat cannot support many more hares, if it can even support this number.

Solutions to natural phenomena are often rather stark. While I stood watching, a flash of wings panicked three hares, and a sharp-shinned hawk swooped away without dinner . . . this time.

Perhaps the deep snow of 1990–91 forced the hares out of this area, but in March 1991, I didn't see a single hare. Perhaps the lone coyote track crossing the thicket told another story.

OCTOBER 8, 1988. Plus thirty and snowing big, heavy flakes that quickly melt, soaking the seven moose almost as rain would. Only the snow on the bull's antlers stays frozen. The moose seem not to notice the snowfall as they browse through the laden willows. Apparently the rut has waned; the bull feeds as intently as the cows. It is not uncommon for large bulls, which may weigh fourteen hundred pounds or more prior to the rut, to lose three hundred pounds over the winter.

I wonder how many of these moose will survive the winter. The bull and the calf probably face the severest challenges — the bull because his strength has been sapped by the rut and the calf because it, like all calves, has little stored fat. Much of the calf's energy must go into growth. It cannot, moreover, reach the higher browse available to mature animals and will have to share the taller plants its mother breaks down.

Even in a mild winter, diet is often insufficient to maintain a moose. So, in large measure, survival hinges on stored fat. But once the usable fat reserves are depleted, the body begins burning muscle for energy. Since muscle has less than half the energy of fat, an accelerating downward slide begins. Once the stored energy is used up, the animal will die. As one scientist has put it, "With wintering wildlife, there is no deficit spending."

Winter 1988–89 turned out to be one of the coldest on record. The "omega block," an intense area of high pressure, stalled over central Alaska, dropping temperatures to record lows for weeks at a time. In the park, January averaged twelve degrees colder than usual. The first three months were without precipitation, clear and cold. At park Headquarters the coldest temperature recorded in January was minus fifty-one, in February, minus thirty-one, and in March, minus thirty-three. Since the park weather station is at Headquarters, other areas within the park, especially in lower elevations, probably experienced colder temperatures. Relatively low snowfall, however, lessened somewhat the impact on wildlife.

OCTOBER 11, 1990. About noon the sun came out; the temperature rose to forty two. Despite the thaw, enough snow remained for good tracking.

Sometime during the night two wolves hunted the shore of Horseshoe Lake. They investigated the castor-scented beaver lodge, then walked most of the shoreline before casting through the timber in search of other prey. A snowshoe hare became the object of pursuit, the circling dash ending in the hiking trail. Judging from the tracks, the two wolves pulled the hare apart, one running a few feet away to consume its share. The story faded as the converging tracks vanished with the melting of the crimson snow.

OCTOBER 17, 1981. Most ponds and small lakes are frozen; a few inches of snow cover the ice. Shelf ice expands along the rivers; slush runs in midchannel. It is foolhardy to attempt to walk on the ice now. Fox, wolf, and coyote tracks cross some ponds, but they are a sucker's lure. Thin ice and open water are hidden by the snow. I resist all temptation to cross the inviting flat surfaces.

A large cache protrudes above the snow in front of a beaver lodge. The ice is likely to be thin there, too, because of the movement of beaver beneath it. Unless it thaws (there's still the chance of a chinook), it is winter for the beaver. Either they are prepared and have stored enough feed in their cache, or they will perish in their ice-locked lodges. In years of light snowfall and continuous cold, even a well-prepared colony may know shortage or starvation if thick pond ice seals off their cache or the pond freezes to the bottom. Twice I have seen starving beaver that have gnawed their way out of the lodge because of food scarcity. They were killed by predators.

NOVEMBER 15, 1990. A heavy snow has been falling over much of Alaska these last few days. Although I am physically far from the park, my thoughts drift to the windswept ridges and snow-drifted valleys. Every winter about this time I wonder how the animals are faring, especially favored ones that I've come to recognize year after year: Savage River's grandfather ram and Igloo Creek's one-antlered moose. And this winter, I wonder about the wolves. They are not confined by invisible sanctuary boundaries and are sometimes not safe even within them.

Perhaps no other wildlife issue draws so much heated debate as wolf control—the killing of wolves for the presumed benefit of other animals. Denali Park's wolves have often been at the core of this controversy.

Prior to 1930, Dall sheep were incredibly abundant in the park as well as throughout Alaska. Various estimates placed the park population as high as 28,000. In the late 1920s, however, park sheep herds began declining dramatically. A few years earlier, wolves had reportedly begun increasing across Alaska at the same time that coyotes expanded their range. Many Alaskans saw a direct connection between increases in these predators and declining sheep populations.

Because the park was established to protect wildlife, especially sheep, many concerned people called for wolf control within the park. By the early 1930s, only fifteen hundred sheep remained in the park. The U.S. Biological Survey began pressing Park Service, saying the park had become a "breeding ground for wolves for the rest of Alaska."

Park wolves and bears could be killed in the park to prevent extermination of other animals, and prior to 1939 a few had been shot or trapped by rangers. But before conducting the large-scale control demanded by the public, the Interior Department ordered a scientific appraisal of the situation. In 1939, Adolph Murie was assigned the task of investigating the wolf–sheep interactions within the park. His study, published in 1944 as *The Wolves of Mount McKinley*, was both hailed as a profound look into predator–prey relationships and condemned as pro-wolf propaganda. The balance of nature theory had little popular support.

Murie found that the harsh winters of 1928 and 1932—the most severe in forty years—had played an important part in the sheep decline. In the winter of 1931–32, remembered as the "Year of the Big Snow," seventy-seven inches fell in just one six-day period. Hundreds of sheep starved. Murie doubted that wolves, though increasing in number, could have held the herds in check until weather played a part. After the die-offs, however, wolves were able to affect a decrease in the surviving population, especially the old, diseased, and young. In 1941, he placed the sheep population at fifteen hundred. When he returned in 1945, he found a remnant population of five hundred. Clearly the situation was critical. The low population might not withstand further impacts.

Instead of silencing the national call for wolf control within the park, Murie's report, particularly his census figures, added fuel to the fire. Papers ran the headline "Wolves Ruining the Park." Both the Boone and Crockett Club and the Camp Fire Club, influential conservation groups, lobbied Congress for wolf control. National legislation, HR5401, a bill "to provide for the protection of Dall sheep, caribou, and other wildlife native to the Mount McKinley National Park," was eventually defeated, but Park Service reluctantly ordered wolf control within the park. In 1945 Murie wrote,

"As a precautionary measure it would be wise to control the Mount McKinley National Park wolves to assist the mountain sheep herds to recover a more favorable status."

In 1946, twelve steel traps were purchased and set at stations along the Park Road. John Colvin arrived on February 18, 1946, to do the wolf control work. To protect foxes and other furbearers, Park Service disallowed poison (then the favored wolf-killing device) in favor of rifles and traps. Colvin managed to kill one wolf. Frank Glaser, working for the U.S. Fish and Wildlife Service, succeeded in killing only two wolves. Rangers killed five in 1946. "Wolf control not effective," Grant Pearson reported, "due to low wolf numbers."

As time passed, Murie found himself in a peculiar position. As park biologist he was both a student of wolves and nominally in charge of killing them. It is clear that Murie wanted to control wolves only as a last resort — to prevent the extirpation of the sheep and to head off legislated control and kill-quotas. "Ade was a true scientist and began the wolf study with an open mind," Louise Murie-MacLeod, his widow, told me. "He never was pro-predator control." Before coming to Alaska in 1939, Murie had weathered a blistering assault for exposing the killing of wolves, cougars, bobcats, coyotes, and bears in Yellowstone. His report absolving the coyote of blame in the reduction of that park's wildlife and calling for the end of all predator control work was as controversial as his Alaskan wolf study.

At times Murie found it necessary to defend himself from both sides. On February 22, 1950, in a letter to Ben Thompson, special assistant to the director, Murie wrote, "The wolf problem has placed me in a difficult position; I have stood in the middle. . . . When I arrived at McKinley in 1945, I learned that wolves had spent considerable time in the park in the winter of 1944 to 1945. To insure no further reduction of sheep numbers, I recommended wolf control. As the situation developed, I am not sure control was needed."

By the end of the 1940s, few wolves were being killed, and the sheep were beginning to come back on their own. A 1949 park report stated that "no wolves were killed . . . due to their scarcity." Wolf control finally ceased at the end of 1952.

Sixty-eight to seventy wolves had been killed in the park. Many more died at the hands of trappers and government control agents using poison just outside the park boundaries. Strychnine and cyanide are indiscriminate killers; foxes often were more victimized than wolves.

Researchers generally agree that 1953 to 1974 was a recovery period for park wolves. The next ten years saw a dip in the wolf population (and, in the eastern part of the park, for moose numbers as well). Sheep populations slowly increased after 1945; today they seem stable at twenty-five hundred.

When caribou, sheep, and moose numbers declined in the 1940s, wolves were not the only hunters afield; humans were active as well. Through ongoing research, Murie began to suspect that poaching on the north boundary had helped depress the sheep population. Frank W. Hynes, then executive director of the Alaska Game Commission, wrote that "1945 was the worst year on record for wildlife . . . thousands of hunters entered the wilderness and slaughtered anything that could be shot." Wanton waste was common.

Perhaps more than at any other time in history, the wolf has a constituency that views it as an important part of the natural process. But even after all of these years, people still call for wolf control in the park. In 1990, the *Anchorage Times* reported that the Denali caribou herd had remained low "because it is subject to heavy predation by bears and wolves." The writer neglected to point out that the herd had been increasing at a healthy 9 percent annual rate despite predation. At the spring 1990 meeting of the Alaska Board of Game, there was much discussion about the impact of wolves on the Denali caribou herd. A newly appointed member asked whether Park Service could be pressured to conduct wolf control within the park to protect the caribou.

In a 1948 field note, Adolph Murie wondered to himself, "Can wolves survive only if they happen to stay out of our way and find a place . . . not wanted by man?"

NOVEMBER 19, 1977. Plus twenty, overcast. Thirty-nine rams and ewes were on the slope above Savage River. Despite the almost complete snow cover, it was easy to find them; they looked somewhat yellow against the snow. I remembered the theory that their white pelage developed, not as camouflage, but as protection from the unrelenting summer heat of the treeless alpine.

Climbing into sheep country in summer is work; in winter it's pure torture. I had a steep slope to climb and fought knee-deep snow as well. I had to stop every five steps to catch my breath. In some places I took two steps up and slid one step back. Expecting cold weather, not the warmth brought by the cloud cover, I was overdressed. For once I was glad to have my big backpack in which to stuff my unnecessary layers of clothing. It took two hours instead of one to reach the band. After an initial look at me, the sheep returned to their activities.

In contrast to the thin summer pelage that gives sheep an almost frail, scrawny look, their thick winter coats make them look huge. The rams looked much larger than their two hundred pounds or so. Even the six-month-old lambs looked big. Their wonderful hollow-hair coats, combined with a layer of fat, offer unsurpassed protection from deep cold and the perpetual alpine wind.

Seven mature rams mingled with the ewes and immature rams. The rut was in full swing; the largest rams guarded estrus females. Even while making the ascent, I saw two rams butting heads. Wherever one ewe went, the largest ram followed, trailed at some distance by two juvenile rams. Each time the ewe stopped to paw at the snow to uncover forage, the ram approached in a head-low display. If the ewe tried to ignore him, he'd strike her with a front leg or attempt to mount her. She seldom snatched more than a bite or two before he forced her to move on. The ram's interest was relentless. Only once, when the ram stopped to smell the ewe's urine (which elicited a prolonged lipcurl), was the ewe able to gather more than a few mouthfuls of dried vegetation.

The sheep's movement across the snowy slope was a classic of wildlife social structure: the ewe, trailed by the largest ram, was followed by two small rams and, well behind, a scrawny, struggling human.

In the fading light of a five-hour day, at the last possible moment before I had to descend, the ram once again approached the ewe. He sniffed at her, then rested his chin on her back. When she did not move, he mounted her in one swift move. In a moment, it was over: the ewe moved away and the ram stood still with a bewildered look.

NOVEMBER 20, 1977. Plus eighteen and snowing hard, the peaks lost in whiteout. I contented myself with an upriver trek on snowshoes. I saw a moose, some willow ptarmigan, and the tracks of a fox.

Everywhere I go, the snow seems different. In the open, the drifts are packed as hard as concrete. In the sheltering timber, the snow has no cohesiveness; I sink in as if floundering in sugar. On the slope yesterday, I slogged heavily through loose snow and walked easily on drifts. (Unlike the heavy, wet snow of late autumn and early winter, midwinter snow that falls in temperatures colder than plus fifteen has little water content; it comes in six-sided wafers or hexagonal columns.) It takes several pots of snow to make one pot of water. This morning I spent half an hour and much of my limited stove fuel to accumulate two quarts of water.

A popular misconception is that sheep move down in winter. In reality, they often go higher, seeking windswept places with exposed forage. Sheep do not do well in deep snow. A heavy snowpack, partially thawed by a midwinter chinook then glazed hard by a cold snap, is especially harrowing for sheep, as well as for other grazers and browsers. They cannot paw through the crust to obtain forage, and their legs are slashed open by the razor-sharp ice. Deep snow is not the norm here, but on occasion it has exacted a toll.

This afternoon as I wandered through the willows, I thought about the sheep. Did I really describe them as looking frail and delicate? With the cold, the snow, the wind, and the darkness—and occasionally, the wolves—I'm astonished there are any sheep at all.

NOVEMBER 21, 1977. Plus ten and clearing when I awoke. Although it is one month until winter solstice, the shortest day of the year, there is little light before ten A.M. After several cups of tea and a leisurely breakfast (if you can call shivering in a cold tent "leisure"), I hiked toward the distant ridge and the rutting sheep.

Where two days ago I'd encountered the small herd, today I counted sixty-five sheep. Ten were rams, perhaps another ten were four- or five-year-olds. Even at a distance, I could see the heavy-horned rams protecting individual ewes and the turmoil as rams chased ewes, rams chased rams, and lambs did their best to stay out of the way. Although I know conception must take place now so the lambs will be born at the optimum time, the timing of the rut still seems odd to me. The sheep have been coping with winter for more than a month. Perhaps some of them are already weakened by cold and poor diet. Now through mid-December, they must face the dual test of the onslaught of the worst weather and the rigors of rut. They probably fare better in early winter than I think. One biologist says that sheep add fat right until the first week in November. Maybe in my own discomfort I exaggerate their predicament.

I'd hoped to follow my previous trail, but the shifting snow had filled it in. Once again the climb was an ordeal—but with an added element. The wind bit and clawed at my exposed flesh, and it was hard to find the right combination of clothing to stay warm and dry. For the millionth time, I questioned my sanity.

Long plumes of wind-driven snow boiled from the peaks to the south. Above me, a ground blizzard began to swirl around the sheep. Once close to the sheep, I huddled in the lee of some rocks for protection while I donned all my clothing. I'd hoped to be able to use color film to record some of the rutting behavior, but that didn't look possible. Not only was I hampered by limited daylight, but the sheep had moved onto a north-facing slope where the sun would not shine. The cold combined with the wind—always the wind—was a real limitation; I had to handle all my gear and film while wearing gloves.

I managed a few rolls of black-and-white film but didn't shoot anything extraordinary—young rams courting disinterested ewes, older rams guarding estrus ewes. Then above the band I saw two mature, evenly matched rams approaching each other in threat display.

One ram turned and moved some yards away, where it stopped to paw at the snow and nibble some grass. His rival, head held high in classic pose, stood motionless where the two had met. The ram scratched at the snow, then pivoted. Both reared to their hind legs and bipedally charged. Still some yards apart, they dropped to all fours. Following a brief pause, both lowered their heads and pawed the snow. Once again they charged, the final hop turning into a powerful lunge that ended in a head-cracking butt. For some minutes, they stood eye-to-eye, studying each other. Then both turned and separated. They pawed at the snow and seemed to feed. Then they whirled again and collided in a butt as loud as two boulders clacking together. In the aftermath, the larger ram lashed his opponent with several hard foreleg kicks. When the pummeled ram tried to turn away, a head butt to his shoulder initiated a chase across the slope.

Soon most of the herd, as well as the two rams, had moved onto a slope too precipitous for me to follow. I watched the chase until it ended. The dominant ram became interested in a ewe at one edge of the scattered herd just as the light began to fail and the wind picked up. Despite my heavy clothing, I could not stop shivering. I headed down, happy to have witnessed the classic battle for dominance: two mature animals fighting for the right to breed, ensuring that only the strongest ram would pass his heritage on to future generations.

DECEMBER 21, 1990. Winter solstice. As the sun slides along just below the southern horizon, only briefly peeking above the lower summits and through mountain passes, its tantalizing glow rekindles the quiet agony of longing for solar warmth and sparkling light.

In these mountains at 63 degrees north latitude, "sunrise" occurs at nine-twenty-eight A.M. and "sunset" at two-nineteen P.M., providing a total of less than five hours of dim light. Today we lose one minute of daylight, tomorrow none, and the next day we will gain one minute. Although it's imperceptible, the Northern Hemisphere will begin to receive more sun. By March we will be gaining six minutes of daylight during each twenty-four hour period. I toast the incredible earth.

I am already planning summer trips: hikes into mountain basins, treks along coastal streams. Sojourns to watch migrating birds, mountain sheep, and lumbering bears. I wonder what the spring and summer will hold. Will the weather be kind, a mixture of sun and rain, or will we have clouds and rain? (A depressing thought on this particular day.) And I wonder what the year will mean to the park, its wildlife, and people. I know I am woefully inadequate as a seer. When the road restrictions were put into place, I bitterly opposed them. I couldn't imagine the wave of visitors predicted by Park Service. Now I am grateful to those who had the foresight I lacked.

I was heartened by a recent conversation with Superintendent Russell Berry. He plans no dramatic changes in park management. He called the shuttle-bus system "one of the best things the National Park Service has ever done in taking steps to preserve a unique resource." He talked at length about the tightrope that Park Service walks as it tries to balance use and preservation. "Both the public and Park Service must work together to assure another seventy-five years of protection," he said. "We need the public's support to keep the visitor transportation system and to balance the uses of the road." Despite pressure from some quarters to increase traffic levels, Berry said he "will not increase bus use without meeting the language of the General Management Plan and will not change it without a monitoring system in place to determine the effects." He vowed to do his utmost to preserve the quality of the park experience.

The wildlife experience in Denali today has changed little in twenty years. I cannot see into the future, but I hope the same will be true twenty years from now. Rams will climb the crags, bears will grub the Toklat soapberry patch, and caribou bulls will spar on the ridges above Wonder Lake. I toast this day, the winter solstice, as I look forward to increasing light—not only on the surface of the earth but in the minds of men and women.

Selected Place Names

Alaskan Range. Proposed in 1868 by William H. Dall.

Anderson Pass. For Peter Anderson, 1910 Sourdough expedition.

Archdeacon's Tower. Named in 1942 by U.S. Army test expedition for Hudson Stuck. (At head of Harper Glacier.)

Bilberg Lake. For Rudy Bilberg, bush pilot. (Northern park addition.)

Brooker Mountain. For Ed Brooker, Sr., miner, postmaster, U.S. commissioner, Kantishna Mining District.

Brooks Glacier, Mount. For Alfred Hulse Brooks, 1902 U.S. Geological Survey (USGS) expedition.

Browne's Tower. For Belmore Brown, artist, climber, and member of 1906 Cook-Parker and 1910 and 1912 Parker-Browne expeditions.

Busia Mountain. For Johnny Busia, miner, Kantishna.

Dan Beard, Mount. For Dan Beard (1850–1941), painter, founder of Boy Scouts.

Capps, Mount. For Stephen Reid Capps, 1916 USGS expedition.

Carlson Lake. For Hjalmar "Slim" Carlson, trapper. (Northern addition.)

Carey Lake. For Fabian Carey, trapper, historian. (Northern addition.)

Cathedral Mountain. Named by Charles Sheldon.

Churchill Peaks. Summits of Mount McKinley named in 1965 for Sir Winston Churchill.

Crosson, Mount. For Joe Crosson, pilot. Second park landing, first glacier landing, first flight over Mount McKinley for scientific expedition in 1932 with S. E. Robbins.

Dall Glacier, Mount. For William H. Dall, 1860s exploration.

Denali Park. Athabascan origin, the "high" one. In 1897 William Dickey named the mountain Mount McKinley for William H. McKinley, Ohio, twenty-fifth U.S. president (1897–1901). It is also known as "*bolshaya gora*" (Russian), "the great mountain."

Dickey, Mount. For prospector William A. Dickey in 1914.

Eielson, Mount. For Carl Ben Eielson, pilot. First park landing.

Eldridge Glacier, Mount. For George H. Eldridge, 1898 USGS expedition.

Foraker, Mount. For U.S. Senator Joseph Benson Foraker, Ohio, in 1899.

Harper Glacier. For Walter Harper, Athabascan, first man on south summit, 1913 Stuck-Karstens expedition.

Healy, Mount. For Captain J. J. Healy, North American Transportation and Trading Company. Healy Creek reported in 1902 by Brooks.

Highway Pass. For caribou migration route, reported six years prior to blazing Park Road.

Herron River, Glacier. For Lieutenant Joseph S. Herron, 1899 U.S. Army expedition.

Hunter, Mount. For Anna Falconnet Hunter, 1906, by her nephew, a traveling reporter. Misapplied by topographer's error.

Huntington, Mount. For Archer Milton Huntington, president, American Geographical Society, 1910 Parker-Browne expedition.

Igloo Creek. Reported by Woodbury Abbey during 1921 park survey; name derived from a "sod igloo" located along the creek.

Karstens' Ridge, Col. For Henry (Harry) Karstens, first park superintendent, member of 1913 Stuck-Karstens expedition. Ridge named by Hudson Stuck; Col, a 10,930-foot pass, by B. Washburn in 1946.

Margaret, Mount. Reported by Woodbury Abbey during his 1921 park survey.

Mather, Mount. For Stephen T. Mather, first director, National Park Service (1917–29).

McGonagall Pass, Mountain. For Charlie McGonagall, 1910 Anderson-Taylor Sourdough expedition, carried fourteen-foot spruce flagpole to 16,000 feet.

Muldrow Glacier. Robert Muldrow, topographer, 1898 Eldridge expedition.

Peters Glacier. For W. J. Peters, USGS, in 1902 by A. H. Brooks. Also named Hanna Glacier in 1904 for U.S. Senator Marcus Alonzo Hanna, Ohio.

Pilgrim Peak. For Earl Pilgrim, miner. (A 4,649-foot peak near Stampede Mine.)

Pioneer Ridge. For Sourdough expedition—Taylor, Anderson, McGonagall, Lloyd—in 1945 by Bradford Washburn.

Polychrome Pass. Name reported and given by C. E. Giffen.

Riley Creek. Local name reported in 1921 by Woodbury Abbey.

Russell, Mount. For Professor Israel Cook Russell, in 1902 by A. H. Brooks.

Ruth Glacier. Named in 1903 by Frederick A. Cook for his daughter.

Sable Pass. Named from Sable Mountain, 1916.

Sanctuary River. Local name reported in 1916 by C. E. Giffen.

Savage River. For Tom Savage, a Cherokee Indian market hunter, in 1916.

Scott Peak. For Lieutenant Gordon Scott, USGS, killed in 1953 plane crash.

Sheldon, Mount. For Charles Sheldon, 1906–8 naturalist expeditions.

Don Sheldon Amphitheater. For Don Sheldon, glacier pilot.

Silverthrone, Mount. Named by U.S. Army test expedition "because of its stately appearance." (At head of Brooks Glacier.)

Stony Hill. Local name reported in 1932.

Taylor Spur. For William Taylor, 1910 Anderson-Taylor expedition.

Tatum, Mount. Robert Tatum, 1913 Stuck-Karstens expedition.

Teklanika River. Athabascan origin.

Thorofare River, Valley. In 1921, because the valley has been an important caribou thoroughfare.

Toklat River. Athabascan origin, "upper" or "headwaters" river.

Wickersham Wall, Dome. For Judge James Wickersham, 1903 summit attempt, Kantishna gold strike.

Wonder Lake. Local name reported in 1916 by topographer C. E. Giffen.

Wright, Mount. For George M. Wright, 1929 founder of wildlife division, National Park Service, in 1943.

Yanert River, Glacier. For Sergeant William Yanert, 1898 U.S. Army expedition.

DISTANCES TO FEATURES ALONG THE DENALI PARK ROAD

	Elevation	Mile
Park Entrance	1600 feet	0
Riley Creek Campground	1650	0.4
Visitor Access Center	1675	0.7
Denali Park Station and Hotel	1700	1.5
Morino Campground	1700	1.8
Park Headquarters	2040	3.4
Savage River Campground	2780	13.0 (12.8)
Savage River Bridge	2550	14.1
Primrose Pullout	3140	17.5
Sanctuary Campground	2400	23.0 (22.0)
Sanctuary River Bridge	2450	23.1
Teklanika Campground	2580	29.6 (29.1)
Teklanika Reststop	2700	30.7
Teklanika River Bridge	2650	31.7
Igloo Campground	2940	34.5 (33.6)
Sable Pass Summit	3900	39.5
East Fork Bridge	3040	43.8 (43.4)
Polychrome Pass	3700	47.4
Toklat Bridge (East End)	3090	53.8 (53.1)

Highway Pass	3980	57.5
Stony Hill Wayside	4080	62.7 (62.2)
Thorofare Pass	3950	65.3
Eielson Visitor Center	3733	66.5 (65.3)
Wonder Lake Junction	2321	84.5
Wonder Ranger Station	2110	86.5
Pre-1980 Park Boundary		87.7
North Face Lodge		88.7
Moose Creek Bridge		88.9
Camp Denali Fork		89.0
Kantishna Roadhouse		90.6

Mileage figures are imprecise odometer readings. Those in parentheses are taken from signboard mileages. The difference reflects variations between vehicle and official measurements. Elevations are approximations and should not be considered exact. Igloo Campground's signboard, for example, gives 2940 as its elevation, though the signboard at the bridge, just a few feet away, gives an elevation of 2975.

SUPERINTENDENTS OF
THE PARK

Henry P. Karstens	1921–28
Harry J. Liek	1928–39
Frank T. Been	1939–43
Grant Pearson (Acting)	1943–47
Frank T. Been	1947–49
Grant Pearson	1949–56
Duane D. Jacobs	1956–60
Samuel A. King	1960–62
Oscar T. Dick	1962–67
George A. Hall	1967–69
Vernon Ruesch	1969–73
Daniel R. Kuehn	1973–78
Frank Betts	1978–80
Robert C. Cunningham	1980–89
Russell W. Berry, Jr.	1989–

From its inception in 1917 until 1921, no funds were provided for administration or protection of the park. On April 12, 1921, Karstens was appointed chief ranger for Alaska, and on July 1, 1921, he was named superintendent of Mount McKinley National Park. Until June 30, 1969, the superintendent also administered Katmai National Monument. Mount McKinley National Park was renamed Denali on December 2, 1980. *When lapses occurred between appointments, interim management was provided by acting, or assistant, superintendents.*

INDEX